£27-50
0359-88

The English Sabbath

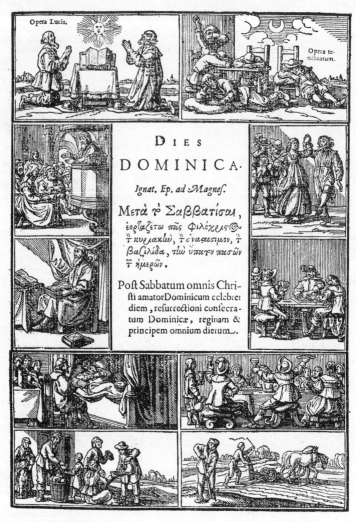

Thomas Young, *Dies Dominica* (Amsterdam?), 1639

The English Sabbath

*A study of doctrine and discipline from
the Reformation to the Civil War*

Kenneth L. Parker

*Monk of St. Andrew's Priory, Valyermo, California
formerly Bankhead Fellow in European History
University of Alabama*

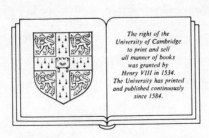

The right of the
University of Cambridge
to print and sell
all manner of books
was granted by
Henry VIII in 1534.
The University has printed
and published continuously
since 1584.

Cambridge University Press

Cambridge
New York   New Rochelle
Melbourne   Sydney

Published by the Press Syndicate of the University of Cambridge
The Pitt Building, Trumpington Street, Cambridge CB2 1RP
32 East 57th Street, New York, NY 10022, USA
10 Stamford Road, Oakleigh, Melbourne 3166, Australia

First published 1988

Printed in Great Britain at
the University Press, Cambridge

British Library cataloguing in publication data
Parker, Kenneth L.
The English Sabbath: a study of doctrine and
discipline from the Reformation to the Civil War.
1. Sabbath – History   2. Reformation – England
3. England – Church history
I. Title
263'.4'0942   BR377

Library of Congress cataloguing in publication data
Parker, Kenneth L.
The English Sabbath.
Bibliography: p.
Includes index
1. Sunday – History of doctrines – 16th century.
2. Sunday – History of doctrines – 17th century.
3. Sunday legislation – England – History – 16th century.
4. Sunday legislation – England – History – 17th century.
5. England – Church history – 16th century. 6. England –
Church history – 17th century. I. Title.
BV133.P37   1988   263'.0942   86-6776

ISBN 0 521 30535 7

In memory of Clyde A. Parker, Sr
AND
in honour of Ernstena P. Parker

Contents

Acknowledgements

Apart from any scholarly merit that this work may possess, it represents an important landmark in my life. It is much more than the fruit of weeks, months, and years spent in libraries, archives, and my cosy room at Leckhampton, Cambridge. It is a reminder of important relationships, the kindness and generosity of others, and major changes in my life. I would be remiss if this book were published without acknowledging the debt owed to so many.

This work is, with some alterations and amendments, the dissertation submitted to the Divinity Faculty of the University of Cambridge, to satisfy requirements for the Ph.D. degree. The completion of this degree was eagerly awaited by my father and mother, who shared my joy after a successful viva on 27 January 1984. My father died three days later in an airplane crash in Greensboro, North Carolina. This book is dedicated to his memory, with grateful thanks from a loving and devoted son. I also wish to honour my mother, who continues to love, support, and encourage her son. No two people have had a more profound impact on my life. As parents, they provided the stimulation and opportunities that made this book possible. No son has been more blessed.

St Benedict stated in his *Rule* that, 'when anyone has received the name abbot, he ought to rule his disciples with a twofold teaching, displaying all goodness and holiness by deeds and by words, but by deeds rather than by words'. This admonition, appropriate for any mentor, was lived out by my Ph.D. supervisor, Dr Eamon Duffy. His rigorous scholarly expectations were only surpassed by the encouragement and enthusiasm he displayed as this study developed. His insistence on thorough and careful research set a high standard to strive towards. Yet this work would not have been completed without his tireless support during several difficult periods of my life at Cambridge. I owe him the deepest thanks for being a challenging mentor, a compassionate pastor, and a very dear friend.

Special thanks are also due to Dr Dorothy Owen and Dr Margaret Spufford. Both found time in their busy lives to provide instruction and encouragement. Dr Owen challenged me with her rigorous standards and infused enthusiasm for a difficult, but rewarding source of historical evidence: ecclesiastical court records. Dr Spufford instilled a respect for *people* in history, and taught me the invaluable lesson that statistics cannot in themselves reveal the nature of life for the 'common sort'. My life has been enriched in many ways by their instruction and counsel.

I owe a great debt to many others who have advanced this work in specific ways. My examiners, Professor Patrick Collinson and Professor Gordon Rupp, provided valuable suggestions for modifying the dissertation for publication. Dr John Morrill read this work several times, and offered insights that caused me to alter several arguments. I am grateful to Dr William Sheils, Dr Norman Jones, and Dr Ralph Houlbrooke, who read and corrected portions of this study that depended heavily on their research. Through conversation and reading of my work, Judith Maltby, Dr Kenneth Fincham, David Hoyle, Dr John Twigg, and Dr Andrew Foster provided stimuli and new ideas which have contributed to the direction and shape of this book. To these and many others who could not be mentioned, I offer thanks. While the deficiencies of this work are my responsibility, much that is worthy of note is due to their advice and counsel.

My life as a researcher was made easier by the kind and helpful service provided in many libraries and archives. I would like particularly to thank the staff of the Rare Books Room and the Manuscripts Room of the Cambridge University Library. I am also grateful to those who work in the public record offices at Chester and Chichester.

In addition to the generous financial support of my parents, this study was funded by Corpus Christi College, which provided a senior research studentship in 1981–2, 1982–3, and 1983–4. The trustees of the Archbishop Cranmer Fund and the Bethune-Baker Fund also awarded grants for specific projects. The History Department of the University of Alabama elected me to the Bankhead Fellowship in European History for 1984–5. This appointment enabled me to prepare the revised text. To those responsible for the generous support received, I wish to express my thanks.

Finally, to Ronald Grubbs, Timothy Kenoyer, Dr Louis Towles, Dr Richard Gould, Mrs Nancy Barcus, Dr David Howard, Professor Katherine Lindley, and Professor Geoffrey Bromiley, many thanks for the time and energy spent, from a grateful and devoted student.

To all these and many more, I wish to express my deepest thanks for their interest, advice, and labours. Their efforts have not only advanced my scholarship, but enriched my life as well.

Valyermo, California　　　　　　　　　　　　Kenneth L. Parker
Third Sunday of Advent
1984

Abbreviations

BL	British Library
CJ	*Commons Journal*
CRO	Cheshire Record Office
CSPD	*Calendar of State Papers: Domestic*
CUL	Cambridge University Library
DNB	*Dictionary of National Biography*
EDR	Ely Diocesan Records
LJ	*Lords Journal*
HLRO	House of Lords Record Office
HMC	*Historical Manuscripts Commission*
MCL	Manchester Central Library
PRO	Public Record Office
SRO	Somerset Record Office
STC	*Short Title Catalogue*
TRHS	*Transactions of the Royal Historical Society*
VA	Visitation Articles
WSRO	West Sussex Record Office

I

The case for a reappraisal

Sometimes it would seem that we regard Protestantism as a Thing, a fixed and definite object that came into existence in 1517...as though Protestantism itself had no antecedents, as though it were a fallacy to go behind the great water-shed, as though indeed it would blunt the edge of our story to admit the working of a process instead of assuming the interposition of some direct agency.

The Whig Interpretation of History, Herbert Butterfield

From the publication of Thomas Fuller's *Church History of Britain* in 1655 to the present, studies of sabbatarianism have treated this doctrine as an important and controversial issue in the post-Reformation period. These studies portray sabbatarianism as a puritan innovation, which that party introduced in an effort to reform the Church from below, having failed to convert the English Church to presbyterianism. This doctrinal 'novelty' is thought to have created a division between Church authorities and puritans by the end of Elizabeth's reign. By denying the importance of ancient or medieval precedents for 'puritan' sabbatarianism and highlighting selected events in the Elizabethan and early Stuart period, these studies have provided a convincing account of 'puritan' doctrinal innovation and agitation for sabbatarian reforms.

When the outlines of these studies are compared, one cannot help noting that they draw their points of reference from the Laudian partisan, Peter Heylyn, in his *History of the Sabbath*, published in 1636. However, this Laudian summary of sabbatarian developments in Elizabethan and Stuart England does not take into account much evidence that suggests a very different story. Heylyn claimed that the notion of a morally binding Sabbath was a puritan invention; yet this doctrine was firmly rooted in the Middle Ages. Heylyn charged puritans with attempting to subvert the established religion with their sabbatarian doctrine; however, there is much evidence which suggests consensus rather than conflict. A reappraisal of these issues may suggest the need to revise our understanding of English sabbatarianism.

While there are many shades of sabbatarian opinion which could be examined, there are two points of view that are relevant for this study. The first is the position which Peter Heylyn treated as the definitive teaching of the Church, ancient and modern. This position treated the fourth commandment as a ceremonial law, abrogated by Christ along with other laws of the Old Testament. The commandment was allegorized and treated as an injunction to rest from sin all our days. Heylyn explained that Sunday was first used in apostolic times and established by Constantine in 321 as the Christian day of worship and rest. This observance was authorized by the Church and regulated by canon law, and was not a divine institution or grounded in scripture.

In contrast, the sabbatarian doctrine Heylyn attributed to Elizabethan puritans, treated the sabbath commandment as a perpetual and moral law, as binding on Christians as the rest of the decalogue. The shift of the day from Saturday to Sunday did not diminish this obligation, for it was divinely instituted to commemorate Christ's resurrection and was not a mere ecclesiastical convention. The whole day was to be kept holy, with public and private exercises of religion and rest from all worldly labours and recreations; for these would distract, and rob God of the time set aside for spiritual works.

Ecclesiastical historians, in attempting to make sense of religious attitudes in the post-Reformation period, have used sabbatarianism as a litmus test of 'puritan' and 'Anglican' leanings. Thomas Fuller explained that, 'all strange and unknown writers, without further examination, passed for friends and favourites of the presbyterian party, who could give the word, and had anything in their treatise tending to the strict observation of the Lord's day'.[1] The eighteenth-century historian, Jeremy Collier, wrote in his *Ecclesiastical History of Great Britain* that, 'the Puritans having miscarried in their open attacks upon the Church, endeavoured to carry on their designs more under covert. Their magnifying the Sabbath-day, as they call Sunday, was a serviceable expedient for this purpose. Preaching the strict observance of this festival had a strong colour of zeal, and gained them the character of persons particularly concerned for the honour of God Almighty'.[2] In the nineteenth century Robert Cox continued this

---

[1] Thomas Fuller, *The Church History of Britain*, 3 vols. (London, 1868), III, 162.
[2] Jeremy Collier, *An Ecclesiastical History of Great Britain*, 9 vols. (London, 1852), VII, 190.

historiographical tradition.[3] Cox's works, and similar studies by W. B. Trevelyan and W. B. Whitaker, were primarily polemical in nature and were produced to defend the strict sabbatarian concerns prevalent in nineteenth- and early twentieth-century Britain.[4] In the last fifty years there has been a tempering of this rigid distinction, but the underlying assumption that sabbatarianism was a puritan innovation and characteristic remains. M. M. Knappen in his short study of the 'Puritan doctrine of Sunday' described it as, 'a bit of English originality and is the first and perhaps the only important English contribution to the development of Reformed theology in the first century of its history'.[5] Winton Solberg concluded in his study of the English Sabbath that 'Sabbatarianism became a distinguishing characteristic of Puritanism as early as the 1590s'.[6] While acknowledging that sabbatarian concerns were shared by 'Anglicans' and 'puritans' in the first fifteen years of Elizabeth's reign, Richard Greaves nevertheless concluded that this matter, 'came to be one of the most hotly disputed spheres of contention by 1603'.[7]

Two conclusions seem to be common to studies of sabbatarianism written by religious historians. The first is that sabbatarianism was a puritan innovation which began to surface in the 1570s and 1580s and was crystallized into a formal doctrine by the 1590s. The second conclusion is that this doctrine was a source of conflict between Church authorities and puritans that led to an open division by 1603.

Political historians in search of the origins of the Civil War have associated the sabbatarian polemics of the 1640s with the tension religious historians have highlighted in the Elizabethan and early Stuart period. Samuel Gardiner noted that this 'puritan inno-

---

[3] Robert Cox, *The Literature of the Sabbath Question*, 2 vols. (Edinburgh, 1865); *Sabbath Laws and Sabbath Duties* (Edinburgh, 1853); *The Whole Doctrine of Calvin about the Sabbath and the Lords Day* (Edinburgh, 1860).

[4] W. B. Trevelyan, *Sunday* (London, 1903); W. B. Whitaker, *Sunday in Tudor and Stuart Times* (London, 1933).

[5] M. M. Knappen, *Tudor Puritanism* (Chicago, 1970, first ed. 1938), p.442. See also: Max Levy, *Der Sabbath in England* (Leipzig, 1933).

[6] Winton Solberg, *Redeem the Time* (London, 1977), pp.59–60.

[7] Richard L. Greaves, 'The Origins of English Sabbatarian Thought', *Sixteenth Century Journal*, 12 (1981), 19–34 (p.33). Also see John Primus, 'Calvin and the Puritan Sabbath: A Comparative Study', in *Exploring the Heritage of John Calvin*, edited by David E. Holwerda (Grand Rapids, 1976); articles by Richard J. Baukham in *From Sabbath to Lord's Day*, edited by Donald Carson (Grand Rapids, 1982); James T. Dennison, Jr, *The Market Day of the Soul* (Lanham, Maryland, 1983).

vation' was resisted because 'all England had been accustomed from time immemorial to consider that at the close of the service the religious duties of the day were at an end'.[8] He was certain of episcopal opposition to sabbatarianism and cited the Lancashire Book of Sports controversy as an example of the conflicts between the authorities and puritans over this issue. J. R. Tanner draws a similar conclusion in his studies of the period.[9] More recently, G. H. Tupling concurred in his article on causes of the Civil War in Lancashire that the sabbatarian controversy was one of the major grievances motivating puritans to revolt.[10]

Christopher Hill has found sabbatarianism useful in his study of seventeenth-century economic history. He explained that 'protestants and especially Puritans elevated the Sabbath, the *regular* day of rest and meditation suited to the regular and continuous rhythms of modern industrial society: they attacked the very numerous and irregular festivals which had hitherto marked out the seasons'.[11]

More recently, social historians have expanded on a notion insinuated by Heylyn and repeated by Collier.[12] This concept, called by some the 'puritan reformation of manners', portrays puritans, thwarted in their efforts to purify the national Church by the queen and bishops, turning to moral reforms on the local level; attacking the excesses of popular culture, the problems of bastardy, and profanations of the Sabbath. These moral reformers are alleged to have found support among constables and justices of the peace, through whom their concerns were translated into county and corporation orders. The use of sabbatarianism in this historiographical model is of great interest, for it lends further

---

[8] Samuel R. Gardiner, *History of England*, 10 vols. (London, 1883–4) III, 248.

[9] J. R. Tanner, *English Constitutional Conflicts of the Seventeenth Century: 1603–1689* (Cambridge, 1928), p.15.

[10] G. H. Tupling, 'Causes of the Civil War in Lancashire', *Transactions of the Lancashire and Cheshire Antiquarian Society*, 65 (1955), 1–32 (p.13).

[11] Christopher Hill, *Society and Puritanism in Pre-Revolutionary England* (London, 1964), p.146. While only cautiously treated in more recent works, Christopher Hill's thesis has become an essential part of any study on the Sabbath. See Solberg, *passim*; Patrick Collinson, 'The Beginnings of English Sabbatarianism', in *Studies in Church History*, edited by C. W. Dugmore and Charles Duggan, 1 (London, 1964), 207–21; Greaves, *passim*, Keith Sprunger, 'English and Dutch Sabbatarianism and the Development of Puritan Social Theology (1600–1660)', in *Church History*, vol. 51, no. 1 (March, 1982), 24–38.

[12] Collier, *Ecclesiastical History*, VII, 190.

support to the notion that this doctrine was a 'puritan' issue and part of their 'party' agenda.[13]

While one need not deny the value of previous studies of sabbatarianism, there is a problem of emphasis which runs through all these works. Although most historians have acknowledged a medieval background to sabbatarian concerns, they have not taken seriously the existence of a developed sabbatarian doctrine which predates the Reformation. Professor Collinson expressed the view of many when he observed that 'the novelty of the new Sabbatarianism lay in the insistence that the strict observance of the Sabbath was a perpetual necessity, part of man's moral obligation'.[14] But it is impossible to isolate Elizabethan sabbatarianism from its medieval origins.

Complaints against the abuses of Sunday were an English concern throughout the Middle Ages, particularly in the fourteenth and fifteenth centuries. This practical concern that the day was misused by working and recreations, was justified by a developed sabbatarian doctrine, based on the fourth commandment and other portions of scripture. Medieval sabbatarianism was promoted by preachers, incorporated into episcopal and secular discipline, and represented in popular art.

The Elizabethan Church restated the long-established sabbatarian teachings of the pre-Reformation era. Complaints against Sunday abuses and the promotion of this doctrine were not limited to 'puritans', but included archbishops Parker, Grindal, Whitgift, and Abbot, as well as Richard Hooker, John Cosin, and many other prominent Church leaders. Episcopal concern is evident from the writings of bishops, their visitation articles, and the enforcement of sabbatarian orders in the diocesan consistory courts. Extreme sabbatarians were censured by both 'puritan' leaders and bishops. The Hampton Court Conference in 1604, which accentuated many differences between Church authorities and precise protestants, revealed a common concern for the reformation of sabbath abuses. A careful study of the Lancashire *Declaration of Sports* controversy of 1617 reveals that James was

---

[13] Keith Wrightson, 'The Puritan Reformation of Manners' (unpublished Ph.D. dissertation, University of Cambridge, 1973), *passim.*; Keith Wrightson, 'Alehouses, Order, and Reformation in Rural England, 1590–1660', in *Popular Culture and Class Conflict, 1590–1914*, edited by E. and S. Yeo (Harvester Press, Sussex, 1981), 1–27.
[14] Patrick Collinson, *The Elizabethan Puritan Movement* (London, 1967), p.436.

not hostile towards a religious observance of Sunday, but desired to see that his subjects had recourse to lawful recreations after divine service. This was not a 'party' issue; for while some 'puritan' sabbatarians endorsed the use of recreations after divine service, Archbishop Abbot opposed the king's declaration. Evidence from the Elizabethan and early Stuart parliaments reveals enthusiasm for strict sabbatarian bills in both the Lords and the Commons. It was not until the early 1630s that an active anti-sabbatarian campaign was launched by a small group of Laudians, who claimed that Sunday observance was a human convention, and that its use was defined and regulated by the Church authorities. While their intention was to emphasize episcopal authority and defend Archbishop Laud's role in re-issuing the *Declaration of Sports* in 1633, their anti-sabbatarian assertions remained a minority view, even among Laudians. The archbishop's harsh suppression of ministers who refused to read the declaration led many Englishmen to conclude that wickedness was being defended by the king's edict while good Christians were being persecuted. Many of the ministers suppressed exhibited none of the recognized traits of 'puritanism', except in their desire to see the Sabbath observed religiously. Yet given the orthodox nature of sabbatarianism, their dissent should not be regarded as 'puritan' reaction, but the opposition of the faithful to a novel teaching which contradicted God's law and the traditions of the English Church.

Because this work challenges a long-established and cherished historiographical orthodoxy, it is important to state explicitly what is not being questioned. This study does not deny the special attention given to this issue by precisionists – especially Elizabethan presbyterians. There is also no attempt to minimize the sharp differences over the extent of this observance: the length of the sabbath day, the activities to be used, the recreations to be avoided, and the institution of Sunday as the Lord's day.

However, this work does challenge the commonly accepted view that the doctrine of a morally binding Sabbath was a late Elizabethan, 'puritan' innovation that divided precisionists from conformists. It also questions the notion that this doctrine was used in a 'puritan' conspiracy to undermine the authority of the established Church. Rejecting the assertion that this doctrine was a long-standing source of tension, this study reveals that sabbatarian doctrine and discipline were used as a theological football during the 1630s, in efforts to justify two different visions of the English Church: in support of the reformed tradition with its emphasis on scripture as the ultimate authority; and in defence of a 'catholic' vision, with Church authorities recognized as interpreters and arbitrators of doctrine and discipline. The irony is that the defenders of this 'catholic' vision resorted to fraudulent means, distorting the doctrinal tradition of the English Church.

It has become fashionable to talk of the pre-Laudian English Church in terms of consensus rather than conflict, and there is a danger in shifting from one unexamined model to another. Nevertheless, consensus is suggested in Elizabethan and early Stuart evidence; for the tensions which did arise concern peripheral issues and not the doctrine of a morally binding Sabbath. The theological works of Church leaders, as well as the sabbatarian discipline promoted by bishops in their dioceses and in parliament confirm the place of this doctrine in the English Church. Unfortunately, Heylyn succeeded in identifying the Church with a position which conflicted with the orthodoxy of the period, resulting in the perpetuation of a historiographical error for 350 years.

2

Medieval sabbatarianism
and Reformation reaction

The argument used to deny the pre-Reformation origins of the sabbath doctrine rests on two basic assumptions. The first is that medieval rigorism in the observance of Sundays and holy days was based solely on the authority of the Church as defined in canon law. A second and related point concerns the way some historians perceive medieval uses of scripture. Solberg observed that 'the Christian Sabbath was one of many non-scriptural elements present in late medieval religion'.[1] The assumption that the protestant slogan *sola scriptura* marked the beginning of a serious use of scripture, particularly in developing a doctrine of the Sabbath, is apparent in many studies. However, these assumptions are difficult to defend when faced with evidence of medieval sabbatarianism which was grounded in scripture, and the uses made of these sources by Elizabethan sabbatarians.

The first issue to be clarified in any study of sabbatarianism is the definition of sabbath observance. In the last fifty years, most historians have agreed that there was a consensus on this matter in the first fifteen years of Elizabeth's reign. Bishops, clergy, and godly laymen shared a concern that parishioners attend services, perform spiritual exercises, abstain from worldly labours, trading, drunkenness, gluttony, and idleness. The most frequently cited evidence for this concern is the homily, 'Of the Place and Time of Prayer', which was one of the homilies prescribed for use in parishes when a sermon by a licensed minister was not delivered. Exhortations and complaints found in the works of Bishop Pilkington, Alexander Nowell, Thomas Becon, William Kethe, and others are cited to illustrate this consensus.[2] But this common view is thought to have been broken by vociferous 'puritan' polemics in the mid-1570s. John Stockwood, Philip Stubbes, John Northbrooke, and others are cited as the 'puritan' spokesmen who are thought to have introduced a new and more rigorous

[1] Solberg, p.15.   [2] Greaves, pp.19, 22; Hill, p.159; Solberg, p.32.

attitude. These men condemned the use of plays, games, church ales, dancing, working, and many other activities on Sundays. They not only exhorted Englishmen to more rigorous sabbath observance, but called on ecclesiastical and civil authorities to issue injunctions and orders that would achieve that end. This alleged innovation is thought to have lacked the support of officials in the established Church, and its proponents were not successful in reforming episcopal discipline or instigating new national laws. Some historians claim that puritans were more successful at the local level, citing as evidence the appearance of county and corporation orders against sabbath abuses which were issued in the last twenty-five years of Elizabeth's reign.

But the complaints which appeared in the 1570s and 1580s, and the sabbatarian orders that followed were part of a long Christian tradition dating back to the early Church and were particularly evident in fourteenth- and fifteenth-century England. From the early centuries of the Church, believers were taught that Sunday should be observed in rest from worldly pursuits and in the performance of spiritual duties. Both ecclesiastical and secular authorities issued regulations against Sunday abuses; and preachers condemned those who misused the day in ordinary labours or recreations. The works of Elizabethan rigorists contained nothing new, for their medieval counterparts taught that Christians had an obligation to devote the day to physical rest and spiritual activity.

MEDIEVAL SABBATH PRACTICE

While much could be said of the early centuries of the Church, the earliest evidence which interests us here is an apocryphal letter from Christ, sometimes called the 'Epistle on Sunday'. This letter, first reported in the sixth century, was alleged to have fallen from heaven and was sent to instruct Christians in the proper observance of the Lord's day. Abuses of Sunday were condemned, and great calamity was threatened if the day was not observed in a godly fashion. Tempest, lightning, sulphurous fire, flying serpents, and invading pagans were potential consequences of these abuses and all offenders were threatened with eternal damnation. The epistle prohibited lawsuits, trading, travelling, domestic labours, grinding corn, racing, shooting, and swimming.

Exceptions were made for cases of danger and acts of mercy.[3]

This epistle was condemned in a sixth-century letter, written by Licinianus, bishop of Carthagena, who rebuked a fellow bishop for his credulity in accepting its authenticity.[4] However, the letter continued to circulate. At the Lateran Council of 745, a report was submitted to Pope Zachary, which stated that a certain Adalbert was promoting a divine epistle concerning Sunday observance. After reading the letter, the pope stated 'this Adalbert you speak of must have taken leave of his senses; and those who use this mischievous letter (*scelerata epistola*) are a pack of silly children'.[5] However, copies of the epistle continued to circulate and survive in Latin, Anglo-Saxon, Old English, and Old Irish, dating from the eighth to the fourteenth centuries; and it was quoted at length in two sermons attributed to Wulfstan, Archbishop of York (1003–23).

Its impact on medieval England is best demonstrated by the sabbatarian campaign of Eustace, abbot of St Germer de Flay.[6] Eustace, a Norman abbot, came to England in 1200 and 1201 to correct the neglect of various religious practices. Chief among his concerns was a reformation of Sunday observance. Roger of Hovedon and other contemporary chroniclers recorded lengthy accounts of the abbot's activities, and verify his use of the 'Epistle on Sunday' to aid his crusade against Sunday markets and servile labours on that day.[7] The chronicler, Roger of Wendover, reported that Eustace and other preachers were dispatched by the pope to read and preach on this epistle, reproving those who use Sunday for any non-religious activities. The truth of that report is uncertain, but the chroniclers were unanimous in crediting him with a successful mission and great reforms in Sunday observance.[8]

[3] J. G. O'Keeffe, 'Cain Downaig', *Ériu: The Journal of the School of Irish Learning*, 2 (1905), 189–214 (pp.195, 197, 201, 203, 211).

[4] Herbert Thurston, 'The Mediaeval Sunday', *The Nineteenth Century*, 46 (July, 1899), 36–50 (p.37).   [5] *Ibid.*, pp.37–8.

[6] *Ibid.*, pp.37–8; J. L. Cate, 'The English Mission of Eustace of Flay', in *Etudes d'histoire dédiées à la mémoire d'Henri Pirenne* (Brussels, 1937), pp.67–89; R. Priebsch, 'The Chief Sources of Some Anglo-Saxon Homilies', *Otia Merseliana*, 1 (London, 1899), 129–47 (pp.129, 130); *Ibid.*, p.190.

[7] T. E. Bridgett, *History of the Holy Eucharist in Great Britain*, 2 vols. (London, 1881), II, 96.

[8] Cate, 'Eustace of Flay', pp.67–9, 74.

Concern over the neglect of the Sabbath was not limited to this Norman abbot, and miraculous signs of God's displeasure with sabbath-breakers can be found in other sources. On his return from a pilgrimage to the Grande Chartreuse in 1200, St Hugh, bishop of Lincoln, rested for a day at St Omer. There he heard the story of a baker who had kneaded his dough on the previous Sunday and baked it on Monday morning. When the loaves were broken, blood flowed from them. St Hugh ordered a loaf to be broken in his presence. The miracle he witnessed was interpreted as a sign of God's anger at this violation of his law of rest.[9] This medieval story and others like it are part of a genre that continued into the Elizabethan and Stuart period, with God's judgement on sabbath-breakers found in earthquakes, famine, and the destruction of whole towns by fire.[10]

Even more interesting are the polemics against sabbath abuses, found in homilies and treatises during the fourteenth and fifteenth centuries. These works, so reminiscent of Elizabethan polemics, provide striking evidence for a continuity of concern over this issue. In 1362, Simon Islip, archbishop of Canterbury, explained in a constitution for his province that God bade Christians to abstain from works on the seventh day and the Church had added other solemn days; but complained that the reverences of earlier centuries

are now turned into blasphemy, seeing that assemblages, trading and other unlawful pursuits are specially followed upon those days; that which was prepared as a summary of devotion is made into a heap of dissipation, since upon these holy-days the tavern is rather worshipped than the Church, gluttony and drunkenness are more abundant than tears and prayers, men are busied rather with wantonness and contumely than with the leisure of contemplation.

He observed that while working folk were glad to be exempt from labour, they expected to be paid and did not 'sabbatize as they should, to the honour of God'.[11]

John Bromyard, a fourteenth-century Dominican, provided a description of the lax observance of his time, which reads like a sabbatarian lamentation of the Elizabethan period. He observed that while Sundays and holy days should be kept religiously, with abstinence from worldly pursuits, few refrained from these

---

[9] Thurston, pp.41–2.
[10] G. G. Coulton, *The Medieval Village* (Cambridge, 1925), pp.530–1.
[11] *Ibid.*, p.256.

activities. However, he was more concerned with the neglect of spiritual duties. Bromyard explained,

But suppose they neither work nor go to markets, yet how little do they do for their souls. They get up late, and come late to church, and wish to be so little there, that they will urge the priest to be quick because they have a friend coming to dinner. If there should be a sermon about their salvation, they excuse themselves from hearing it, by saying it is getting too late for them to remain...Even the short time that they cannot help remaining in the church they spend in unnecessary talk, forgetting that the house of God is the house of prayer. Then they go away to dinner or to the tavern, and there they are in no hurry, for some spend the whole rest of the day and even till late at night, like the Amalecites eating and drinking and as it were keeping a festival day.[12]

Tippling, dancing, and other pastimes were condemned by these medieval rigorists. One homilist, like his Elizabethan counterpart, condemned those that 'spendeth yvel the tyme that God hath sent hem...running on the holidays to wrestlings, markets, fairs...and dances, to bede-ales, bede-wines and shootyngs, and other such vanities, idle without profit of ghostly fruit'. In place of these, he exhorted his hearers to perform public and private spiritual exercises, and devote a portion of the day to acts of mercy.[13] Robert, abbot of Brunne, in his penitential, *Handlyng Synne*, condemned plays, carols, wrestling, and field sports as desecrations of Sunday.[14]

A very interesting form of evidence for late medieval sabbatarianism are church wallpaintings, which portray Christ on the cross, with the symbols of his crucifixion replaced by ordinary tools of trade and implements used in domestic labour. In some examples these tools simply surround the body; in others the implements inflict wounds on the corpus. These figures, often described as St Sunday, were found in many parishes throughout England and Europe. Their purpose was to impress on laymen the injury inflicted on Christ when his day was misused in worldly pursuits.[15]

---

[12] Bridgett, II, 234. This is a reference to I Kings 25:16.

[13] G. R. Owst, 'The People's Sunday Amusements in the Preaching of Medieval England', *Holborn Review*, n.s., xvii (1926), 32–45 (pp.32–3).

[14] Bernard Manning, *The People's Faith in the Time of Wyclif* (Cambridge, 1919), p. 128; Robert Mannyng, *Handlyng Synne*, edited by Frederick J. Furnivall (London, 1862), p.33.

[15] Christopher Woodforde, *The Norwich School of Glass-painting in the Fifteenth Century* (London, 1950), pp.191–2; Gertrud Schiller, *Iconography of Christian Art*, 2 vols. (London, 1971–2) II, 204; E. Clive Rouse, *Discovering Wall Paintings*, (Shire Publications, 1968 and 1980), p.42; A. Caiger-Smith, *English Medieval Mural Paintings*, (Oxford, 1963), pp.55–8; E. W. Tristram, *English Wall Paintings of the Fourteenth Century*,

The canons and statutes of medieval councils and synods supported the sabbatarian discipline promoted by preachers. One of the earliest ecclesiastical declarations was issued by the second Council of Macon in 585. This statement prohibited labour on the Lord's day, and ordered that 'all be occupied with mind and body in hymns and the praise of God'.[16] The Anglo-Saxon Council of Clovesho, held in 747, ordered that

Sunday is very solemnly to be reverenced; therefore we command that no man dare on that holy day to apply to any worldly work unless for the preparing of his food, except it happen that he must of necessity journey. Then he may ride, or row...on the condition that he hear his mass, and neglect not his prayers.[17]

Other Anglo-Saxon canons appeared in the tenth and eleventh centuries, defining the length of Sunday and prohibitions on markets, work, and carrying goods. In the Northumbrian Priests' Law, the penalties for these violations were fines for freedmen and flogging for slaves.[18] Canons appeared in the thirteenth century requiring priests to warn parishioners against the sin of attending markets and other places of commerce on Sundays and major feast days. Any clergy who countenanced such behaviour were liable to canonical censure and laymen were threatened with excommunication.[19] Fifteen statutes and canons concerning the observance of Sunday and the suppression of markets were issued during the thirteenth century, illustrating an interest which persisted to the end of the Middle Ages.[20]

Concern over proper observance in the fifteenth-century was illustrated by Thomas Arundal, archbishop of Canterbury at the turn of that century. In 1413, he complained to the mayor and the aldermen of London that barbers were violating the sabbath rest. The archbishop observed that these tradesmen,

(London, 1955), p.121. Thanks to Dr Graeme Lawson and Mr Dave Park for these references.

[16] J. A. Hessey, *Sunday, its Origins, History, and Present Obligation* (1860), pp.116–17.

[17] Bridgett, I, 194.

[18] *Councils and Synods: A.D. 871 –1066*, edited by Dorothy Whitelock, M. Brett and C. N. L. Brooke, 2 vols. in 4 (Oxford, 1981), I pt I, 225, 393–4, 463.

[19] James L. Cate, 'The Church and Market Reform in England during the Reign of Henry III', in *Medieval and Historiographical Essays in Honor of James Westfall Thompson*, edited by Cate and Anderson (Chicago, 1938), p.38.

[20] *Councils and Synods: A.D. 1205–1313*, edited by F. M. Powicke and C. R. Cheney, 2 vols. in 4 (Oxford, 1964) II, pt I, pp.35, 174, 194, 204, 297, 320, 410, 461, 465, 647; *Councils and Synods: A.D. 1205–1313*, II, pt 2, pp.1020–1, 1063, 1096–7, 1117; John R. H. Moorman, *Church Life in England in the Thirteenth Century* (Cambridge, 1945), p.69; Thurston, p.40; Bridgett, II, 233; Coulton, *Medieval Village*, p.2.

being without zeal for the law of God and not perceiving that the Lord hath blessed the seventh day and made it holy, and hath commanded that it shall be observed by no abusive pursuit of any servile occupations, but rather by a disuse thereof, in their blindness do keep their houses and shops open on the seventh day, the Lord's day, namely, and do follow their craft on the same, just as busily and in the same way as on any day in the week customary for such work.

He threatened offenders with excommunication and suggested that a city order should support his decree, exacting heavy fines on all offenders. The intensity of Arundal's concern is further demonstrated by his request to the pope that his ordinance be confirmed *ex certa scientia*.[21]

The Church was not alone in its efforts to regulate Sunday observance. Rulers in England from the seventh to the fifteenth centuries issued strict regulations which enforced sabbath discipline.[22] Perhaps the most interesting of these was a statute issued by Henry VI in 1448 against Sunday markets and fairs. Henry condemned such events as abominable offences against God and his saints, who are 'always aiders and singular assisters in our necessitites'. Participants were condemned for not remembering 'the horrible defilement of their souls in buying and selling, with many deceitful lies and false perjury, with drunkenness and strifes, and so especially withdrawing themselves and their servants from divine service'.[23]

Many more examples from homilies, penitentials, canons, and statutes could be cited to illustrate the sabbatarian concerns of the episcopate, clergy, and secular authorities. However, enough evidence has been presented to demonstrate that the rigorist polemics and regulations of the Elizabethan period were not new, but part of an identifiable social and religious pattern that had existed in England for centuries. While making no pretence to provide a comprehensive study of medieval attitudes towards Sunday observance, one may conclude nevertheless that from the earliest centuries of Christianity, the Church taught that believers

---

[21] Thurston, pp.45–6; James Wylie, *The Reign of Henry V*, 3 vols. (Cambridge, 1914), I, 243; British Library, Cott. MS Cleop.c.4, fol. 216. Arundal's successor, Henry Chichele, also issued orders against Sunday labours. See Hessey, p.121.

[22] Coulton, *Medieval Village*, pp.530–1; *Councils and Synods: A.D. 871–1066*, I pt I, pp.101, 310, 311, 478, 440–1; Cate, 'Market Reform', pp.49–51; W. B. Whitaker, *Sunday in Tudor and Stuart Times* (London, 1933), p.13; W. Denton, *England in the Fifteenth Century* (London, 1888), p.219.   [23] Bridgett, II, 235; Thurston, p.45.

should rest from worldly pursuits on Sunday and devote the day to spiritual exercises. This conclusion is supported by Bernard Manning's study of fourteenth-century English religion. He observed that 'when modern writers adduce the "freedom" of the old English Sunday as proof of the easy "liberal" attitude of the medieval Church they are guilty of the fundamental mistake of imagining that the Church sanctioned what it was obliged – after many protests – to tolerate'.[24]

Elizabethan and early Stuart sabbatarians recognized their continuity with these medieval predecessors and did not hesitate to use medieval canons and statutes to support the doctrine they preached. In John Deacon's complaint against pedlars selling on Sunday, published in 1585, he explained,

You imagine the ordinary good lawes of our Land have hitherto had no regard at all for the Sabaoth, wherin you are fully deceived. For, if the penaultie appointed for the breache heerof were dulye inflicted upon the offenders, I beleeve they would saye they had law enough for their mony. Now, for proofe heerof, besides other good lawes, peruse the statute at large of Henry the sixt, and the same will tel you, that if any Faires and markets be kept upon good Friday, Corpus Christi day, the Ascension day, All Saints day, Whitson day, Trinitie daye, or any other Sondaye, goods or Mercandies in them be showed: the owners thereof shall forfeit all their said goods so showed to the Lord of the Libertie, etc.[25]

Deacon's use of a fifteenth-century law to support his plea for reforms in the use of Sunday markets and fairs clearly illustrates that Elizabethan sabbatarians were not only aware of pre-Reformation rigorism, but cited these precedents to strengthen their arguments. The use made of these regulations in the sabbatarian works of Nicholas Bownde, John Sprint, Robert Cleaver, and many others confirms the self-conscious incorporation of medieval precedents in works by Elizabethan and Stuart protestants to justify their position and prove the continuity of sabbatarian discipline.

Perhaps the most unexpected use of medieval evidence is the attention given to St Sunday wallpaintings. Despite our assumptions about protestant iconoclasm, these paintings were cited by some post-Reformation sabbatarians with approval. In a letter written to Samuel Ward of Sidney Sussex College, Nicholas

[24] Manning, p.124.

[25] John Deacon, *A Treatise, Intituled, Nobody is My Name, Which Beareth Everi-bodies Blame* (London, 1585), sig.G9v.

Estwick, rector of Warkton, Northamptonshire, expressed concern that the recreations approved by the 1633 Book of Sports were rarely used without some occasion of sin. He observed that,

I can scarcely believe, that they [the approved sports] and the sanctification of the Sabbath are compatible in our villages and do greatly fear that a godly man heerafter may give that censure which Doctor Jackson hath averred in Print. He saw on Wickam Church in Buckinghamshire the Picture of Saint Sunday on the walls many times stabbed through and he gave his interpretation thereof that Christ hath received of Christians more wounds on Sunday than he did of the Jews.[26]

This use of a medieval painting is one of the most striking examples of the ease with which post-Reformation sabbatarians appropriated medieval precedents to support their position.

The account presented above provides a context for the sabbatarian polemics of the Elizabethan period. Medieval homilies, penitentials, and ecclesiastical and secular regulations illustrate that the post-Reformation developments were not unique or spontaneous. The use made of medieval evidence by protestant sabbatarians confirms that these writers were not only aware of these precedents, but did not hesitate to use this material to prove continuity. Medieval and Elizabethan sabbatarians shared a common concern that the day be spent in worship and private devotions, with rest from all worldly labours and trading and abstinence from recreations and popular celebrations.

Nevertheless, it is not enough simply to demonstrate the continuity of preoccupations with sabbath observance between the medieval and post-Reformation Church of England. The historiographical tradition being criticized here rests on the conclusion that post-Reformation sabbatarianism was founded on a fundamentally different theological base than that of the medieval Church. The concern of churchmen in medieval England rested, it is claimed, on the Church's law, while the doctrine of 'puritans' was founded on the law of God, as set forth in the decalogue and other portions of the Old and New Testaments. This assumption must now be examined.

[26] Bodleian Library, Tanner MS 71, fol. 186.

MEDIEVAL SABBATARIAN DOCTRINE

In his *History of the Sabbath*, Peter Heylyn claimed that medieval Sunday observance was based on ecclesiastical authority, with prohibitions on labour and recreations, and the requirement to use spiritual exercises on that day imposed on Christians by canon law. He observed that the Reformation brought a relaxation of these 'legalistic' restrictions, but this observance continued to be based on Church authority, making no great distinction between Sundays and holy days. With this as a foundation, Heylyn asserted that in the 1580s and 1590s puritans developed a new sabbatarian doctrine based on scripture, claiming that the fourth commandment was a moral law and as binding on Christians as the rest of the decalogue. He emphasized their rejection of Church authority in this matter and noted that their refusal to accept holy days had caused these sabbatarians to clash with ecclesiastical authorities, who opposed this 'puritan' innovation.

Subsequent studies of sabbatarianism have accepted Heylyn's account of this matter. Christopher Hill observed that 'the Bible had been read for centuries without sabbatarian inferences being drawn by significant sections of the population'.[27] Although Solberg was more cautious, he concluded that while 'none of the constituent elements was entirely novel...the theory as a whole marked a significant break with the past'.[28] Professor Collinson and others have expressed similar views.[29]

However, a closer examination of patristic and medieval sabbatarianism suggests a very different conclusion. In the first three centuries of Christianity, theologians like Irenaeus, Justin, and Tertullian, adopted the method of the Sermon on the Mount, interpreting the sabbath precept as a spiritual rest from sin.[30] But during the fourth century this allegorical interpretation gave way to an analogical explanation, with theologians applying the sabbath laws of the Old Testament to the Christian Sunday. Ephraem Syrus, Eusebius of Caesarea, and other theologians of that century elaborated this analogy.[31] The notion that Old Testament prohibitions against sabbath labours applied to the

---

[27] Hill, p.146.   [28] Solberg, p.58.   [29] Collinson, *Puritan Movement*, p.436.
[30] Willy Rordorf, *Sunday* (London, 1968), pp.102–4.
[31] *Ibid.*, pp.169–71; Roger Beckwith and Wilfrid Stott, *This Is the Day* (London, 1978), p.76.

Christian observance of Sunday was a theme which ran thoughout the Middle Ages. The Christian casuistry developed by early medieval theologians drew comparisons between Jewish and Christian practice: if Jews kept their Sabbath strictly, how much more should Christians observe the Lord's day in abstinence from worldly labours and in spiritual exercises.[32]

This observance was regarded as a divine institution, rooted in scripture and confirmed by the many miracles performed on the Lord's day. While secular and ecclesiastical authorities issued canons and statutes to regulate the day, they were human agents, administering divine law. Although Christians were freed from the observance of the Saturday Sabbath and the more rigorous prohibitions of the Old Testament laws, the sabbath precept still required Christians to set aside time for worship and to rest from their ordinary labours so that spiritual duties could be performed. The second Council of Macon in 585 cautioned against judaizing practices in Sunday observance; but defended the prohibition of ordinary labours, noting that the Lord's day is a day of perpetual rest, a teaching shadowed out for Christians in the seventh day rest of the law and prophets.[33] A sixth-century homilist implied this obligation when he observed that,

There are people who with charitable intention indeed, say on Sunday, 'Come on, let us today help the poor with their work'. They do not consider that wherein they would do well, they do in fact commit a sin. Do you wish to help the poor? Then do not rob God of his day.[34]

The author of the 'Epistle on Sunday' did not use the Mosaic sabbath laws, but claimed that the day was divinely ordained because of the miracles performed on Sunday. Twenty-three miracles were noted, including the creation of heaven and Christ's conception, birth, and resurrection.[35] This became a common means of proving the divine institution of Sunday in medieval theology, and was to remain so in Reformation and post-Reformation sabbatarianism as well.

But the application of Jewish sabbath laws remained an important part of medieval justifications for strict Sunday observance. Canons issued during the reign of Charlemagne against servile work on Sunday were based on the 'precept of the Lord'.[36]

[32] Rordorf, p.172.   [33] Hessey, pp.116–7.   [34] Rordorf, p.169n.
[35] O'Keeffe, p.199.   [36] Hessey, pp.117–8.

In the twelfth century, Bernard, abbot of Clairvaux, grounded both Sunday and holy day observance in the sabbath precept: '*Spirituale obsequium Deo praebetur in observantia sanctarum solemnitatum, unde tertium praeceptum contexitur*'.[37] In the same century, Petrus Alphonsus referred to the Lord's day as the Christian Sabbath.[38] This analogical interpretation, combined with accounts of the many miracles which explained the change of the Sabbath from Saturday to Sunday, became the most common theological explanation of this doctrine in the early medieval period. However, while this approach remained a part of Church teaching throughout the Middle Ages and early Modern period, thirteenth-century scholastic theologians introduced a new explanation which was to influence not only medieval theology, but protestant theology as well.

The scholastics discarded the allegorical and analogical interpretations of the sabbath precept, defining instead the moral and ceremonial parts of this law. Thomas Aquinas presented the most thorough explanation of this concept in his *Summa Theologica*. He stated that,

the commandment to keep holy the sabbath is partly moral, partly ceremonial. It is moral in that man should set aside some time in his life for concentration upon the things of God...But it is a ceremonial precept on the grounds that in this commandment a particular time is determined in order to signify creation.[39]

Aquinas explained that the sabbath commandment logically followed from the other precepts of the first table, for by it men were firmly established in genuine religion. The commandment was given to man under the symbol of God's rest from creation, a day set aside for the worship of God. He divided the duties of this precept in two parts: that one should worship God and rest from servile labours. He excluded from servile labours those activities required for bodily health, for one's self, neighbour, or beast, and in the avoidance of damage to property.

However, Aquinas made a distinction between the moral obligation to set some time aside for worship and a direct transfer of Jewish sabbath obligations to the Lord's day. He explained that, 'in the New Law the keeping of Sunday supplants that of the

---

[37] *Ibid.*, pp.119–20.   [38] *Ibid.*, p.120.
[39] Thomas Aquinas, *Summa Theologica*, 2a2ae, 122, 4 (Blackfriars Edition, 1972, p.305).

Sabbath, not by virtue of the precept of the law, but through determination by the Church and the custom of the Christian people'.[40] The strict observance of the Old Law was not as binding on Christians, partly due to necessity, and because the strictest part of this practice was a figure in the Old Law which is not part of the New Law.

Aquinas' position was to be crucial for all subsequent developments of sabbatarianism, and it is vital that it should be correctly understood. In this discourse, he made the sabbath precept part of the Christian's moral obligation, but explained that the day had been shifted from the Jewish *Sabbath* to the Christian *Sunday*, and thus avoided the obligation of observing all the Jewish sabbath laws. This Thomistic distinction between the moral and ceremonial parts of the sabbath precept was accepted by nearly all subsequent sabbatarian writers. It was this scholastic distinction which became the framework for most Elizabethan and Stuart treatments of this doctrine. However, Thomas was silent concerning the reasons for changing the day from Saturday to Sunday, making no use of the biblical 'precedents' employed by earlier sabbatarians to explain the shift of days. Yet this omission does not necessarily mean that Thomas acknowledged the Church's power to change the day to any other time of week. This ambiguity persisted in medieval statutes and canons.

Examples of this problem can be found in the canons of the Lambeth Council in 1281, the synodal constitutions of Exeter in 1287, and in the canons of the Synod of York in 1466.[41] These ecclesiastical laws emphasized the moral obligation to keep some time for worship, but reserved for the Church the right to set the time and regulate the activities of the day. The canon issued at York in 1466 stated that:

By this [commandment] the observance of the Christian worship is enjoined, which is of obligation alike on the clergy and laity. But it is to be known here that the obligation to keep holyday on the legal Sabbath, according to the form of the Old Testament, wholly expired with the other ceremonies of the law. And that under the New Testament it is sufficient to keep holyday for the Divine worship on the Lord's Days, and other solemn days ordained to be kept as holydays by the authority of the Church; wherein the manner of keeping holy day is to be taken, not from the Jewish superstition, but from the directions of the Canons.[42]

[40] *Ibid.*, p.309.
[41] *Councils and Synods:* A.D. *1205–1313*, II, pt 2, 1020–1.   [42] Hessey, p.126.

While Thomas was silent, other theologians spoke out. These writers treated Sunday observance as a divine institution, which the Church had no authority to modify or change. Robert Mannyng, abbot of Brunne in the early fourteenth century, made this point in his penitential. In his exposition of the sabbath precept, Mannyng set Sunday apart from other holy days, explaining that,

> Of al þe festys þat yn holy chyrche are
> Holy sunday men oghte to spare;
> Holy sunday ys byfore alle fre
> Þat euere ȝyt were, or euere shal be.
> For þe pope may þurghe hys powere
> Turne þe halydays yn þe ȝere
> How as he wyl, at hys owne wyl,
> But, þe sunday shal stondë styl.[43]

This distinction between Sunday as a divine institution and holy days as creations of the Church, is also found in a fifteenth-century English exposition of the decalogue.[44] The author of *Dives and Pauper*, after explaining the moral and ceremonial parts of the sabbath precept, stated that Sunday succeeded the Sabbath, because of the miracles performed on that day and noted that Holy Church, through the teaching of the Holy Ghost, 'hath ordeynyd the Sonday to ben halwyd for the reste that mankende schal takyn aftir sexe agys of this world on the Sonday, whiche rest and Sabat nevyr schal hav ende'.[45] This sabbatarian view was implicit in Archbishop Arundal's letter against the barbers of London in 1413. He condemned these tradesmen for 'being without zeal for the law of God, and not perceiving how that the Lord hath blessed the seventh day and made it holy, and hath commanded that it shall be observed by no abusive pursuit of any servile occupations'.[46]

Attempts to emphasize the moral obligation to keep the Christian Sabbath sometimes took extreme forms; with some sabbatarians claiming that it was a greater sin to work on Sunday than to kill a man. This notion was derived from the scholastic concept that sins against God had a malice not intrinsic to sins

---

[43] Robert Mannyng, p.27.
[44] James F. Royster, 'A Middle English Treatise on the Ten Commandments', *Studies in Philology*, 6 (1910), 5–39 (p.20).
[45] *Dives and Pauper*, edited by Priscilla H. Barnum (London, 1976), 1 pt 1, 267.
[46] Thurston, p.46.

against man. This extremist view was ridiculed by Erasmus in *Praise of Folly*, noting that these sabbatarians claimed 'that it is a lesser crime to butcher a thousand men than for a poor man to cobble his shoe on a single occasion on the Lord's day'.[47] Precisely this form of radical sabbatarianism was to persist into the Elizabethan period and has often been singled out as a manifestation of the 'new', 'puritan' doctrine of the Sabbath. However, Elizabethan and Stuart sabbatarians dissociated themselves from such extremes, regarding them as judaizing tendencies.[48]

The most striking evidence of this developed medieval doctrine of a morally binding Sabbath is found in two fifteenth-century treatises. These treatises combine the moral-ceremonial interpretation of the sabbath precept, with a defence of Sunday as the divinely ordained day of worship and rest. One of these works, a short Latin treatise, thought to have been written by a German Carthusian, begins with references to four texts of scripture that direct Christians to obey the decalogue. Among these texts was Christ's injunction 'if you would enter eternal life, keep the commandements'.[49] The writer found reasons for keeping the sabbath precept in divine law, natural law, the statutes of the Church, and the end of the precept: to provide a time for men to rest from their worldly labours and worship God. These points were supported by several references to scripture,[50] the *Summa Theologica*, and Church Councils. The imprimatur at the end of the treatise testifies to the theological soundness of this fifteenth-century sabbatarian doctrine.[51]

The other work is an English treatise, also dating from the fifteenth century, which addresses the question, 'How mighte we change our saboth from saterday to sunday'. This writer provided a scholastic explanation of the ceremonial and moral parts of the sabbath precept, stating that keeping the Saturday Sabbath was ceremonial and passed away. But he denied that to keep some time did not mean keeping any time or any day. The Holy Ghost had instructed the Church to keep Sunday, through the many miracles performed on that day. The writer concluded by stating that Christ

[47] Erasmus, *Praise of Folly*, translated by Betty Radice (Penguin Books, 1971), p.155–6.
[48] Collinson, 'English Sabbatarianism', p.208; Greaves, 'Origins', p.26.
[49] Matt. 19:17.
[50] Ex. 20, Lev. 23, Matt. 12, Acts 1, I Macc. 2, Matt. 6, Prov. 11, Ex. 23, John 7.
[51] British Library, Additional MS 18007, fols.149–52v. I wish to thank Dr Damian Leader for his assistance with this source.

had claimed power over all things, and had appointed the Lord's day by his actions.[52]

It is simply not possible to draw any fundamental theological distinction between the medieval and post-Reformation doctrines of the Sabbath. The moral obligation to keep the Sabbath was a concept as familiar to the fifteenth-century Englishman as the seventeenth-century protestant. Much more attention could be given to the medieval antecedents of this doctrine; but enough evidence has been presented here to demonstrate that Heylyn's account of medieval sabbatarianism is wrong. While Elizabethan polemics against Sunday abuses have been treated as the precursors of a 'new' theological development, they were in fact part of a religious and social pattern which had existed in England for centuries. The sabbatarian orders of the post-Reformation period have been identified as signs of subversive 'puritan' activity; yet sabbatarians found ample precedent in medieval tradition. Although early medieval sabbatarianism had been fostered by the spurious 'Epistle on Sunday', theological developments from the thirteenth century to the seventeenth century made use of many passages of scripture to defend the sabbath doctrine. No fundamental distinction can be made between medieval and post-Reformation sabbatarianism based on the use of biblical texts; for scripture was the foundation for this doctrine in both periods. It must be emphasized that post-Reformation sabbatarianism did not appear until after an initial rejection of this doctrine by the early reformers. However, their objections had less to do with the doctrine itself, than with the way Catholic apologists used it in polemics.

REFORMATION REACTION

The early sixteenth century reformers on the continent and in England rejected the Catholic Church's claim to be the only true source of spiritual authority and orthodox teaching. Among the many doctrines called into question was the Church's teaching that believers are morally bound to observe Sunday and required to use the spiritual exercises prescribed and enforced by ecclesiastical authorities. Emphasizing Christian freedom, many early reformers rejected the scholastic concept of a morally binding Sabbath as unscriptural and a hindrance to Christian liberty. Yet the transition

[52] British Library, Harl. 2339, fols. 104v-116r.

from ecclesiastical 'subversives' to 'establishment figures' caused some first generation and most second and third generation reformers to reassert the divine imperative to observe one day in seven. This was particularly true in Zurich and Geneva. These two protestant centres, which exercised a profound influence on the Elizabethan Church, adopted the scholastic interpretation of the sabbath precept. Our purpose here is to examine how continental and English reformers explained sabbath observances, tracing the movement from allegorical and analogical interpretations back to the scholastic explanation of this observance.

Luther and Calvin

With Luther's appeal to *sola scriptura* in evaluating the validity of doctrine, came many theological problems. One which he had to face in the early years of the Reformation was extreme sabbatarianism. With greater attention being given to the Bible, came an increased interest in the implications of Old Testament laws on Christians. Some protestants gave particular attention to the sabbath regulations. Luther's volatile former associate, Andrew Karlstadt, took up this issue while under the influence of the Zwickau prophets, and published in 1524 the first protestant treatise on the Sabbath, entitled *Von dem Sabbat und gebotten Feyertagen*. Karlstadt divided his study into two parts, the first emphasizing the importance of a day of rest, and incorporating many of the Mosaic regulations on this matter. The second portion concerned the inward 'sabbath rest', in which Christians must devote their time in 'Langweiligkeit, Mussigkeit, Gelassenheit'. He asserted that, 'It were well for a man that on the sabbath he sat with his head in his hands and abased himself, and confessed his unholiness and sinfulness with lamentation'.[53]

While Karlstadt's sabbatarianism proved a problem in Wittenberg, a much more extreme position was developing in Silesia and Moravia, with the sabbatarian Anabaptism of Oswald Glait and Andrew Fischer. These men called for a return to the Saturday Sabbath, along with other Jewish practices which they claimed were laws binding Christians as well as Jews.[54]

---

[53] Gordon Rupp, 'Andrew Karlstadt and Reformation Puritanism', *Journal of Theological Studies*, n.s. vol. 10, (1959), 308–26 (pp.318–19).

[54] Martin Luther, *Works*, edited by Jaroslav Pelikan (St Louis, 1960), 2, p.361; G. H. Williams, *The Radical Reformation* (London, 1962), pp.257, 401.

Luther was careful to counter this literalism in his commentaries, sermons, and treatises on various matters, adopting two Augustinian arguments to deal with the problem of the sabbath precept and laws relating to the Sabbath. In one argument he denied that the sabbath precept applied to Christians in its literal sense, because reverencing the seventh day had no place in natural law, the rule written on the hearts of all men. However, Luther did argue that this precept was important as a shadow of our eternal rest from sin. Luther made much of this allegorical interpretation, explaining that what the Jews lived out in an arid, external legalism, Christians were to transform into an inward sabbath, resting from sin every day of the week. Yet, because of man's need to set aside specific times for worship and reflection, Luther encouraged his followers to use faithfully those times appointed by religious and civil authorities for corporate worship and meditation.[55]

While Luther's treatment of the Sabbath was intended to emphasize his concepts of interior religion and Christian liberty, they had other ramifications. Most significant for this study was the implicit rejection of scholastic claims that the Church was the vehicle of the Holy Ghost in transferring the Sabbath from Saturday to Sunday. By presenting Sunday observance as an ecclesiastical convention, he reduced to human tradition what had formerly been regarded as a divine institution. His rejection of the moral-ceremonial interpretation of the sabbath precept, in favour of an allegorical interpretation left no basis for the divine institution of a particular day or any moral imperative to observe it.

Like Luther, John Calvin taught that the principal meaning of the sabbath precept was found in the believer's obligation to rest from sin. However, unwilling to reject the emphasis on external observance found in this commandment, he incorporated the concept of a 'spiritual rest' and a day of worship into an analogical

[55] Luther, *Works*, 2, pp.361–2; Luther, *Works* (St Louis, 1960), 9, pp.81–2; Luther, *Works* (St Louis, 1963), 26, p.330; Luther, *Works*, edited by E. T. Bachmann (Philadelphia, 1960), 35, pp.164–6; Luther, *Works*, edited by Conrad Bergendoff (Philadelphia, 1958), 40, pp.93–4; Luther, *Works*, edited by Jaroslav Pelikan (St Louis, 1956), 13, p.25; Luther, *Works*, edited by James Atkinson (Philadelphia, 1966), 44, pp.71–2; Luther, *Works*, edited by H. C. Oswald (St Louis, 1972), 17, p.293; Luther, *Works*, edited by Franklin Sherman (Philadelphia, 1971), 47, pp.92–3; Luther, *Works*, edited by E. W. Gritsch (Philadelphia, 1966), 41, p.67.

interpretation of this precept. Throughout his commentaries, the Sabbath was treated as the outward sign of a spiritual mystery, our rest from sin, which was revealed by Christ. The true 'sabbatism' of Christians is a spiritual rest from sin every day of the week.[56] Yet in his *Institutes*, 'Catechism', and 'Commentary on Genesis', Calvin stated that the allegorical treatment of the Sabbath was only a portion of this precept's meaning. While the principal object of this commandment was a spiritual rest from sin, two other points could be found.

One of the practical objectives of this precept was the 'preservation of ecclesiastical polity', by meeting corporately at certain times to worship and perform spiritual exercises. While emphasizing that Christians 'should have nothing to do with a superstitious observance of days', Calvin explained that, 'religious meetings are enjoined [on] us by the word of God; their necessity, experience itself sufficiently demonstrates'. Because the purpose of the sabbath rest is to free Christians for spiritual duties, 'we have an equal necessity for the Sabbath with the ancient people, so that on one day we may be free, and thus the better prepared to learn and to testify our faith'.[57] The by-product was the rest given to servants. Calvin explained that this portion of the precept stipulated that some relaxation should be given to those under the power of others on appointed days of worship.[58]

In his commentary of Genesis, Calvin explained that resting every seventh day had a symbolic importance; for the number seven represents perfection.[59] However, Calvin denied that the Church was in bondage to a seventh day rest. He also rejected the scholastic division of this precept into ceremonial and moral parts. He explained that by using this description of the three objects of this commandment,

we get quit of the trifling of the false prophets, who in later times instilled Jewish ideas into the people, alleging that nothing was abrogated but what was ceremonial in the commandment...while the moral part remains, viz., the observance of one day in seven. But this is nothing else than to insult the Jews, by changing the day, and yet mentally attributing to it the same sanctity; thus retaining the same typical distinction of days as had place among the Jews.[60]

---

[56] John Calvin, *The Whole Doctrine of Calvin about the Sabbath and the Lord's day*, edited by Robert Cox (Edinburgh, 1860), pp.17, 25–6, 42, 62, 63, 69–70.

[57] *Ibid.*, pp.8, 77, 81–2.   [58] *Ibid.*, pp.8, 78, 82.

[59] *Ibid.*, p.7.   [60] *Ibid.*, pp.83–4.

He explained that the Sabbath had been abolished and the Lord's day appointed to avoid superstitious observance and to retain order and decency in the Church. Sunday had not been chosen by the early Christians without good reason; for Christ's resurrection on that day accomplished the true rest symbolized by the Jewish Sabbath and served as a warning to Christians against adhering to that shadowy ceremony.[61] However, Calvin did not acknowledge any obligation to continue Sunday observance. There are accounts which suggest that Calvin even had consultations about transferring the day of worship from Sunday to Thursday to make this point. While these stories are of doubtful authenticity, they do not conflict with his attitude towards the keeping of a particular day.[62]

Calvin, like Luther, attempted to interpret the sabbath precept in a manner which excluded the moral-ceremonial categories established by the scholastics. Yet his emphasis on the 'spiritual rest' did not lead to a neglect of the practical aspects of this precept. Calvin regarded the day of worship and rest for servants as a divine imperative, basing this obligation on an analogical interpretation of this precept, using the rationale that if these practical provisions were necessary for the Jews, they are needed by Christians as well. In this way, Calvin avoided the moral-ceremonial categories while nevertheless asserting the divine imperative to observe the practical points of this commandment. Thus Calvin concurred with Luther in condemning the scholastic interpretation, while justifying his own emphasis on the external worship and rest needed to structure a Christian society.

Geneva after Calvin

While Calvin rejected the moral-ceremonial interpretation, those who followed him in Geneva did not. Theodore Beza, Calvin's successor, used this explanation in his interpretation of the sabbath precept, stating that

the fourth commandment, concerning the sanctification of every seventh day, was ceremonial, so far as it respected the particular day of rest and legal services; but that, as regards the worship of God, it was a precept of the moral law, which is perpetual and unchanging during the present life. That day of rest had stood, indeed, from the creation of the world to the resurrection of our Lord, which

---

[61] *Ibid.*, p.83.   [62] *Ibid.*, p.IV.

being as another creation of a new spiritual world (according to the language of the prophets), was made the occasion (the Holy Spirit, beyond doubt, directing the apostles) for assuming instead of the Sabbath of the former age, or the seventh day, the first day of this world...Therefore the assemblies of the Lord's day are of apostolical and truly divine tradition.[63]

Beza claimed that this apostolic and divine institution was tarnished by the legalism of later tradition, till Sunday observance degenerated into 'mere Judaism'.[64]

Beza's summary of the scholastic interpretation, with its emphasis on the moral and perpetual nature of this precept and divine institution of Sunday, stands in stark contrast to the teaching of Calvin. Yet this interpretation became the established position of Geneva. In a work entitled *Proposition and Principles of Divinitie*, students of the Geneva Academy endorsed the scholastic interpretation, with the Netherlander Jan Utenbogaert defending this position. The Welsh extremist, John Penry, translated this work, which was published in Edinburgh in 1591.[65] It asserted that the sabbath precept began with God's rest after creation on the seventh day. Despite man's fall this commandment continued; but the provisions found in that law were both moral and ceremonial. The ceremonial parts were temporary, to teach the law, while the moral parts endured forever. The ceremonial side of this precept was the appointing of the Saturday Sabbath, the sacrifices to be performed on that day, and the strict rest from all servile labours. Calvin's summary of the divine imperatives was used to describe the moral side of this precept. Sunday was established by the apostles, guided by the Holy Ghost, as a memorial of Christ's resurrection. Unlike Calvin, it was concluded that this apostolic tradition must be perpetually observed. Holy days were allowed, but it was thought that these should be few, to avoid abuse and superstition.[66]

While Luther's impact on English protestantism was fleeting, those who succeeded Calvin in Geneva exercised a profound influence on Elizabethan theology. Dr R. T. Kendall has suggested that Beza and later Calvinists influenced the way English theologians used and interpreted Calvin, referring specifically to

---

[63] *Ibid.*, p.88.   [64] *Ibid.*, p.88.
[65] Collinson, 'English Sabbatarianism', p.214.
[66] *Propositions and Principles of Divinity*, translated by John Penry (Edinburgh, 1591), pp.78–9.

Calvin's doctrine of predestination.[67] The same observation can be usefully applied to later Genevan teaching on the Sabbath. Using the scholastic interpretation, Beza and later Calvinists reasserted a concept their master had specifically rejected. The impact of this shift is evident in Elizabethan sabbatarianism.

Zurich

If one searched for the continental centre which exercised the greatest influence on the Elizabethan Church, Geneva's greatest rival would be Zurich. This city, which welcomed the future bishops Sandys, Pilkington, Parkhurst, and others, not only provided refuge from Marian persecution, but also supplied encouragement and advice when the English refugees returned to roles of leadership in the Elizabethan Church. Ulrich Zwingli's successor, Heinrich Bullinger, not only influenced the leaders of the English Church, but his collected sermons, known as the *Decades*, were translated into English and under Whitgift became required reading for all clergy below the status of M.A. These homilies were also prescribed for use in parishes when a licensed preacher was not present to give a sermon.[68] Bullinger used the scholastic interpretation in his sermon on the fourth precept, making his work crucial for any study of Elizabethan sabbatarianism.

Bullinger rejected Luther's notion that sabbath observance was given to the Jews and not to the gentiles, noting that 'Remember' in the sabbath precept harked back to an earlier commandment given first to the ancient fathers and renewed in the decalogue. In his sermon on *The Ceremonial Lawes of God*, Bullinger explained that,

the Sabbath was observed by a natural and divine law ever from the first creation of the world: and is the chiefe of al other holy daies. For it was not then first ordeined by Moses, when the ten commandements were given by God from heaven. For the keeping of the Sabbath was received of the Saintes immediately from the beginning of the worlde.[69]

Bullinger found three 'significations' in this precept: first, the spiritual and continual sabbath, which is the believer's rest from

[67] R. T. Kendall, *Calvin and English Calvinism to 1649* (Oxford, 1979), *passim*.
[68] Collinson, 'English Sabbatarianism', p.211.
[69] Henry Bullinger, *Fiftie Godlie and Learned Sermons* (London, 1577), p.351.

sin and submission to God; second, the outward institution of religion; and third, the reminder that God alone sanctifies those who worship his name. He treated the first and third points very briefly and devoted most of his study to the outward institution of religion.[70]

Because the worship of God cannot be without a time, Bullinger explained that God appointed a certain time for his people to abstain from their ordinary occupations so that they might attend to spiritual matters. These spiritual labours were the public reading and exposition of scripture, public prayers and common petitions, the administration of the sacraments, and 'the gathering of every man's benevolence'.[71] God gave six days for labour, but required one day for himself. Bullinger noted that this precept specifically charged the heads of household to enforce this precept, by giving rest to those under his care, so that they might have bodily refreshment and time for spiritual exercises. This rest included beasts and cattle as well as servants. God gave his own example in his rest on the seventh day after creating the world. Denying that the sabbath rest was a hindrance to men's worldly affairs, Bullinger asserted that because God blessed the sabbath day, he would honour those who kept his precept. Those who despised the sabbath rest and used their ordinary labours were condemned, explaining that they 'do erre from the truth, as far as heaven is wide'.[72]

Bullinger explained that the sabbath precept was ceremonial and abrogated in so far as it was joined to Jewish ceremonies and tied to a certain time. However, it was perpetual in its provision for the exercise of true religion and godliness, establishment of seemly order in the church, provision for Christian charity, and rest for families, giving time to instruct one's household in true religion. The primitive Church changed the sabbath day to avoid the appearance of imitating the Jews, and changed it to the first day of the week in memory of Christ's resurrection. He explained that,

Although we doe not in any parte of the Apostles writings, find any mention made that this sundaye, was commaunded us to be kept holy, yet for because in this precept of the first table: we are commaunded to have a care of religion and the exercising of outwarde godlinesse, it would be against al godlinesse and Christian charitie, if wee would denie to sanctifie the Sunday: especially, since

[70] *Ibid.*, pp.136–44.   [71] *Ibid.*, p.137.   [72] *Ibid.*, pp.138–9.

the outward worship of god can not consist without an appointed time and space of holy rest.[73]

Bullinger did not claim that Sunday was a divine institution, adopting instead the position held by Aquinas. He grudgingly conceded that this precept might apply to the major feast days as well, but rejected those holy days held in honour of 'anie creatures', explaining that 'the Lorde will have holie dayes to be solemnized and kept to himselfe alone'.[74]

Bullinger took care to explain that the Sabbath was not broken by labour performed for any urgent necessity. The Sabbath was made for the preservation, not the destruction of man. Labour necessary for the preservation of life and property was not a violation of the Sabbath. Yet he warned against the use of labours under the pretence of necessity, when men 'exercise the works of greedie covetousnes, and not of sincere holinesse'.[75]

Bodily labours were not the only way men violated the Sabbath. The Lord's day was abused by pursuing 'fleshly pleasures', using dicing, drinking, dancing, and idleness, doing the works of the devil rather than giving themselves to God's service. Even good men and women violated this day if they did not enforce the observance on Sunday in their own household.[76]

Bullinger charged the Christian magistrate with the responsibility to enforce this observance in his jurisdiction. He explained that,

The peeres of Israell, and all the people of God, did stone to death (as the Lord commaunded them) the man that disobediently did gather stickes on the sabboth daie. Why then should it not be lawful for a Christian Magistrate to punish by bodily imprisonment, by losse of goods, or by death, the despisers of religion, of the true and lawfull worship done to God, and of the sabbath day?[77]

Bullinger's use of the scholastic explanation, his denunciation of sabbath abuses, and plea to secular authority for the reformation of these violations, reads like a blue-print for the sabbatarian works of Lancelot Andrewes, Nicholas Bownde, Lewis Bayly, John Dod, and many other Elizabethan and Jacobean sabbatarians. References to his homily in English expositions of the sabbath precept illustrate the influence he exercised; while the use of his *Decades* in parishes must have had a direct impact on the clergy and laity alike.

[73] *Ibid.*, p.140. [74] *Ibid.*, p.140. [75] *Ibid.*, pp.143–4.
[76] *Ibid.*, p.142. [77] *Ibid.*, p.141. Also see p.143.

Further examination of second and third generation reformers confirms the widespread use of the scholastic interpretation.[78] Like Bullinger, the Zuricher Joannes Wolphius asserted the moral nature of the sabbath precept in 1585.[79] Zacharias Ursinus of Heidelberg also used the scholastic interpretation in his work.[80] Zanchius of Neustadt, a close friend of Edmund Grindal, emphasized the perpetual and moral character of the sabbath precept.[81] The works of Emmanuel Tremellius, Peter Martyr, Franciscus Junius, and many others further illustrate that protestant theologians made use of analogical or scholastic interpretations of this commandment.[82] Their influence on English developments is evident from the numerous citations and quotations found in sabbatarian works.

The English reformers

Like their continental counterparts, the early reformers initially adopted a polemical Lutheran position, rejecting the medieval doctrine. As they gained control of the Church, protestant leaders passed through a transitional stage, represented by the *Bishops' Book*, which marked a practical shift towards external observance, justified on analogical grounds. While this was not a coherent position in Henrician and Edwardine formulations, second and third generation English reformers incorporated the analogical and scholastic interpretations in their expositions of the sabbath precept. Their works provided the foundation and substance of the sabbatarianism found in the Elizabethan period.

In 1528 Thomas More, then a privy councillor, wrote against Luther and Tyndale in his *Dialogue Concernynge Heresyes and Matters of Religion*. Prominent among the concepts he attacked was Luther's appeal to *sola scriptura*. More observed that 'this one

---

[78] Professor Collinson's survey of sabbatarian views held by the continental theologians confirms the use of analogical or scholastic interpretations by second and third generation protestants. (Collinson, 'English Sabbatarianism', *passim*.)

[79] Collinson, 'English Sabbatarianism', p.214; Johannes Wolphius, *Chronologia* (1585), pp.91–7.

[80] While Ursinus was more cautious in his treatment than some other protestant theologians, he nevertheless acknowledged the moral side of this precept. (Collinson, 'English Sabbatarianism', p.212; Zacharias Ursinus, *The Summe of Christian Religion*, Oxford, 1587.)

[81] Collinson, 'English Sabbatarianism', p.213.

[82] *Ibid.*, pp.212–15.

poynt is the very fond foundacion and ground of all his great heresyes, that a man is not bounden to beleve any thing but if it may be proved evidently by scripture'. He explained that Luther used this position to deny any doctrine he wished to reject, noting that 'no scripture can be evident to prove any thing that he lyst to deny'.[83]

More used the sabbath precept as an example of Lutheran inconsistency, explaining that on this basis the Church of Christ must be condemned for sanctifying Sunday rather than the Saturday Sabbath, instituted by God among the Jews. He concluded this point by using the scholastic explanation and arguing that the Church was the Holy Ghost's agent in changing the day, observing that 'I wene no man thinke, that ever the church woulde take upon them to chaunge it without speciall ordinaunce of God, whereof we find no remembraunce at all in holy scripture'.[84] Expressing the same point in his *Responsio ad Lutherum*, published in 1523, More explained that

They [Lutherans] will argue that this is an optional matter [keeping the Lord's day], since no particular day has been defined by any scriptures, except perhaps the sabbath. But if someone should say that it is the business of the church, governed by the Holy Spirit, to determine which day should be especially dedicated to God and that she has decided on Sunday, they will answer that the papist church has decided this.[85]

More was not merely attacking a foreign heresy, for among the English reformers William Tyndale was explicit in his support of Luther's view of the Sabbath. In Tyndale's *Answere unto Syr Thomas Mores Dialogue*, published in 1530, he complained that Christians, like the Jews, had come to believe that they were justified by abstaining from bodily labours, becoming servants of the day.[86] He denied that Christians are bound by any day, noting that

As for the Saboth, a great matter, we be Lordes over the Saboth and may yet chaunge it into the monday or any other day, as we see neede, or may make every tenth daye holy daye onely if we see cause why, we may make two every weeke, if it were expedient and one not inough to teach the people. Neither was there

[83] Thomas More, *The Works of Sir Thomas More* (London, 1557), p.161.
[84] *Ibid.*, p.161.
[85] Thomas More, *The Complete Works of St. Thomas More*, edited by J. M. Headley (New Haven, 1969), v pt. 1, 209.
[86] William Tyndale, John Frith, Robert Barnes, *The Whole Workes of W. Tyndall, John Frith, and Doctor Barnes* (London, 1573), p.274.

any cause to chaunge it from Saterday then to put difference betwene us and the Jews, and least we should become servauntes unto the day after their superstition. Neyther needed we any holyday at all, if the people myght be taught without it.[87]

Tyndale was not alone in emphasizing Christian liberty in this matter. In Robert Barnes' account of his examination before five bishops in 1526, he gave a spirited defence of the Christian's liberty to work on Sunday. He claimed that the command to abstain from bodily labours was given only to the Jews, and cited Augustine, Tertullian, and Jerome in defence of his position. He also quoted Pope Gregory the Great, who declared that those who taught that Christians must abstain from bodily labours on Sunday were 'the prechers of anti-Chryst'.[88] John Frith, in his treatise on baptism, published in 1533, used the Sabbath as an example of an Old Testament ceremony that was abolished by Christ. He explained that the day was changed to emphasize the point that 'we are free and not bounde to any day, but that we may do all lawful workes to the pleasure of God and profite of our neighbour'.[89]

Thomas More refuted these arguments for Christian liberty in *The Confutation of Tyndale's Answer*, published in 1532. He objected to Tyndale's attempt to make the change of the sabbath day a slight matter. He found none of the reasons for changing the day from Saturday to Sunday satisfactory. He particularly objected to the notion that it separated Christian practice from Jewish superstitions, noting that some Christians persisted in superstitious practices despite the change of days. Asserting that there could be no more compelling reason than that Christ himself set aside that day as a memorial of his resurrection, he accepted Tyndale's point that the Church made Sunday, and therefore could change it; but turned the argument against his opponent, explaining that,

it [the Church] made it by the spirite of God, so it may breake it by the same spirite. That is to wyt that as it made it by the spirite of God, so it may breake it by the same spirite. That is to say that as god made it; so himselfe may breake it, if it shall please him.[90]

---

[87] *Ibid.*, p.287.

[88] Robert Barnes, *Supplication* (n.p.[1534]), fols. 23r-25r. For Pope Gregory's statement see *Corpus Juris Canonici* (Graz, 1959), p.1355.

[89] Tyndale, Frith, and Barnes, *Works*, p.96.   [90] More, *Workes* (1557), p.493.

More's argument struck at the root of the conflict; for Tyndale could not accept late medieval teaching on the Sabbath, without also acknowledging that the Church was guided by the Holy Spirit in establishing a new day of worship. Tyndale's use of Luther's allegorized 'sabbath rest' was not simply a part of his emphasis on interior religion and Christian liberty; for its principal purpose was to support his polemics against the spiritual authority of the 'papistical' Church.

Thomas Cranmer used the sabbath precept for similar purposes in his *Confutation of the Unwritten Verities*, written in 1547.[91] He observed that Catholics used the shift from a Saturday Sabbath to Sunday observance as an example of the Church's power to change God's laws, noting that if 'the church hath authority to change God's laws, much more it hath authority to make new laws necessary to salvation'. To confute this position, Cranmer used the arguments of Luther and the early English reformers, stating that the outward bodily rest was ceremonial and had nothing to do with the gospels. It was the spiritual rest from sin, signified by the outward rest which still applied. 'This spiritual sabbath, that is, to abstain from sin and to do good, are all men bound to keep all the days of their life, and not only on the sabbath-day. And this spiritual sabbath may no man alter nor change, no, not the whole church'.[92] He cited Paul, Augustine, and Jerome to confirm his opinion on the ceremonial nature of the outward rest. He concluded by arguing that the shift to Sunday was an ecclesiastical convention, explaining that 'you may easily perceive that the church hath not changed the special part of the sabbath, which is to cease from vice and sin; but the ceremonial part of the sabbath only...in place whereof the Church hath ordained the Sunday'.[93]

This treatise and the works of Tyndale, Barnes, and Frith appear to support Heylyn's argument that the Henrician and Edwardine church 'restored' the early Church's allegorical interpretation of the sabbath precept, and established Sunday and holy day observance on the authority of the Church. However, it should be clear from our discussion that the matter is not so simple. These

[91] Thomas Cranmer, *Miscellaneous Writings and Letters*, edited by John Cox (Cambridge, 1846), p.5.
[92] *Ibid.*, p.61.   [93] *Ibid.*, p.61.

works were polemical attacks against the legalism of the medieval Church, and the Sabbath was being used as an example of the Church's unfounded claim to spiritual authority. These essentially Lutheran arguments were not intended to explain the observance of Sundays and holy days, but were part of a polemic against the claims of the 'papistical' Church. Their polemical context makes the anti-sabbatarian views of Tyndale, Barnes, Frith, and Cranmer an unreliable indicator of the official teaching of the Henrician and Edwardine Reformation. Indeed official pronouncements on the Sabbath in these years show a marked difference between the polemical Lutheran position of anti-Catholic writings and the practical instructions on sabbath observance intended for the guidance of the laity. The allegorical position does appear in these official works, but is overshadowed by analogical and scholastic explanations of the sabbath precept.

The *Bishops' Book*, published in 1537, struck a cautious balance, separating the fourth commandment from the other nine, explaining that while the other precepts were moral laws which bound both Christians and Jews, the sabbath precept applied only to the Jews in its requirement that men rest from bodily labours on the seventh day. However, the spiritual rest from sin signified by external rest was binding on Christians. Believers are to 'rest from carnal works of the flesh, and all manner of sin...not for every seventh day only, but for all days, hours, and times'.[94]

However, in addition to this spiritual rest, it was stated that, 'we be bound by this precept at certain times to cease from all bodily labour, and to give our minds entirely and wholly unto God'.[95] On Sundays and holy days, Christians were to hear and learn God's word, acknowledge their sins and God's goodness and mercy, worship corporately and give thanks for his benefits, receive the sacraments, visit the sick, and instruct their children in the faith. Christians were not bound to these duties on the Saturday Sabbath of the Jews, but on Sundays and holy days, which had been appointed by the Church to provide time for men to give themselves wholly to God. Yet Christians were cautioned not to be superstitious in abstaining from necessary labours on the holy days, noting that, 'we should offend, if we should for

---

[94] *Formularies of Faith* (Oxford, 1825), p.143.   [95] *Ibid.*, p.143.

scrupulosity not save that [which] God hath sent for the sustenance and relief of his people'.[96]

Those who neglected their spiritual duties without necessity were condemned and preachers were directed to teach that God is offended by men 'who will not cease and rest from their carnal wills and pleasure, that God may work in them after his good pleasure and will'. Those who passed the holy days in dancing, idleness, gluttony, riot, at plays, and other vain pastimes, as well as men who were present at worship but occupied with worldly thoughts, were to be condemned for misusing these days of worship.[97] While these instructions rested on ambiguous theological grounds, this exposition implied an analogical explanation of the fourth precept. Although the commandment was separated from the other nine 'moral' laws, the need to keep Sundays and holy days in rest from worldly labours and use of spiritual exercises was treated as a Christian obligation, and those who broke this law with work or worldly recreations offended God. This emphasis on Christian duty was necessary as the reformers laboured to organize Church practice and inculcate the reformed faith in Englishmen. Like Calvin, they found it necessary to justify this practice and impress on laymen the importance of this obligation.

In 1543 the *Bishops' Book* was revised and reissued as *The Necessary Doctrine and Erudition of a Christian Man*. Though a product of Henry's conservative shift, the exposition of the sabbath precept was substantially that of the *Bishops' Book*, with one significant exception; for the distinction between Sundays and holy days found in late medieval sabbatarianism was reintroduced. This study explained that the Jewish Sabbath had been succeeded by Sunday, in memory of Christ's resurrection, while the holy days were appointed by the Church. Although the early reformers initially used Luther's position, by 1543 the official teaching of the Church contained a distinction between the Lord's day and holy days, directing laymen to take literally the precept's directive to rest from worldly occupations and use spiritual exercises. This shift towards a more traditional interpretation is all the more striking given Cranmer's crucial role in this phase of the Reformation.[98]

The same transition is found in the *Injunctions*, issued by Edward

[96] *Ibid.*, pp.143–5.   [97] *Ibid.*, p.146.   [98] *Ibid.*, p.307.

VI in 1547. The holy day injunction implied the ancient practice and divine institution of the Sunday, stating that 'as the people be commonly occupied the work-day, with bodily labour, for their bodily sustenance, so was the holy-day at the first beginning godly instituted and ordained, that the people should that day give themselves wholly to God'.[99] The word 'holy-day' leaves ambiguous an important point and indicates that no firm judgement had yet been established. However, reference to the antiquity of this observance and its divine institution implies that Sunday was particularly intended here.

The sad state of this observance was lamented, noting that some did not go to church at all, and others were satisfied to attend public worship, using the remainder of the day in worldly pursuits. This injunction instructed subjects to be occupied on holy days in public and private prayers, acknowledging offences committed and seeking reconciliation for the same, receiving the sacraments and spending the day in sober and godly conversation. Yet the clergy were ordered to instruct the people that they might with a safe conscience labour in harvest time, warning that 'if for any scrupulosity, or grudge of conscience, men should superstitiously abstain from working upon those days, that then they should grievously offend and displease God'.[100]

The analogical interpretation was clearly presented in the catechism Edward VI commissioned Bishop Ponet to write. Ponet used the notion of a spiritual rest to emphasize the outward observance. Noting that the word 'sabbath' means rest, he explained that this rest is 'a figure of that rest and quietness, which they have that believe in Christ'. This trust in Christ is reflected in the ceremonies and religious exercises used on the Sabbath, for 'they are tokens and witnesses of this assured trust'. Christians ought to 'keep holily and religiously the sabbath day; which was appointed out from the other [days] for rest and service of God'.[101] Ponet's linking of the 'spiritual sabbath' with the outward exercises of the Sundays and other holy days contradicted the polemical rejection of external observance found in the works of Luther and the early English reformers.[102] By the end of

---

[99] Edward Cardwell, *Documentary Annals*, 2 vols. (Oxford, 1839), I, 15.

[100] *Ibid.*, p.16.

[101] John Poynet, *A Short Catechism* (London, 1553), fols. 5r-v, 46v-47r.

[102] Although Cranmer's *Unwritten Verities* dates from this period, it is important to note that it was not published until 1582 and had no apparent influence on the sabbatarian developments in the Edwardine Church.

Edward's reign, the analogical interpretation was firmly established in the official teaching of the English Church.[103]

However, the scholastic interpretation was not absent from
theological developments in the Edwardine period. John Hooper,
bishop of Worcester and close friend of Heinrich Bullinger, used
the scholastic explanation in his *Declaration of the Ten Holy
Commandments*, published in 1548. He divided this study into the
physical and spiritual reasons for sabbath keeping. Physically,
sabbath observance is important because it provides refreshment
for man and beast. This rest allows both master and servant to
regain bodily strength for work during the week. Spiritually, it
is necessary to abstain from labour so that while the body rests
men may learn and know God's will. Through this spiritual
labour, men can leave the adversity of sin and gain strength to
withstand the temptations of the week. God sanctified the seventh
day for these reasons. Hooper explained that while no day is holier
than another, the Sabbath had been set aside for holy activities;
and was properly observed when Christians attended public
services, showed charity to others, and permitted beasts and
servants to rest on that day. He condemned those who used sports,
games, markets, and fairs as sabbath-breakers.[104]

Hooper justified his teaching by explaining that the fourth
commandment was a law containing some ceremonial elements
abrogated by Christ, and some moral elements that endured.
Sabbath observance was not a law of man but expressly commanded by scripture. While the day was changed, the moral
obligation to keep the day strictly remained in force. Hooper, like
the medieval scholastics, denied that the Sabbath depended on
human authority, but was established by God. All Christians are
morally bound to observe the Sabbath in rest from worldly
occupations and in the performance of spiritual exercises.[105]

Hooper challenged the polemical point made by Thomas More

---

103 Martin Bucer did much to re-enforce the analogical interpretation of the fourth
commandment in English theology. For a summary of his influence see Kenneth L.
Parker, 'The English Sabbath: 1558–1640', unpublished 1984 Cambridge Ph.D. thesis,
pp.61–3. Also see Martin Bucer, *Common Places of Martin Bucer*, translated and edited
by D. F. Wright (Abingdon, Berkshire, 1972), p.90; Martin Bucer, 'De Regno
Christi', in *Melanchthon and Bucer*, translated by Wilhelm Pauck (Philadelphia, 1969), pp.
158–62, 251–2, 282; P. D. L. Avis, 'Moses and the Magistrate: A Study in the Rise
of Protestant Legalism', *Journal of Ecclesiastical History*, 26, no.2 (1975), 149–72 (p.
161).

104 Hooper, *The Holy Commandments*, p.337.   105 *Ibid.*, pp.341–2.

and others that Sunday had been established by the Holy Ghost through the Church, claiming that this observance was based on scripture. He explained that, 'this Sunday that we observe is not the commandment of man, as many say, that would, under the pretence of this one law, bind the church of Christ to all other laws that men hath ungodly prescribed unto the church; but it is by express words commanded [in scripture] that we should observe this day (this Sunday) for our sabbath'.[106] By basing the divine institution of Sunday on scripture, he answered the assertions of More and other Catholics. While such a clear statement on the institution of Sunday was not to reappear in the published works of the early Elizabethan period, Hooper's work was read and influenced the sabbatarian developments of the Elizabethan period.[107]

Early protestant reaction against the sabbath doctrine was marked by practical rather than theological priorities. This issue was peripheral in the Catholic-protestant debates, but proved useful in scoring points in conflicts over ecclesiastical authority and the use of scripture as the ultimate rule of doctrine and practice. However, as the reformers struggled with the problems of practical theology, analogical and scholastic interpretations were reasserted to justify the external observance enforced by the Church. While the divine institution of Sunday remained an ambiguous point in this transitional period, doctrinal formulations and royal injunctions left no doubt that this observance was a divine imperative and binding on all Christians. Soon after Elizabeth's accession, the scholastic interpretation was reasserted as an authorized teaching in the reformed Church of England – and remained a virtually undisputed doctrine until the 1630s.

---

[106] *Ibid.*, p.342. Hooper cited I Corinthians 16:2 in support of this assertion.
[107] Edmund Grindal, *The Remains*, edited by W. Nicholson (Cambridge, 1843), pp.215–16.

3

Early Elizabethan sabbatarianism: 1558–82

In 1636 Peter Heylyn finished his study of the early Elizabethan period by noting that 'upon due search made, and full examination of all parties, we find no Lords day Sabbath in the book of Homilies: nor in any writings of particular men, in more than 33 years after the Homilies were published'.[1] His conclusion has never been seriously tested, with studies of sabbatarianism leaping from the Queen's Injunctions to the complaint literature of the 1570s. The search for theological developments starts with the Dedham Classis debates, and Nicholas Bownde's *Doctrine of the Sabbath*, published in 1595, is presented as the first published work on the morally binding nature of the fourth precept. It is already apparent that this was not the case. Indeed the study of early Elizabethan sabbatarianism reveals that the Church promoted analogical and scholastic interpretations through its teaching and encouraged sabbatarian rigorism in its discipline.

There were disputes between Church officials and disaffected precisionists; but these conflicts were over the institution of the Lord's day, holy days, the proper use of the Sabbath, and penalties to be exacted for sabbath abuses. However, this discord stemmed from differing views of Church authority and interpretations of scripture, and does not detract from the fundamental consensus on the divine imperative to observe one day in seven. This chapter will explore sabbatarian developments in the Church from the Elizabethan settlement to the formation of the Dedham Classis in 1582, and in particular the Church's role in promoting sabbatarian teaching and discipline. This emphasis is important, for by it the pessimistic conclusions found in complaint literature will be put in proper perspective, demonstrating that the 1580s and 1590s were not a period of theological creativity, but one of elaboration.

[1] Heylyn, *History of the Sabbath*, p.249.

THE CHURCH AND THE SABBATH

In his exposition of Haggai, published in 1560, James Pilkington, the soon to be consecrated bishop of Durham, complained of the lax application of reforms in England. He observed that, 'poor cities in Germany, compassed about with their enemies, reform religion thoroughly without any fear, and God prospereth them. And yet this noble realm, which all princes have feared, dare not'. Pilkington noted that magistrates see so much out of order and so little hope of correcting the problems that they 'let the whip lie still... and everyone do what he list'. Chief among his concerns were the neglect of church and the popularity of alehouses. 'For come into a church on the Sabbath day, and ye shall see but few, though there be a sermon, but the alehouse is ever full'. He lamented the diligence of the wicked to do the deeds of Anti-christ, while Christian rulers and officers were so cold in setting up true religion, 'that neither they give good examples themselves in diligent praying and resorting to the church, nor by the whip of discipline drive others thitherward'. He called every Englishman to 'keep himself in God's school house and learn his lesson diligently'.[2]

This lack of sabbatarian discipline was not for want of laws. The Queen's Injunctions of 1559 provided a practical, though not theologically justified, prescription for the observance of holy days. Parishioners were to spend these days in

hearing the word of God read and taught, in private prayers, in acknowledging their offences unto God, and amendment of the same, in reconciling themselves charitably to their neighbors... in often times receiving the communion of the very body and blood of Christ, in visiting the poor and sick, using all soberness and godly conversation.

The prohibition of ordinary labours was tempered with the Edwardine provision which warned that men should not hesitate to work after service time in the harvest period, warning that, 'if for any scrupulosity or grudge of conscience men should superstitiously abstain from working upon those days, that then they should grievously offend and displease God'.[3] These restric-

[2] John Strype, *Annals of the Reformation*, 7 vols. (Oxford, 1824), 1 pt 1, pp.270–1; James Pilkington, *The Works of James Pilkington*, edited by James Scholefield (Cambridge, 1842), pp.6–7.

[3] David Wilkins, *Concilia Magnae Britanniae et Hiberniae*, 4 vols. (London, 1737), IV, 184; W. H. Frere (ed.), *Visitation Articles and Injunctions*, Alcuin Club Collections XVI, 3 vols. (London, 1910), III, 15.

tions were amplified in 1560 by Richard Cox, bishop of Ely, in *Interpretations and Further Considerations of Certain Injunctions*, a document later revised by Archbishop Parker.[4] Of particular concern was the restriction of commercial activities. Cox stipulated that, 'On Sunday there be no shops open, nor artificers going about their affairs worldly; and that all fair and common marts falling upon Sunday, there be no shewing of any wares before the service be done'.[5] These restrictions were incorporated into the diocesan discipline of Canterbury, Norwich, and elsewhere in 1560 and 1561,[6] and were to appear frequently in visitation articles through the rest of this period.

These regulations were not devised in a theological vacuum. Thomas Becon presented a scholastic explanation of the fourth precept in his *New Catechism*, published in 1560. The ceremonial side of this law was defined as the external rest required on the Saturday Sabbath which was abrogated by the coming of Christ. However, he explained that Christians remain morally bound to assemble at church on days appointed by Christian rulers, to pray corporately, give thanks for his benefits, hear his word, receive his holy mysteries, and abstain from all worldly things and servile labours, except in times of necessity. Becon's theological treatment of this precept owed much to the work of Hooper and Bullinger, and was part of the tradition exploited in the 1580s and 1590s.

This explanation of the fourth precept was so commonly known that Archbishop Parker used it in a letter to Elizabeth in 1559, as part of his argument for the moral and perpetual nature of the second commandment. He explained that,

If by virtue of the second commandment images were not lawful in the temple of the Jews, then by the same commandment they are not lawful in the Churches of the Christians. For being a moral commandment, and not ceremonial, (for by consent of writers only a part of the precept of observing the Sabbath is ceremonial) it is a perpetual commandment, and bindeth us as well as the Jews.[7]

The English Church produced an officially sanctioned sabbatarian doctrine in 1563. In that year, the convocation approved the second *Book of Homilies* for use in parishes when no sermon was

---

[4] Strype, *Annals*, 1 pt 1, p.318.
[5] Frere, III, p.69; Strype, *Annals*, 1 pt 1, p.319.
[6] Visitation Articles for Canterbury 1566 and Norwich 1561, and the anonymous *Interrogatories* 1560; Frere, III, 93; John Strype, *The Life of Matthew Parker*, 3 vols. (Oxford, 1821), III, 31.
[7] Matthew Parker, *Correspondence of Matthew Parker*, edited by John Bruce (Cambridge, 1853), p.81.

prepared. These homilies had been planned by the Edwardine episcopate, but were written in the early 1560s by a group of Elizabethan bishops, and were intended to ground laymen in the reformed religion. Although not initially given the status of official Church teaching, these homilies came to be regarded as an authoritative compendium of orthodox theology.

The homily 'Of the Place and Time of Prayer' is often treated as an historiographical anomaly. Christopher Hill went so far as to call it 'that very "Puritan document"'.[8] However, he acknowledged that the sabbatarian developments of the 1590s would not have been effective without it, noting that, 'respect for the Sabbath was part of the common protestant heritage, summed up in the Homily "Of the Place and Time of Prayer"'.[9] While William Haugaard was reluctant to claim that the *Homilies* 'defined' doctrine for the English Church,[10] the testimony of such opposites as Peter Heylyn and Archbishop James Ussher illustrates the high regard given to these works. Heylyn described the Homilies as 'part of the publicke monuments of the Church of England, set forth and authorized... [in] the fourth [year] of that Queenes reigne',[11] and he treated the homily 'Of the Place and Time of Prayer' as official Church teaching. Ussher, in a letter written in the mid 1630s, supported John Ley's doctrine of a morally binding Sabbath, noting that 'this is to be held undoubtedly the Doctrine of the Church of England. For if there could be any reasonable doubt made of the meaning of the Church of England in her Lyturgy, who should better declare her meaning than herself in her Homily?'[12]

The homily 'Of the Place and Time of Prayer' could not have been a satisfactory source of authority for either of them, for it left several crucial questions unanswered. While the author dealt with the ceremonial aspects of the fourth precept, he did not use the scholastic explanation of the moral obligations which endured, but adopted an analogical interpretation instead. He also was silent on the institution of Sunday and the use of holy days.

However, the writer left no doubt that the sabbath precept was

[8] Hill, *Society and Puritanism*, p.159.
[9] *Ibid.*, p.169.
[10] William Haugaard, *Elizabeth and the English Reformation* (Cambridge, 1968), p.276.
[11] Heylyn, *History of the Sabbath*, p.244.
[12] James Ussher, *The Judgement of the Late Archbishop of Armagh and Primate of Ireland* (London, 1657), p.106.

a divine imperative to keep one day in the week free from ordinary occupations and devoted to the things of God. He explained that,

God hath given express charge to all men, that upon the sabbath-day, which is now our Sunday, they should cease from all weekly and work-day labour, to the intent that like as God himself wrought six days, and rested the seventh, and blessed and sanctified it, and consecrated it to quietness and rest from labour; even so God's obedient people should use the Sunday holily, and rest from their common and daily business, and also give themselves wholly to heavenly exercises of God's true religion and service.[13]

The author explained that God not only commanded this observance, but stressed the importance of this practice by resting on the seventh day, after creation. Those who kept this day were not only following God's express command, but were marking themselves out as 'loving children' of God.

Sunday observance was presented as a Christian tradition which began after Christ's ascension, and was used instead of the Saturday Sabbath as a memorial of Christ's resurrection. From the days of the early Church 'God's people hath always, in all ages, without any gainsaying, used to come together upon the Sunday, to celebrate and honour the Lord's blessed name, and carefully to keep that day in holy rest and quietness'.[14]

He equated many of the Old Testament sabbath laws with the Christian Sunday and cited as a warning the case of the man who was stoned for picking up sticks on the Sabbath.[15] Those who worked, travelled, traded, and participated in popular festivals were condemned as violators of God's holy day. The writer called such people to

repent and amend this grievous and dangerous wickedness, stand in awe of the commandment of God, gladly follow the example of God himself, [and] be not disobedient to the godly order of Christ's church, used and kept from the apostles' time until this day.[16]

Sunday was to be spent in spiritual exercises at church, hearing the Word read, expounded and preached, and receiving the sacraments.[17]

The author explained that the observance of a Saturday Sabbath and forbearance of working in times of necessity were ceremonial sides of this precept and did not bind Christians. However, that

---

[13] *Homilies*, edited by G. E. Corrie (Cambridge, 1850), pp.341–2.

[14] *Ibid.*, p.343.   [15] Numbers 15:32–6.

[16] *Homilies*, pp.343–4.   [17] *Ibid.*, pp.345–7.

which was part of natural law endured. 'Whatsoever is found in the commandment appertaining to the law of nature, as a thing most godly, most just, and needful for the setting forth of God's glory, it ought to be retained and kept of all good Christian people'.[18]

Christopher Hill was quite right to acknowledge this homily as the foundation on which Nicholas Bownde and others built. Yet it must also be acknowledged as the primary source of sabbatarian teaching in the Elizabethan and early Stuart period; for no other sabbatarian work was more accessible to the people. As William Haugaard has observed, 'thousands of Englishmen grew up and lived their lives with the weekly sound of its [the *Homilies*'] contents droning past their ears and occasionally impressing its teaching upon their minds'.[19] Given this evidence, it is difficult to regard the sabbatarian developments of the 1570s and 1580s as the product of over-zealous and divisive 'puritanism'. Instead it appears to be the legitimate expression of godly churchmen who witnessed every Sunday the transgression of a doctrine preached from the pulpit.

Another source of sabbatarian teaching endorsed by the 1563 Convocation was the *Catechism* of Alexander Nowell.[20] This work was examined by a committee of bishops which included John Jewel, and was approved unanimously by the lower house. The *Catechism* did not appear in print until 1570, after many revisions, but was endorsed by archbishops Parker and Grindal as the only officially approved catechism for use in schools and parishes.[21] Nowell's treatment of the fourth precept demonstrates no originality; for he did little more than synthesize the work of Calvin and Ponet. Using Calvin's three divisions in interpreting this precept analogically, Nowell explained that this law applied to Christians, because it established and maintained an ecclesiastical discipline and order, provided rest for servants, and was a figure of our spiritual rest from sin. But like Ponet, he emphasized that this figure is manifested by men's sabbath activities: assembling to hear Christian doctrine, making public prayers, giving thanks for benefits received, and using God's holy mysteries. This

---

[18] *Ibid.*, pp.341–2.   [19] Haugaard, p.276.
[20] Dean of St Paul's and prolocutor of the convocation's lower house.
[21] Alexander Nowell, *A Catechism*, edited by G. E. Corrie (Cambridge, 1853), pp.v–vii; Edward Cardwell, *Synodalia*, 2 vols. (Oxford, 1842), I, 128; Edmund Grindal, *The Remains*, edited by W. Nicholson (Cambridge, 1843), pp.142,152; Haugaard, pp.277–90.

spiritual rest is a holy vacation, when men rest from worldly works and studies, and do the works of God.[22]

The well-defined sabbatarian doctrines found in the *Homilies* and Nowell's *Catechism* were augmented by the marginal notes found in the English translations of the Bible used in parishes. The most popular of these was the Geneva Bible, produced by the Marian exiles in the 1550s. In this translation a very high regard for the fourth precept was displayed, with a note explaining that 'the whole keping of the Lawe standeth in the true use of the Sabbath, which is to cease from our workes, and to obey the wil of God'. The comment on Deuteronomy 5:13 stated that, 'since God permitteth six daies to our labours, that we ought willingly to dedicat the seventh to serve him wholy'. The marginal comments to many other passages reinforce the position that Sunday observance was a divine imperative.[23] Although the marginal comments of the Bishops' Bible are thought to be less radical, the comments on Exodus 20:8-11 did not diverge from the position found in the Geneva Bible.[24] The Latin translation of Emmanuel Tremellius, who was Hebrew professor at Cambridge, also supported the sabbatarian opinions that were current in England, and was used in the sabbatarian works of the later Elizabethan period.[25]

A further search of sabbatarian literature in this early period reveals no deviation from the analogical or scholastic explanation of the sabbath precept. The posthumously published works of John Rogers and John Bradford, and the studies of two conformists like Edmund Bunny and Christopher Shutte, as well as the work of a precisionist like John Knewstub, illustrate consensus rather than division.[26] Indeed these works used sabbatarian doctrine to justify their exhortations to rest from worldly occupations and devote Sundays to spiritual duties. Continental works which were translated and published in this period also supported

---

[22] Nowell, pp.128-30; Strype, *Annals*, 1 pt 1, p.518.

[23] *Geneva Bible* (Geneva, 1560), Ex. 31:14; Deut. 5:13; Psalm 92:1-2,4; Isa. 56:2.

[24] *Bishops' Bible* (London, 1568), Ex. 20:8-11.

[25] Collinson, 'Beginnings', p.213.

[26] Edward Dering, 'xxvii *Lectures or Reading, upon...Hebrues*', in *Works* (London, 1597), sig. s2v-s3v; John Bradford, *Godly Meditations upon the Ten Commandments* (London, 1567) fol.12v; John Rogers, *The Summe of Christianitie* (n.p., 1560), fol.12v; John Knewstub, *The Lectures of John Knewstub upon the Twentieth Chapter of Exodus* (London, 1577), pp.63-76; Christopher Shutte, *A Compendious Forme and Summe of Christian Doctrine* (London, 1581), sig. B8v.

this doctrine. Notable among these were works by Heinrich Bullinger and Wolfgang Musculus, which were placed in parishes by episcopal authority.[27]

In his work against Cartwright, published in 1574, John Whitgift, then master of Trinity College, Cambridge, included the fourth commandment among the moral laws which remained in force. Responding to Cartwright's claim that this precept bound Christians to spend one day in worship and six in ordinary labours, Whitgift argued that six days were permitted for labour but that the Church had authority to establish holy days and enforce observance of them. The moral obligation to observe one day in seven was never in question.[28] In 1576 Whitgift was consulted by a minister from Essex concerning a group who claimed that the whole law of Moses was abolished, freeing Christians from any obligation to the moral law. Whitgift responded that,

We have nothing to do with Moses's ceremonial and judicial laws: whereof the one was given for a certain time, the other for a certain nation. But touching the moral law, which is the perfection of the law of nature, and afterwards was written in tables of stone being the rule of God's justice, that remaineth for ever. Secondly, we are indeed free, but not from the obedience of the law, but from the curse of the law.[29]

The evidence presented above can leave one in no doubt that the analogical and scholastic interpretations were firmly rooted in the teaching of the Elizabethan Church. The *Homilies*, Nowell's *Catechism*, as well as other theological works confirm this conclusion. But there were several areas of ambiguity that did cause disputes. The institution of Sunday as the Lord's day, the use of holy days, the regulation of sabbath activities, and the penalties for sabbath abuses were contentious issues that were never fully resolved. However, these conflicts had more to do with differing views of ecclesiastical authority and scripture than with sabbatarianism. Like the disputes between Tyndale and More, English-

[27] Thomas Cooper, bishop of Lincoln, ordered the use of Bullinger's *Decades* in 1577, and Richard Cox ordered the use of Musculus' *Commonplaces* in 1571. *Elizabethan Episcopal Administration*, edited by W. P. M. Kennedy, Alcuin Club Collections XXVI, 3 vols. (London, 1924), II, 45–6; Frere, III, 301. Also see Rudolf Gualter, *A Hundred, Three Score, and Fifteen Sermons Upon the Acts of the Apostles* (London, 1572), p.521.

[28] John Whitgift, *The Works of John Whitgift*, edited by J. Ayre, 3 vols. (Cambridge, 1852), II, 569–71, 593–5. Also see Matthew Hutton's position found in a letter to Whitgift in 1589. John Strype, *The Life and Acts of John Whitgift*, 3 vols. (Oxford, 1822), III, 224.   [29] Strype, *Whitgift*, I, 151–2.

men in the Elizabethan and early Stuart period argued over the source of authority in these matters. Some asserted that the Church could impose no discipline that was not positively affirmed in scripture, and sought the imposition of the judicial laws of the Old Testament, which would have meant the death penalty for sabbath-breakers. Others argued that the Church had authority to establish days of worship and claimed that the judicial laws of the Old Testament were abrogated. However, there were few who denied the morality of the decalogue – and the sabbath precept was not excluded. Disputes over application were always a problem, and those who lacked the authority to enforce observance were often critical of the intentions and effectiveness of those who did. However, the reports of malcontents are not the most reliable sources of information when studying English sabbatarianism, for tensions over peripheral issues have obscured the consensus on sabbath doctrine.

THE INSTITUTION OF THE LORD'S DAY

The institution of the Lord's day proved to be the least contentious sabbatarian concern; for in the early Elizabethan period no extraordinary claims were made for that day. While the homily 'Of the Place and Time of Prayer' clearly emphasized Sunday observance and Nowell's *Catechism* stressed the divine imperative to keep one day in seven, these works did not present Sunday as a day divinely appointed. This was also true of works by John Rogers, Edmund Bunny, John Knewstub, Christopher Shutte, Thomas Becon, and others.[30] In 1574 John Whitgift asserted that scripture had not appointed a particular day, explaining that Christians observed Sunday because it was 'appointed by the Church'. But he denied that this observance should ever be altered, explaining: 'I do not think that that which the church hath

---

[30] J. Rogers, fol.12v; Edmund Bunny, *The Whole Summe of Christian Religion* (London, 1576), fols. 46–52; Knewstub, pp.63–76; Shutte, sig. B8v; Thomas Becon, *Catechism*, edited by J. Ayre (Cambridge, 1844), pp.80–4; Thomas Becon, *A New Postil* (London, 1566), fols.130–2; Thomas Becon, *The Demaundes of Holy Scripture* (London, 1577), sig. c6r-v; Stephen Bateman, *The New Arrival of the Three Gracis* (London, [1580?]), sig. D6r; Gualter, p.521; Wolfgang Musculus, *Commonplaces* (London, 1563), pp.60–3; Henry Bullinger, *Fiftie Godlie and Learned Sermons* (London, 1577), pp.137–8; Peter Martyr, *Commonplaces* (London, 1583), fols. 8v-9r. The marginal comments in the Geneva Bible and Bishops' Bible supported this emphasis as well. *Geneva Bible*, Acts 20:7, I Corinthians 16:1, Revelation 1:10; *Bishops' Bible*, Exodus 20:8–11.

once determined, and by long continuance proved to be necessary, ought to be altered, without great or especial consideration'.[31] Like Whitgift, other writers explained that Sunday observance was an ancient tradition, established as a memorial of Christ's resurrection; but no direct claim has been found for the divine institution of that day in the theological writings of the 1560s and 1570s.

HOLY DAYS

The place of holy days in the English Church was a more controversial matter which has complicated the study of sabbatarianism; for Heylyn and others have argued that these days were treated as equal to the Lord's day, explaining that both were established by the Church's authority. However, this was not the teaching of the Elizabethan Church. Bishop Pilkington complained in 1560 that 'every day in the year is called by the name of some saint, and not in all countries alike, but as every country is disposed to worship their saints'. He observed that 'in the New Testament I find no days named, but the first of the Sabbath, etc., and the Lord's day, which I take to be the Sunday...Thus superstition crept into the world, when men began to forget calling on the true and only God, and made them gods of every dead saint as they list'.[32] Evidence from the 1560s and 1570s illustrates the distaste for holy day observance at all levels of the Church.

This is most apparent in the proceedings of the 1563 Convocation. In the preliminary papers drawn up for the convocation, the 'General Notes' restricted the number of holy days to those found in the Prayer Book and recommended the punishment of those observing abrogated holy days.[33] Members of the lower house of the convocation wanted to go even further. A third of the members subscribed to the 'Seven Articles' which requested reforms in the Prayer Book and clerical dress. The seventh article recommended the elimination of all saints' feasts and holy days bearing the names of creatures, explaining that these days led to superstitious practices – a very Bullingerian clause. If these days were not abrogated it was suggested that after sermons or common prayers 'for the better instructing of the people in

[31] Whitgift, *Works*, I, 200, 202.   [32] Pilkington, p.17.
[33] Strype, *Annals*, I pt 1, p.475.

history' that they should be allowed to 'occupy themselves in a bodily labour, as of other working days'. This petition was signed by the prolocutor of the lower house, Alexander Nowell, as well as six cathedral deans, thirteen archdeacons, and fifteen others.[34]

On 13 February 1563, a revised version of six articles was presented to the lower house. The first of these articles recommended, 'that all the Sundays in the year, and principle feasts of Christ, be kept holy days; and all other holy days to be abrogated'. Along with this article were recommendations to remove organs, omit the sign of the cross at baptism, use surplices only in service time, and that the minister face the people when reading divine service. Most hotly disputed was the article concerning kneeling at communion. Unfortunately, the evidence is too sketchy to know if there was discord over the proposed abolition of saints' days, but these articles were narrowly defeated: fifty-eight votes for acceptance and fifty-nine against. Success in the lower house would not have established these reforms; their passage would have been followed by considerations of the bishops and the assent of the queen. Nevertheless, this event is significant, for it illustrates that many in the Church made a clear distinction between Sundays, along with the major feasts of Christ, and other holy days of the year. Heylyn's assertion that Sundays and holy days were not differentiated is simply not true.[35]

Even more striking are the sabbatarian bills sent by the upper house of the convocation to parliament for enactment. These bills, which were either drafted or approved by Bishop Grindal and commended to the upper house by Archbishop Parker, applied a strict prohibition on ordinary activities to Sundays and principal feast days, with the conspicuous omission of saints' days.[36] Although the bills were not enacted by parliament, they are a significant indicator of episcopal attitudes towards the place of holy days in the English Church.

Indeed, other evidence in this early period points to a low view of holy days; for these days were either treated as *adiaphora* or opposed as popish remnants in the Church. The *Homilies* emphasized Sunday observance; and Nowell's *Catechism* made no reference to holy days. Although Thomas Becon encouraged men

---

[34] Strype, *Annals*, I, pt I, pp.501–2; Haugaard, p.64; Collinson, *Puritan Movement*, p.66.
[35] Strype, *Annals*, I, pt I, pp.502–6; Haugaard, pp.64–5. Heylyn, *History of the Sabbath*, p.239.   [36] Strype, *Annals*, I, pt I, pp.529–32.

to observe those holy days appointed by the 'rulers of Christ's church', he was among those in the lower house who voted for the abolition of all saints' days.[37] John Northbrooke, in his complaint against dicing, dancing, and plays, observed that, 'Holy dayes (as they are termed) were invented in old time for pastimes ...For the Pope appointed them (and not God in his worde) and that onely to traine up the people in ignorance and idlenesse'.[38] While Northbrooke's condemnation of holy days has been treated as the more extreme view of his period, Pilkington and other bishops shared his attitude.

Yet the episcopate has often been presented as the enthusiastic defender of holy days against 'puritan' opposition. Hill cited a case presented before Grindal in 1567 as an example of episcopal support for holy day observance.[39] However, the bishop's distaste for holy days suggests a different interpretation. One can imagine Grindal's discomfort when the separatist William White observed at his trial that while God commanded man to work six days and keep one day of worship, 'the prince's law saith, "Thou shalt not labour [six] days, but shall keep the popish holy-days"...In the church of England there is none but the pope's discipline'. Grindal defended holy days as *adiaphora*, noting that not all popish practices were ungodly. When he implied that White's attitude towards holy days was heretical, another defendant named Robert Hawkins retorted that John Hooper stated in his commentary on the decalogue that 'holy-days are the leaven of antichrist'. The transcription ended here with a note that the subject was changed. This account is hardly convincing evidence of episcopal support for holy days, and Grindal's early activities lead one to doubt Hill's interpretation of this event; for it is apparent that Grindal was obliged to enforce ecclesiastical discipline which he did not favour.[40]

A more significant example used to illustrate official support for holy days is the pamphlet battle waged between Thomas Cartwright and John Whitgift over the *Admonition to the Parliament*.[41] Among the many reforms in church discipline and government which the *Admonition* promoted, was the abolition of

---

[37] Becon, *Catechism*, p.83; Strype, Annals, 1 pt 1, p.504.
[38] John Northbrooke, *A Treatise* (London, 1577), fols. 11v-12r.
[39] Hill, *Society and Puritanism*, p.154.   [40] Grindal, pp.201, 215-16.
[41] Written by John Field and Thomas Wilcox in 1572.

saints' days. These were thought to encourage superstition and violated God's command that men should labour six days a week.[42] A work entitled the *Second Admonition* was written in support of Field and Wilcox, who were imprisoned for their tract. While it is almost certain that Cartwright was not the author, he actively supported and defended its contents. The affair was treated very seriously by the secular and ecclesiastical authorities; and John Whitgift was appointed as the Church's spokesman. His last, massive response to Cartwright's criticisms contained a long section defending holy days; for Whitgift recognized that Cartwright's rejection of holy days challenged the authority of the hierarchy to establish religious practices and discipline not based on scripture.

Cartwright's argument was simple and straightforward. God commanded Christians to devote six days to labour and one day to worship. By clinging to popish remnants, the Church not only contradicted the law of God but maintained the superstitious practices of many. He denied the Church's right to set aside weekdays in which men had to forgo their necessary labours and devote the day to spiritual duties. As the Church was commanded by God only to observe the seventh day, it should not restrain the liberty of men on other days of the week. Cartwright cited the works of Bullinger, Bucer, and Hooper, as well as John Calvin, and challenged the Church to prove from scripture that such a practice was commanded by God.[43]

Whitgift replied that the fourth commandment *required* one day of worship and *permitted* six days of labour. He explained while God commanded men to give one day in seven wholly to his service, that 'the meaning of this commandment is not so to tie men to bodily labour, that they may not intermit the same to labour spiritually'.[44] He agreed that to observe any day superstitiously was evil, but denied that the use of holy days was a hindrance to true religion. Whitgift stated that,

Holy-days as they be now used, be rather means to withdraw men not only from superstition of the days themselves, but from all other kinds of superstition whatsoever: for then is God in the public congregation truly worshipped, the sacraments rightly ministered, the scriptures and other godly homilies read, the

---

[42] *Puritan Manifestoes*, edited by W. H. Frere and C. E. Douglas (London, 1954), p.24; John Field and Thomas Wilcox, *Admonition to Parliament* (London, 1572), sig.B2r.
[43] Whitgift, ii, 565–7, 569, 572, 574, 575, 585, 587, 591.   [44] *Ibid.*, pp.565, 593.

word of God faithfully preached; all which be the chief and principle means to withdraw men, not only from superstition, but all kind of error likewise.[45]

He did not accept that all things used by papists should be abrogated, observing that if that were done, 'there would be a marvellous alteration both in the church and in the common weal'.[46] He stated that while God gave liberty to work six days a week, he also established in the Old Testament special feast days which fell on those days. Following this example, the Church appointed special days of remembrance. He rejected Cartwright's claim that men were at liberty to use

> not one tittle in the six week days as they wished, explaining that, God's word doth restrain either the magistrate, or the church, from turning carnal liberty to the spiritual service of God, or bodily labour to divine worship... As the same God that gave this commandment hath done before in the old law, so may the churches likewise, for the increase of godliness and virtue, and edifications appoint some of those days to be bestowed in prayers, hearing the word, and ministration of the sacraments, and other holy actions.

Although the Church had no authority to release men from spiritual duties and obligation to rest from worldly occupations on the seventh day, it did have the right to establish additional days for spiritual labours.[47] Whitgift explained that the use of these days was not contrary to scripture, stating that 'to honour God, to worship him, to be edified by the stories and examples of saints out of the scriptures cannot be but consonant to the scripture'.[48]

When examining the arguments presented by Cartwright and Whitgift, it is important to note that three crucial issues were not contentious. First, both men worked from the assumption that the observance of one day in seven was a divine imperative, established by God in the fourth commandment. Second, they accepted that this commandment required men to rest from worldly occupations and devote that day to spiritual labours. Third, their discord over holy days grew out of the recognition that these days were ecclesiastical conventions and had no basis in scripture. These points are crucial, not only because of Whitgift's role as Church spokesman in this affair; but also because of his supposed opposition to sabbatarian developments at the end of Elizabeth's reign. However, even more important, he illustrated that while bishops enforced the same discipline for Sundays and holy days, the theological basis for these observances were understood to be fundamentally different.

PATTERNS OF OBSERVANCE

While the evidence above illustrates a theological division over the use of holy days, it conversely accentuates the consensus on the strict observance of Sunday; for the dispute was over the application of sabbatarian regulations to the weekdays and not the use of these restrictions on Sunday. The common concern of both the leaders of the Church and their critics was that Sunday be observed according to the fourth precept of the decalogue. Whether the writers used an analogical or scholastic explanation, their objective was to emphasize the Christian's obligation to perform spiritual exercises and rest from worldly occupations on that day. These spiritual exercises consisted of assembling at church for corporate prayer and hearing God's Word, receiving the sacraments, giving alms, and instructing children and servants in the fundamentals of the faith. All worldly things and weekday labours were to be shunned to prevent any distraction from the spiritual labours of that day.[49]

Special attention should be given to the activities proscribed by these writers; for the complaint literature of the 1570s has been treated as works containing frameless sabbatarian principles that were not theologically defined until the 1590s.[50] The sabbatarian works of the 1560s and 1570s prohibited the use of one's ordinary labours, except in times of necessity or as an act of mercy. Unnecessary travelling was to be avoided, as well as carrying burdens. These sabbatarian writers condemned the selling of food and drink during service time; and most rejected the use of trading on Sunday, though a few made allowances for markets and fairs which did not begin until after service time. Recreations were a more controversial matter, with some sabbatarians allowing the

---

[49] Becon, *Catechism*, pp.82–3. Knewstub, pp.72–3; Bullinger, *Sermons*, pp.137–8; Musculus, pp.62–3; Nowell, p.129; Bradford, fol. 12r; Rogers, fol. 12v; Shutte, sig.B8v; Gualter, p.521; John Bridges, *A Sermon* (London, 1571), p.111.

[50] Patrick Collinson, *The Religion of Protestants: The Church in English Society 1559–1625* (Oxford, 1982), p.199.

use of some sports and pastimes, but there was an almost universal rejection of plays, dancing, excessive drinking, and blood sports.[51]

Thomas Becon must have been an inspiration to later Elizabethan sabbatarians, for he not only used the scholastic explanation of the fourth precept, but also had definite notions of what should be avoided on Sundays. Ordinary labours and trading at markets and fairs were treated as violations of this day of rest, for they were distractions from the spiritual duties of that day. In addition he emphasized that one must not misspend the day idly in lewd pastimes, 'in banqueting, in dicing and carding, in dancing and bearbaiting, in bowling and shooting, in laughing and whoring, and in such like beastly and filthy pleasures of the flesh'.[52]

The author of 'Of the Place and Time of Prayer' was no less severe. He lamented the disregard of Sunday observance, and described two types of sabbath-breakers. The first type consisted of those who went about their business, regardless of its urgency, travelling, carrying burdens, and trading on Sunday, treating it as any other work day. But the other type was worse,

> For although they will not travel nor labour on the Sunday, as they do on the weekday; yet they will not rest in holiness, as God commandeth; but they rest in ungodliness and filthiness, prancing in their pride, pranking and pricking, pointing and painting themselves, to be gorgeous and gay: they rest in excess and superfluity, in gluttony and drunkenness, like rats and swine: they rest in brawling and railing, in quarrelling and fighting: they rest in wantonness in toyish talking in filthy fleshliness; so that it doth too evidently appear that God is more dishonoured and the devil better served on the Sunday than upon all the days in the week besides.[53]

With this message coming from the pulpit, one need not search further for the inspiration of the complaint literature in this period.

These examples illustrate that practical sabbatarian concerns in the early Elizabethan period were often presented as part of a well-defined Sabbath doctrine. While the 1580s and 1590s brought a growing interest in this matter, advocates of strict observance built on foundations established by the teaching and discipline of the early Elizabethan Church. The conflicts which did arise had

---

[51] Knewstub, pp.72–3; Becon, *Catechism*, p.80; Bullinger, *Sermons*, p.142; Musculus, pp.64–7; Nowell, pp.128–9; Bradford, fols.11v, 14r-15r; J. Rogers, fol. 12v; Shutte, sig.B8v; Gualter, p.521; *Homilies*, pp.343–4.

[52] Becon, *Catechism*, p.80.

[53] *Homilies*, pp.343–4.

less to do with sabbatarian concerns than with differing views of Church authority and the use of the judicial laws of the Old Testament.

JUDICIAL LAWS AND THE SABBATH

Disputes over the interpretation of scripture have already been illustrated in the differences over holy days. Cartwright argued that what scripture did not prescribe was forbidden, while Whitgift asserted that where scripture was silent the Church has authority to provide guidance. Cartwright's position was quite rightly treated as an attack on ecclesiastical authority. Yet more threatening was his claim that the Mosaic judicial code was perpetual and binding. While Whitgift and Cartwright agreed that the moral law endured and the ceremonial law was abrogated, they clashed over the application of Old Testament judicial laws and penalties in English society. Like Aquinas, Luther, Calvin, Bullinger, and others, Whitgift argued that these laws were established by God for one nation in a particular time and place. They did not bind the Christian magistrate or limit his power to make laws and assign penalties.[54] The seventh of the 39 Articles affirmed that 'the Law given from God by Moses, as touching Ceremonies and Rites do not bind Christian men, nor the Civil precepts thereof ought of necessity to be received in any commonwealth'. But in the 1570s, Cartwright and others objected to this teaching. Bishop Sandys of London complained to Bullinger in August 1573 that 'foolish young men' were disturbing the peace of the Church, and outlined their presbyterian programme. Among the points of contention was that 'the judicial laws of Moses are binding upon christian princes, and they ought not in the slightest degree to depart from them'.[55]

While Cartwright claimed that some parts of the judicial law were limited to the Jews, he denied that 'any magistrate can save the life of blasphemers, contemptuous and stubborn idolaters, murderers, adulterers, incestuous persons, and such like, which God by his judicial law hath commanded to be put to death'.[56]

---

[54] Avis, *passim.*; C. H. and K. George, *The Protestant Mind of the English Reformation, 1570–1640* (Princeton, N.J., 1961), pp.231–2.

[55] *The Zurich Letters*, edited by Hastings Robinson (Cambridge, 1842), pp.295–6.

[56] Whitgift, *Works*, I, 270. Cartwright's arguments were reprinted with Whitgift's responses.

The death penalty also applied to sabbath-breakers.[57] Humphrey Roberts complained that 'if one do steal, or comit murder, the laws of the Realm doth punish with death. But for Idolatry, swearing, and breaking of the Sabbath day, there is no punishment. And yet, the same God which said: Thou shalt not steal, said also...Thou shalt remember to keep holy the Sabbath day'.[58] While Charles George dismissed this adherence to the judicial laws as 'one of Cartwright's wildest anachronisms',[59] this view attracted a surprising number of adherents and influenced the early legal codes in the colonies.[60]

Whitgift argued that the Church had the right to determine many things, including matters 'which appertain to the external discipline and government of the church; which are to be varied according to time, persons, and place'.[61] He explained that if the judicial laws of Moses were used, many laws of the land would be abrogated; and the prince's prerogative to pardon offenders condemned to death would be abridged:

> To be short, all things must be transformed: lawyers must cast away their huge volumes and multitude of cases, and content themselves with the books of Moses: we of the clergy would be the best judges; and they must require the law at our hands...And so, while we make them believe that we seek for equality among ourselves, we seek indeed regal dominion over them'.[62]

Whitgift cited Musculus, Calvin, Beza, and others in his argument against Cartwright and concluded that 'this doctrine of yours not only tendeth to the overthrowing of states of comonwealths, but is contrary also to the truth, and opinions of learned men, and those especially of whom you yourself make greatest account'.[63]

The tensions created by this emphasis on the judicial laws have gone largely unnoticed. But they are critical to our understanding

---

[57] *Ibid.*, p.201.

[58] Humphrey Roberts, *An Earnest Complaint of Divers Vain, Wicked, and Abused Exercises, Now Commonly Practised on the Sabbath Day* (London, 1572), sig.B2v; see also John Stockwood, *A Very Fruitful Sermon* (London, 1579), p.50. These men were not writing without precedent, for Bucer recommended in *De Regno Christi* that the death penalty be applied to false teachers, blasphemers, sabbath-breakers, murderers, adulterers, rapists and others. He asked, 'who would approve of men wishing to be more merciful and just than God? If a magistrate is appointed to punish the wicked and anointed thus by God, how could he possibly discharge his duty more correctly than by punishing most rigorously what God has decreed to be offences with the penalties he has likewise decreed'. (Avis, p.161.)

[59] George, p.232.   [60] Solberg, pp.137–8.

[61] Whitgift, *Works*, I, 271.   [62] *Ibid.*, p.273.   [63] *Ibid.*, pp.273–7, 278.

of sabbatarian complaints in the 1570s; for if death was considered the most appropriate penalty for obstinate sabbath-breakers, a 12*d* fine or confession made in a white sheet before the parish must have seemed a mockery of God's justice. The efforts of bishops and secular officials could never measure up to the expectations of these precisionists; for their complaints were not just against officials who failed to implement existing laws, but also expressed the frustration that more rigorous penalties were not prescribed. Ecclesiastical and secular officials naturally reacted against this criticism as unwarranted and a threat to the established order. Here again, conflicting views of scripture and Church authority are the necessary background to understanding sabbatarian complaints in this period; for the discord was not fundamentally over the sabbath doctrine, but whether the Church could prescribe more lenient penalties for sabbatarian offences than the judicial laws allowed. With this in mind, it is important to use caution when interpreting contemporary complaints that bishops and secular officials were indifferent to sabbatarian doctrine and discipline. Indeed evidence from this period illustrates that much attention was devoted to this matter. Balancing this picture requires the study of visitation articles to ascertain the policy of Church officials, and consistory court records to evaluate the attitudes of parish officers who were the most important link in implementing ecclesiastical discipline.

VISITATION ARTICLES AND INJUNCTIONS

Any study of the discipline exercised by the Elizabethan spiritual courts is complicated by many factors. The first problem is the survival of injunctions and visitation articles, which stipulated the matters to be reported. While several thousand sets of articles must have been produced between 1558 and 1640, fewer than four hundred have survived.[64] Churchwardens and other parish officials were required to report on the moral, spiritual, clerical, and administrative deficiencies in their communities, using these articles as a guide for their enquiry. The contents of these articles are important, for they set the moral and spiritual agenda for a given jurisdiction and can illustrate the concerns of the ecclesiastical official who drafted them, although one can rarely be certain

[64] See *STC* entries.

of authorship. A comparison of these documents confirms the standardization of some articles, which appeared in many dioceses over several decades; but they also reveal the concerns of particular officials, who appended special notices or included uniquely worded articles. They are an invaluable aid in the search for trends in the ecclesiastical discipline, providing evidence of the shifting emphases in the discipline administered by ecclesiastical officials.

An examination of thirty-six visitation articles and injunctions used in fifteen dioceses and one archdeaconry in England and Wales between 1558 and 1583 reveals five areas of concern relating to Sunday and holy day observance.[65] First and foremost was the detection of recusant Catholics, by enforcing church attendance and requiring parishioners to receive communion at least once a year. These articles followed the pattern set by the Queen's Injunctions of 1559 and became a standard matter of enquiry throughout the Elizabethan and early Stuart period. While they were applied to recusant protestants as well, fear of Catholic subversion made church attendance a first test of religious loyalty and a means of detecting malcontents. Bishops were not only active in enforcing church attendance through their spiritual courts, but supported church attendance bills in parliament as well.

Ecclesiastical officials also sought to suppress trading on Sundays. Bishop Cox, in his *Interpretation and Further Considerations of Certain Injunctions*, extended the restrictions in Article xx, stating that: 'On Sunday there be no shops open...and that all fairs and common marts falling upon Sunday, there be no showing of any wares before the service be done'.[66] The legislation commended by the upper house of the 1563 Convocation to parliament went even further, requiring those persons and corporations holding patents for Sunday fairs and markets to move the event to the day before or after. Any buyer or seller who transgressed this law was to forfeit half the goods in question and those offending three times were to be imprisoned for fourteen days without bail.[67] The bill never passed parliament; and although it was read again in the 1566 parliament, it was not successful.[68] Promotion of this

[65] See bibliography heading 'Visitation articles'.
[66] Frere, III, 60; Strype, *Annals*, I pt I, p.319.
[67] Strype, *Annals*, v. I pt I, pp.529–32.
[68] Strype, *Annals*, I pt 2, pp.238–9; John Strype, *Grindal* (Oxford, 1821), pp.478–81.

legislation by Bishop Grindal and Archbishop Parker emphasizes the ecclesiastical support for this measure; for Church officials lacked the power to enforce such penalties on their own authority, and desired the help of secular regulations and enforcement. However, Church officials did attempt to stop trading during service time and prohibited the use of churchyards for that purpose. Parker used Cox's article in his 1566 Advertisements, as did Bishop Cooper in 1571, while similar articles were issued by bishops Parkhurst, Sandys, Cox, and others.[69] In 1565 Thomas Bentham, bishop of Coventry and Lichfield, prohibited all Sunday markets on pain of excommunication;[70] and in 1577 John Whitgift, then bishop of Worcester, enquired 'whether on Holy days and especially on the Sabbath days...any in your parish open shops for sale of wares'.[71] Episcopal attempts to suppress Sunday trading persisted throughout the Elizabethan and early Stuart period, and became a frequently reported offence in Ely diocese during Lancelot Andrewes' episcopate in the 1610s.[72]

Another sabbatarian concern found in early Elizabethan articles was the suppression of Sunday and holy day labours. These articles prohibited carrying loads, artisans using their crafts, and other ordinary labours. In 1561 Bishop Parkhurst of Norwich enquired whether any man, 'geveth himself or causeth his [servants] to labour bodelie or to attende their occupacion on the sabboth daie hindring both themselves and theyrs, therby to learn gostly things'.[73] Thomas Cooper's injunctions for Lincoln in 1571 ordered that, 'on the Sundays and Holydaies, ther be no shops open, nor Artificers commonly going aboute their worldly affayres'. In the same year he enquired, 'whether any do violate or breake the Sabboth day or holly daies with their manuall labours'.[74] The article which Whitgift used in 1577 was even more specific, searching out,

Whether on Holy days and especially on Sabbath days...any...use on those days their occupations as in brewing, baking, cutting down of corn or grain, or labouring in their artificial trades; [and] whether your butchers, walkers, fullers, or bargemen, do use their occupations or trades.[75]

Like Whitgift's view of the fourth precept, this article does not fit the anti-sabbatarian caricature found in Thomas Rogers'

[69] Frere, III, 176, 106, 308; Ely VA 1573; Lincoln VA 1571. [70] Frere, III, 169.
[71] Kennedy, II, 60; this article is drawn from those produced by John Aylmer.
[72] See Table 1b. [73] Norwich VA 1561.
[74] Lincoln VA 1571. [75] Kennedy, II, 60.

account of events in 1599. The same is true of Thomas Cooper who is also presented as an anti-sabbatarian bishop, because he defended the bishop condemned by Martin Marprelate for bowling on Sunday.[76] Bishops Robert Horne of Winchester, Richard Cox of Ely, and others used similar articles.[77] Like the suppression of recusants and Sunday trading, working was an episcopal concern throughout this period, and an interest which increased over time.

The fourth matter relating to Sundays and holy days was the attempt to regulate alehouse activities and popular pastimes. Episcopal efforts were usually limited to closing alehouses during service time and suppression of unlawful games. Parkhurst's 1569 Norwich article on this matter was similar to many others, enquiring 'whether there be any Inne kepers, Taverne, or Alehouse kepers that maintaine eating and drinkinge in them uppon any Sonday or holiday in the time of preaching or common praier'. In Parker's 1574 metropolitical visitation articles for Winchester, he enquired 'whether Innes, Tavernes, victayling and typling houses or gamying places be patent or entred into in service or preaching tyme'. Richard Cox went much further, condemning popular festivals and prohibiting their use on Sundays. At the end of his 1579 visitation articles, Cox issued the following order:

Because the Saboth day is so fondly abused in going unto Fayres and visiting frendes, and acquaintances, and in feasting, and making of good chere, in wanton dawnsing, in lewd maygames sometyme continuing riotously with Piping all whole nightes in barnes and such odde places, both younge men and women out of their fathers and masters howses, I charge all my parishes within my Dioces, and charge the Churchwardens, Sidemen, and ministers to see that no such disorders be kept upon the Sabaoth day, commonly called the Sundayes, as they will answere uppon their othe.[78]

While Cox's order was one of the the most dramatic of those found in this early period, his concern was not exceptional; for of the thirty-six documents examined, twenty-nine contained articles against the use of alehouses, drinking, and popular pastimes on Sunday.[79]

---

[76] He argued that if man may prepare food on the Sabbath, that he could also use 'some convenient exercise of the body, for the health of the body'. Thomas Cooper, *An Admonition to the People of England* (London, 1589), p.57.

[77] Winchester VA 1570; Ely VA 1573; Frere, III, p.93.   [78] Ely VA 1579.

[79] Included in this number are three blank sets used in various parts of the country.

While the enforcement of these regulations may not have been consistent and vigorous throughout the country, there can be no doubt about the importance placed on sabbatarian discipline by early Elizabethan bishops; for only Marmaduke Middleton at St David's and Edmund Guest of Rochester failed to include a question on at least one of these issues,[80] and most sets of visitation articles included two or more of the concerns discussed above. Indeed bishops were actively implementing sabbatarian discipline long before the complaint literature of the 1570s and their interest persisted throughout the Elizabethan and early Stuart period. The failure of their efforts was due primarily to the problems inherent in administering the spiritual courts.

The principal difficulty was receiving full and accurate presentments. To remedy this problem, bishops not only enquired about church attendance, trading, working, and the use of alehouses and pastimes on Sunday, but also demanded a report on the diligence of churchwardens in detecting these faults. In the 1560s the question usually concerned the collection of 12*d.* for non-attendance, imposed by the Queen's Injunctions. But in the 1570s more specific orders were added, requiring churchwardens and swornmen to leave the church and search the parish during service time, and report all who absented themselves 'negligently or wilfully from their parish Church or Chappell, or un-reverently...use themselves in time of divine service'. Bishops also enquired whether parish officials failed to report offenders because of 'any private corrupt affection', and whether they had abused the Sabbath themselves, by staying 'at home, or in some Taverne, or Alehouse, or else about some worldly business or at Bowles, Cardes, Tables, or other gaming'.[81] These reports were to be made by current parish officials against their predecessors; a system which could lead to vindictive behaviour or collusion, and often did. This social pressure was noted by Sir Owen Hopton of Suffolk in the Commons debate on the 1571 church attendance bill. He observed that churchwardens 'beinge simple men and fearinge to offende, would rather incurre the daunger of perjurie than displease some of their neighbours'.[82] This problem, plus

---

[80] St David's VA 1583; Rochester VA 1565.   [81] York VA 1571.

[82] J. E. Neale, *Elizabeth and Her Parliaments, 1559–1581* (London, 1953), p.389; *Proceedings in the Parliaments of Elizabeth I, 1558–1581*, edited by T. E. Hartley (Leicester, 1981), I, 202.

the ineffective penalties of suspension, excommunication, and small fines indicate the difficulties faced by the most conscientious bishop.

Clearly, early Elizabethan bishops were active in establishing sabbatarian discipline in the Church; and their formulations became the standard for over fifty years. Edmund Grindal's metropolitical visitation articles for 1571 were particularly important as a model. Although precisionists desired more severe penalties, the discipline established by ecclesiastical officials would have satisfied most sabbatarians. Those who complained of lax enforcement of these regulations had a valid case. However, this had more to do with administrative failure than the good intentions of ecclesiastical officials. The problems of effectively implementing sabbatarian discipline are easily seen when examining consistory court records.

CONSISTORY COURT RECORDS

The study of ecclesiastical visitation articles and injunctions is instructive, but one can never be certain that they were implemented without examining consistory court records. This task is daunting because of the mountains of evidence surviving and the difficulty of interpreting them.[83] In this study we will examine the operation of consistory courts in Ely and Norwich under bishops Richard Cox and John Parkhurst; a comparison which is useful for several reasons. Because East Anglia has been regarded as a 'puritan' stronghold in this period, these diocesan court records offer an opportunity to test the connection between precisionist sympathies and the sabbatarian zeal of parish officers and court officials. The crucial role of Cox in formulating sabbatarian discipline and the similarity of Parkhurst's sympathies make them ideal candidates for a study of episcopal administrative effectiveness.[84] Cox and Parkhurst had travelled the same spiritual road, nurtured in Henrician and Edwardine protestantism, and matured by the hardships of their Marian exile. Although both

---

[83] For a description of Court procedure, see Dorothy Owen, *The Records of the Established Church in England* (London, 1970), *passim*.

[84] Another important factor was the accessibility, quality, and quantity of Ely court records, as well as the availability of Dr Ralph Houlbrooke's work on the Norwich records.

men could claim the same pedigree, their activities on the continent marked out the differences between them. While Cox battled for adherence to the Prayer Book at Frankfurt and assumed a role of leadership there, Parkhurst enjoyed a gentle, scholarly life at Zurich, under the protection of Rudolf Gualter, Zwingli's son-in-law.[85] When Elizabeth appointed Cox to Ely in 1559, he soon demonstrated administrative abilities both in his diocese and in the national Church. Parkhurst's performance as bishop of Norwich demonstrated his incompetence in both spheres.[86]

Their differences are particularly evident when examining their consistory courts. The bishops in English and Welsh dioceses depended on two levels of administration in these courts. While parish officials detected and reported moral, spiritual, liturgical, and administrative offences stipulated in visitation articles and injunctions, the bishop's commissaries and chancellors presided over his courts and punished offenders. These courts handled cases between private parties as well, but attention here will be limited to *ex officio* cases brought before the courts by churchwardens, ministers, and other parish officers, as well as local informers. Bishops rarely presided over their courts, and Cox and Parkhurst were not exceptions.[87]

For this reason, the reliability of commissaries and chancellors was essential if the bishop's disciplinary policies were to be effectively implemented. While Cox proved an able judge of men and selected qualified officers to run his courts, Parkhurst was hampered by both diocesan administrative structures and his inability to direct the actions of his subordinates. Between 1576 and 1580, Thomas Ithell, Robert Conwaye, Thomas Legge, and Richard Bridgwater presided over Cox's courts. All four proceeded to LL.D. and ran the courts efficiently, implementing their bishop's disciplinary policy by punishing offenders presented.[88]

---

[85] *The Letter Book of John Parkhurst*, edited by R. A. Houlbrooke (Norfolk Record Society, 1974 and 1975), p.23.

[86] Houlbrooke, *Parkhurst*, pp.23–53.

[87] There is no record of Cox presiding between 1576 and 1580. EDR D/2/10a; EDR D/2/10; Houlbooke, *Parkhurst*, p.31. See also Dorothy Owen, 'The Records of the Bishop's Official at Ely: Specialization in the English Episcopal Chancery of the Late Middle Ages', in *The Study of Medieval Records*, edited by D. A. Bullough and R. L. Storey (Oxford, 1971), pp.189–205.

[88] EDR D/2/10a; EDR D/2/10; J. A. Venn, *Alumni Cantabrigienses* (Cambridge, 1927), for Thomas Ithell, Robert Conwaye, and Richard Bridgwater; see *DNB* for Thomas Legge.

In Norwich, archdeacons held office for life and appointed their own officers, leaving Parkhurst with little control over the men who ran his consistory courts. They demonstrated scant interest in his reforming efforts and little was accomplished through the courts.[89] His chancellors were no better; for they were either ignorant of canon law, hostile to his reforming policy, or possessed a disagreeable temperament. The disarray of his finances and courts brought rebukes from Archbishop Parker, and in 1567 a metropolitical visitation. But Parkhurst never managed to control his underlings.[90] In 1573 he implored his chancellor to move more quickly against those who had disturbed evening prayer at St Simon's, Norwich, noting that 'if we shall continue slow and negligent in reforming, the blemish and discredit will light upon us both at the length, and that more heavily than will be well borne'.[91] Parkhurst spent his later years longing for the Arcadian days of Zurich.

The success of Cox and failure of Parkhurst in managing their courts are sterling illustrations of how two bishops with similar concerns might produce very different results; for the type of discipline applied had more to do with the co-operation of parish and court officers than with the disciplinary policy of the bishop. Consensus at all three levels was crucial for the effective implementation of the bishop's orders. This is particularly evident when examining sabbatarian concerns; for both bishops attempted to enforce church attendance, regulate alehouse activities, and prohibit trading and working on Sundays and holy days.[92] Their courts obtained large numbers of sabbatarian presentments from parish officials; but while Parkhurst's court officials rarely took action against offenders, Cox's officials regularly imposed a fine or ordered offenders to do penance.

The negligence of Parkhurst's commissaries in punishing recusants for non-attendance brought a rebuke from the Privy Council, which he passed on to his officials stating, 'the faulte hereof resteth in you as the eye of the bysshop within your circuit'.[93] He had good reason to complain, for while eighty-seven sabbatarian offenders were presented in five deaneries of the archdeaconry of

[89] Houlbrooke, *Parkhurst*, p.27.   [90] *Ibid.*, pp.30–2.

[91] Strype, *Annals*, II pt 1, 329–30; Houlbrooke, *Parkhurst*, pp.161–2.

[92] Norwich VA 1561, 1569; Ely VA 1571, 1573, 1579.

[93] Houlbrooke, *Parkhurst*, pp.93–4.

Norwich in 1569–70, sixty-seven were either dismissed or were never punished. Of those that were punished, five were ordered to do penance, and fourteen were charged a fine or given a commuted penance. One person was successfully purged of the charge by the testimony of neighbours.[94] Although the number of sabbatarian presentments was second only to sexual offences, Parkhurst's commissaries were negligent in applying effective punishments.

The pattern was different in Ely. Between 1576 and 1580 Cox's courts dealt with 259 sabbatarian cases, with commissaries assigning fines and penances, or giving admonitions to 169 offenders. Forty-four offenders were able to certify their innocence or exceptional circumstances, while sixteen were last recorded as excommunicated or suspended. Only thirty offenders escaped without punishment or an appearance in court.[95]

However, Cox's consistory courts also had administrative problems. While his court officials regularly punished the sabbatarian offenders presented, these cases amounted to less than fifteen per cent of the 1,675 presentments and were predominantly cases of non-attendance and Sunday labours. With Cox's interest in suppressing Sunday trading and popular festivals, it is striking that no such cases appear between 1576 and 1580 throughout the diocese.[96] This omission illustrates that ultimately the courts could only succeed in reforming behaviour if parish officials made accurate presentments. As Sir Owen Hopton noted in 1571, social pressure worked against such honesty.

Indeed churchwardens suffered enough with the presentments they did make. Stephen Kercher of St Peter's parish, Cambridge, was presented in 1579 for seldom attending church and reviling parish officials. It was reported that when they came to collect the statutory penalty, Kercher 'sayd he wolde breake his pate that cam to fitche any distresse oute of his house'. His case came before Richard Bridgwater nine times, and Kercher was excommunicated twice before confessing his fault and paying the fine.[97] In 1580 Thomas Wells, churchwarden at Foxton, presented Allin Hall for being absent one Sunday. Shortly thereafter he was presented again for quarrelling and brawling with Wells. It was reported that

[94] R. A. Houlbrooke, *Church Courts and the People* (Oxford, 1979), p.281.
[95] EDR D/2/10a; EDR D/2/10.
[96] EDR D/2/10a; EDR D/2/10.   [97] EDR D/2/10, fol. 201v.

Hall abused the churchwarden, 'saying that he was no honest man, nor fytte to be in that office...and did use diverse other quarelling and brawling words'.[98]

Given such pressures it is little wonder that parish officers did not present offenders. In 1580 six parish officials from Cottenham were presented for not reporting those who worked on St James' day. Their testimony conflicted, with some stating that they had seen no one work, while others observed that they would have to 'presente all the towne'; but all refused to supply names.[99] When churchwardens from Fen Ditton and Parsons Drove were presented in 1576 for not reporting non-attendance, both sets accused their scribes of not recording their presentments accurately.[100] In other cases the parish officers simply claimed that there were no violations.[101] However, informers sometimes reported such omissions if successive parish officials did not. In 1579, an informer reported that

many have deserved by reason of wilfullnes and otherwise to have paid the forfeiture mentioned in the xith article [of Cox's visitation articles] how be it we cannot learne that it hathe ben taken from us of longe time. For yf it have ben trewlye taken accordinge to Statute either the poore box shoulde have ben better stowed with mony or ells the churche many times better filled with people.[102]

Parish officials were in an unenviable position, caught between local pressures and their sworn duty to report offences to the church courts.

When presentments were made, factors other than sabbatarian zeal sometimes motivated the officers' actions. Vindictive behaviour was a real problem for the courts, for parish officials and informers occasionally settled scores with their enemies by presenting them for offences they may or may not have committed. In 1578 Francis Lubson from Elm was presented for pulling hemp on Sundays and holy days. Lubson replied that a Mr Blythe had presented him because of 'sum displeasure between them'. Parish officials confirmed this and the case was dismissed.[103] In other cases, sabbatarian charges seem to have been thrown in to increase the list of offences. Robert Palmer, vicar of Eltisley, was presented

98 *Ibid.*, fols. 229r,239r.   99 *Ibid.*, fol. 224v.
100 EDR D/2/10a, fol. 31v; EDR D/2/10, fols. 11r, 15v, 31v.
101 EDR D/2/10, fols. 17v, 26v, 28r-v.
102 *Ibid.*, fol. 154.   103 EDR D/2/10a, fol. 70v.

in 1576 for not catechizing, not saying divine service at regular times, running an alehouse in the vicarage, and many other things. As if to emphasize his negligent behaviour, Palmer was also presented for playing cards during evening prayer time, forcing parishioners to forgo the service. The vicar rather feebly claimed that this had happened only once. Conwaye ordered him to do penance for these transgressions.[104] In other cases sabbatarian charges were coupled with failure to pay parish dues or turn over church property held while in office.[105]

The existence of papists and separatist protestants contributed to a growing disregard for the spiritual courts, and even conforming laymen were not always intimidated by the penalties of suspension or excommunication. The small fines imposed and public acts of penance assigned often failed to induce the contrition desired. The case of Allin Hall illustrates this point. Yet Ely was more successful than other dioceses in imposing penalties and taking cases to a conclusion. The reappearance of Stephen Kercher's case nine times in six months indicates that even recalcitrant offenders were often brought to submission. Norwich courts were rarely as successful, with many cases left uncompleted; and the situation was even worse in dioceses with a high recusant population. In Chester diocese, wholesale excommunications left many unmoved, with effective discipline being exercised only in protestant strongholds like Manchester.[106]

All these problems emphasize that the type of discipline exercised by the spiritual court can rarely be simply attributed to the ideological commitment of the bishop. A multitude of factors, which included social pressures and intimidation, as well as the ineptitude, apathy, or corruption of officials, complicated the picture. These complications must be recognized before consistory court records can be evaluated responsibly.

However, despite the many complicating factors in interpreting these records, they nevertheless illustrate that in many cases parishioners respected diocesan discipline and demonstrated cont-

[104] EDR D/2/10, fol. 14r-v.
[105] EDR D/2/10a, fol. 10v; EDR D/2/10, fol. 79v.
[106] Cheshire Record Office, EDV1/6d; *The Manuscripts of Lord Kenyon: HMC, Fourteenth Report, Appendix, Part IV* (London, 1894), p.587; Roger C. Richardson, 'Puritanism in the Diocese of Chester to 1642' (unpublished Ph.D. thesis, University of Manchester, 1968), p.352; W. B. Whitaker, *Sunday in Tudor and Stuart Times* (London, 1933), pp.38–9; Edward Baines, *The History of...Lancashire*, 2 vols. (London, 1868), I, 183.

rition for offences committed. When Fabian Wrighte of Whittlesey was presented in 1578 for mowing barley before morning prayer, it was reported that he was 'greved when he was towlde of his falte'. He confessed that the work was performed because his barley was in danger of being destroyed by the village herd. Wrighte was admonished and his case dismissed.[107] Peter Lynge of Barrington was presented in 1576 for carting on the sabbath day in service time. He confessed that he had fetched half a load of tythe corn to save it from the village herd of hogs and cattle. Assuring the court that his labours had been necessary, Lynge explained that, 'but for loseinge the [barley] he had let that stand still untyl the Munday followeinge'.[108] When Jeremy Manninge was presented in 1579 for not hearing service at Trumpington on Whitsun Sunday, he claimed that he had not been wilfully absent. He explained that on Whitsun Eve he had been at a fair twenty-three miles from home. Because 'he woulde not travell uppon Whitson Sundaye he came home that nighte', arriving around two hours after midnight. Drenched from a storm, he went to bed very sick and could not go to church the next day.[109]

These examples are important illustrations of lay attitudes towards the Sabbath; for in each case there was no question of their obligation, and each man exhibited an awareness of his sabbath duty. In Manninge's case, his effort to avoid a Sunday journey had resulted in illness. The central issue in Wrighte's case was not whether labour could be used on Sunday but whether his labours could not have waited till Monday. These laymen clearly knew and understood their duty on the Sabbath and holy days.

Wilful disobedience was punished and exceptional circumstances resulted in the dismissal of those accused. But there is no indication that laymen questioned the right of the Church to enforce attendance and prohibit Sunday labours. Observance of the Sabbath was part of the layman's definition of a good Christian. The mistress of John Wood, a minister at Marden, was uncertain whether adultery was a sin, but could affirm that she was no 'swearer, saboath breaker, [or] contemner of God's holy word and sacraments'.[110]

[107] EDR D/2/10a, fol. 75v.
[108] EDR D/2/10, fol. 60r; see similar cases, *Ibid.*, fols. 4v, 18v, 226r.
[109] *Ibid.*, fol. 173r.
[110] Collinson, *Religion of Protestants*, p.107.

By contrast, Cox's efforts to prohibit Sunday trading and festivals resulted in no presentments. His attempts to regulate alehouse activities produced only ten presentments between 1576 and 1580. Like Owen Hopton, one might blame the churchwardens who feared to 'displease some of their neighbours';[111] however, a more fundamental truth belies that answer. The Church had tried for centuries to suppress these activities with little success, for laymen resisted such control. Clinging to popular religious practices, some lay people were unwilling to accept such limitations and passively – or aggressively – resisted. Philip Stubbes, in his *Anatomy of Abuses*, summarized lay attitudes well. In the dialogue between Philo and Spud, Philo condemned maygames, feasts, piping, tennis, cockfighting, hawking, hunting, football, and other Sunday pastimes, and provided a theological justification similar to that found in the *Homilies*. Spud responded that

You will be deemed too Stoical, if you should restrain men from these exercises upon the Sabbath, for they suppose that that day was ordained, and consecrated to the end and purpose to use what kind of exercises they think good themselves.[112]

While a precisionist like Stubbes or a bishop like Cox might have been contemptuous of such an attitude, this caricature resembled the attitude of many. Faced with popular resistance to such reforms, it is little wonder that the disciplinary efforts of bishops did not succeed. Even in the efficiently run courts of Ely, parish officials vetoed Cox's efforts by their silence. While the complaint literature of the 1570s decried the failure of authorities to enforce a strict observance, Parkhurst and Cox illustrate that the best of intentions did not bring success. Yet they also indicate that the Church was not indifferent or negligent in this matter. Indeed the English Church, its teachings, and its discipline established the precedent followed by later sabbatarians; and this influence was not limited to Church discipline, but extended to secular regulations at the local and national level.

[111] *Parliaments*, Hartley, p.202.
[112] Phillip Stubbes, *The Anatomy of Abuses* (London, 1583), sig.L2v.

PARLIAMENT AND THE SABBATH

Thomas Barnes, in his essay on the 1633 Book of Sports controversy noted that 'the painstaking researches of the historians of Parliament have established that from early in Elizabeth's reign, the Commons assumed an increasingly Puritan complexion'.[113] This observation is part of an introduction which associated the religious legislation of Elizabeth's parliaments with the 'preciser sort' of protestant who is thought to have become increasingly disaffected with the Church in the early seventeenth century. Sabbatarian legislation is particularly implied here as a precursor to the controversies which occurred in the 1630s. However, this interpolation of sabbatarianism as one of the first seeds of strife cannot be supported by parliamentary evidence; for in the early Elizabethan parliaments bishops and clergy not only co-operated in promoting sabbatarian legislation but initiated such bills as well.

Alexander Nowell's sermon at the opening of parliament in 1563 urged the members to pass strict legislation against sabbath abuses. He stated that 'the Lord's day, which now is so diversly abused, is to be looked unto: for on that day, taverns, alehouses, and other unruly places be full, but the Lord's house empty; which crime before this hath been punished with death'.[114] He urged that a law be passed to restore this discipline, noting that men have six days for their own use, but must dedicate the seventh to the Lord.[115] The Lord Keeper's speech also urged the creation of such legislation.[116] Drafts for this legislation passed through the hands of Grindal and Parker, were approved by the convocation's upper house, and commended to parliament.[117]

These measures did not pass in 1563, nor did a bill against Sunday trading succeed in 1566. However, it is interesting to note that a successful private act fulfilled the intentions of the general bills in at least one locality. This act, entitled 'For Keeping of Thursday Market at Battle in Sussex', licensed Viscount Montague to move the Battle market from Sunday to Thursday. The

[113] Thomas Barnes, 'County Politics and a Puritan Cause Célèbre: Somerset Churchales, 1633', *TRHS*, 5th series, 9 (1959), 103–22 (p.103).

[114] A reference to Old Testament judicial laws.

[115] Nowell, p.226.

[116] *Parliaments*, Hartley, p.82.   [117] Strype, *Annals*, I, pt 1, pp.529–32.

justification for this action was that 'yt ys more Convenyent for thenhabitants of the sayde towne, and other of the Queenes Majesties Lovinge Subjectes to attende devine Service on the Sondayes then the sayd Market'.[118]

While most of these regulations were incorporated into episcopal injunctions and visitation articles, they never became national laws. However, the important point to note is that the initiative was taken by Church officials, contradicting the polemical accounts found in complaint literature and later Laudian propaganda.

The sabbath bills of the 1571, 1572, 1576, and 1581 sessions focused on church attendance, and were aimed primarily at recusant Catholics. The failure of these bills in the first three sessions was due primarily to Elizabeth's reluctance to exert pressure on English Catholics, and her veto was used against the advice of the highest secular and ecclesiastical authorities. Unfortunately, accounts critical of bishops have obscured this point. Thomas Norton, parliamentarian and translator of Calvin,[119] complained in 1584 that recusants were not being punished 'because the Bishops object to lay justices having power in this matter, and so do not give them support'. He asserted that the bishops had failed to do their duty in this matter and condemned them for implying that 'the Queen has hindered such execution in the past'.[120]

However, Norton's criticism was not entirely justified, for many bishops were active in this matter. The bill on church attendance and receiving communion was the first bill read at the 1571 parliament. J. E. Neale observed that, 'the Puritan leaders must have been delighted when the Speaker chose this bill to inaugurate the session'. However, even Neale concluded that this bill was not part of the 'puritan' programme. Clearly, contentious and divisive issues were being raised, as evidenced by the extreme

---

[118] Strype, *Annals*, 1, pt 2, pp.238–9; also Strype, *Grindal*, pp.478–81. I am grateful to Dr Norman Jones for the Battle Market reference.(HLRO, Original Acts, 8 Eliz. no.34.)

[119] *The House of Commons: 1558–1603*, edited by P. W. Hasler, 3 vols. (London, 1981), III, 145–9.

[120] *The Seconde Parte of a Register*, edited by Albert Peel, 2 vols. (Cambridge, 1915), 1, 191; see also Collinson, *Religion of Protestants*, p.151. Michael Graves' article has established that Norton was not a puritan leader and anti-establishment figure, as Neale has portrayed him; but was in fact working closely with the Privy Council and the bishops. (Michael Graves, 'Thomas Norton the Parliament Man: An Elizabethan M.P., 1559–1581,' *The Historical Journal*, 23, 1980, 17–35.)

protestant views found in the *Admonition*. However, it would be a mistake to associate this bill with 'puritan' scheming.[121]

This bill, which was in substance the measure approved by the convocation in 1563, stipulated that 'every man borne and resyding within this realme sholde on every festyvall day repaire to the church to the devine service upon payne of xxxsh', and required that communion be received at least once a year under the penalty of a 100 marks fine.[122] The reason for the bill seems fairly clear, with the papal bull and the Northern Rebellion fresh in the minds of those in parliament,[123] but its origins are unknown. Bishop Sandys stressed the need for this action in his sermon before parliament, explaining that it was the duty of Christian princes 'to compel every subject to come and hear this word [scripture], lest the church by this evil example should be greatly offended'.[124] Burghley also favoured the bill. While Neale denied that it was a bishop's bill or a formal government measure, he did not rule out the possibility that some Privy Councillors may have devised it.[125] Unfortunately, Neale's search for anti-episcopal attitudes and puritan plots in the 1571 parliament confused this issue.

Professor Elton has observed that 'what is often called puritanism by historians was to contemporaries just zealous protestantism and a sensible fear of Rome'. He also noted the important role played by Privy Councillors in managing the activities of the Commons, and cites the 1571 religious bills as an occasion when leading members of the Commons solicited support from the bishops.[126] These factors must be taken into account when examining the 1571 parliament.

When the bill received its second reading on 6 April, Sir Thomas Smith, a close friend of Lord Burghley and a Privy Councillor, was the first to speak in support of the legislation, suggesting that the bishops be consulted on certain points. This

[121] Neale, *Parliaments: 1559–1581*, pp.192–3; *Parliaments*, Hartley, pp.199,245.
[122] The fine for non-attendance at church varies in surviving accounts, with amounts of 12*d.* and 12 pounds also given. Neale, *Parliaments: 1559–1581*, p.192n; *Parliaments*, Hartley, pp.204, 205n, 245; Strype, *Annals*, 1, pt 1, pp.529–32.
[123] Neale, *Parliaments: 1559–1581*, p.191.
[124] Edwin Sandys, *Sermons*, edited by John Ayre (Cambridge, 1841), p.46.
[125] Neale, *Parliaments: 1559–1581*, pp.191–3.
[126] G. R. Elton, 'Parliament in the Sixteenth Century: Functions and Fortunes', *The Historical Journal*, 22 no.2 (1979), 255–78 (pp.271, 273–4).

seems to have been in compliance with the Lord Keeper's request that the bishops be consulted about religious measures presented to the Commons.[127] William Fleetwood, another Burghley man, was the second to speak in favour of the bill; although he moved that the penalty of the statute should not go to the informer. He noted that 'evilles and inconveniences' grew out of this practice, for it resulted in 'private gaine to the worst sort of men'. He also objected to Smith's suggestion that the bishops be consulted, citing King Edgar's sabbatarian laws to prove that 'the princes in the parliaments have made ecclesiastical lawes and constitucions'. He concluded by requesting that the bill 'be committed to some of the House and not to expect the bushopps, who perhappes would bee slowe'.[128]

Neale interpreted this motion as an open act of defiance, in which Fleetwood 'proclaimed himself a rebel and probably got into bad odour with authority'. But P. W. Hasler's description of Fleetwood presents him as Burghley's friend, and a loyal supporter and promoter of his politics in parliament. Although Neale implied that Fleetwood was hostile to the episcopate, Bishop Pilkington wrote of Fleetwood with approval, stating that 'if I might have such a helper I would not doubt by God's help to conquer many things'.[129] A more likely explanation would be that Fleetwood was attempting to protect the house's jurisdiction; for it was highly irregular to refer a bill to the bishops before the Commons had finished its work.[130] The bishops had already demonstrated their eagerness for the passage of such legislation in 1563, and Sandys' sermon openly promoted this measure. So it is unlikely that he was concerned that the episcopate would disapprove of such a bill. At any rate, Neale's attempt to taint Fleetwood's motion with rebellious sentiments seems unfounded.

The bill appeared in a new form on 9 April, with a provision appended to exempt gentlemen with chapels, ambassadors, strangers, sick men, and imprisoned persons, as well as a proviso for times of plague. Thomas Snagge expressed concern that the old law on church attendance and these new measures could be used

---

[127] *Parliaments*, Hartley, p.201; Neale, *Parliaments: 1559–1581*, pp.186, 195–6. Smith's role in the 1571 parliament was to assist Burghley in guiding the Commons, which his elevation to the peerage prevented. *House of Commons*, Hasler, III, 400–1.

[128] *Parliaments*, Hartley, pp.201–2.

[129] Neale, *Parliaments: 1559–1581*, p.196; *House of Commons*, Hasler, II, 133–4.

[130] I am grateful to Dr N. Jones for this observation.

against those who were well intentioned; for one could be fined for non-attendance at church, but also be liable for a much larger sum if one remained at a service which was not conducted according to the Prayer Book.[131]

Edward Aglionby, who owed his seat to the influential Earl of Warwick, moved that no exemption be made for any gentlemen, noting that laws should demonstrate equity between the prince and the poor man. No doubt he also had in mind the freedom this measure would have given recusant gentry. In addition he objected to the provision requiring that all receive communion once a year, arguing that 'it was not convenient to enforce consciences'.[132]

Strickland approved of Aglionby's first objection, but rejected the second, explaining that 'consciences may bee free, but not to disturbe the common quiett' and asserted that 'the sword of the prince for lacke of lawe must not bee tyed'. James Dalton supported Strickland's position, arguing that 'the matter of conscience did not concerne the law makers, nether were they to regard the error, curiositie or stiffnecknes of the evill, ignorant or froward persons'.[133]

On 20 April the bill received its second reading and Aglionby repeated his position, arguing for the enforcement of church attendance but against requirements for receiving communion. He explained that to 'come to the church, for that it is publique and tendeth but to prove a man a Christian, is tollerable and convenient...for that by religion onely a man is knowne and discerned from brute beastes'. But he denied that it was lawful to coerce the consciences of others.[134] However, John Agmondesham and Thomas Norton supported both parts of the bill, and carried the Commons with them, for the next day the bill was read and committed. It was engrossed on 30 April and passed the Commons on 4 May.[135] The bill finally passed the Lords on 25 May, after several conferences with the Commons, of which little is known. However, one interesting insight is provided by the

[131] *Parliaments*, Hartley, p.205; Neale, *Parliaments: 1559–1581*, pp.212–13.
[132] *Parliaments*, Hartley, pp.205–6; *House of Commons*, Hasler, 1, 329.
[133] *Parliaments*, Hartley, p.206; Neale, *Parliaments: 1559–1581*, pp.212–13.
[134] *Parliaments*, Hartley, pp.240, 248.
[135] Neale, *Parliaments: 1559–1581*, p.215; *Parliaments*, Hartley, pp.240–1, 248–50.

French ambassador, who reported that some noblemen had found it intolerable that bishops and ministers had become so arrogant that they now wished to subject the nobility as well as the people to their authority – an obvious reference to the refusal to exempt gentlemen's private chapels.[136]

Elizabeth vetoed the bill. Apparently the more controversial requirement to receive communion was the reason for her action, keeping her promise not to open windows into men's souls. Neale regarded it as a striking example of personal monarchy, for her action was taken despite the support of the Privy Council, both houses of Parliament, and most, if not all, of the bishops.[137]

Any residual doubt of this official support can be dispelled by examining the events at the 1572 parliament. Despite the tensions created by the *Admonition*, and the polarization of religious opinion, the sabbath bill of 1571 reappeared in the Lords, with Archbishop Grindal and other bishops backing the measure. Although nothing is recorded in the *Lords Journal*, Grindal's letter to Lord Burghley of 2 June explains the situation. He reported that 'I and some other bishops, according to the order taken by the Higher House, were yesternight with the Queen's Majesty, to move her Highnes that the bill for coming to divine service might by her assent be propounded.' Although he intended to read the bill to her, Elizabeth ordered that the bill should be delivered to Burghley, and Grindal sought the Secretary's support. The queen evidently refused to let the bill go forward, for no further action was taken.[138]

Grindal did not give up. In the first week of the 1576 session, the newly enthroned archbishop of Canterbury re-introduced the bill in the Lords. After the second reading it was sent to a committee which included Burghley, Sussex, Bedford, and Leicester, as well as bishops Sandys, Cox, Cooper, and Curtis. Although the evidence is unclear, it seems reasonable to suggest that Elizabeth intervened again; for a new bill was drafted with the restricted title, 'for coming to church'. This bill was read once

[136] Neale, *Parliaments: 1559–1581*, pp.215–16; *CJ*, i, 91–2; *LJ*, i, 683, 688, 695–7; Bertrand de Salignac de la Mothe Fénélon, *Correspondance diplomatique…1568–1575*, edited by A. Teulet, 7 vols. (Paris, 1838–40), IV, 106; *Parliaments*, Hartley, pp.253–5.
[137] Neale, *Parliaments: 1559–1581*, p.216.
[138] *Ibid.*, pp.304, 349; Fénélon, p.225; SP/10/88, no.5.

and disappeared from the records. It appears that again the queen's will proved stronger in this matter than the desires of the bishops and leading peers of the realm.[139]

It was not until 1581 that strong measures on church attendance were passed; and these were part of a bill directed specifically at Catholic recusants. On 27 January Sir Walter Mildmay, Chancellor of the Exchequer, made an impassioned speech against the seditious nature of papists and the dangers of not suppressing their activities. His motion for stringent controls on Catholics was well received and committees were formed to draw up bills.[140] Thomas Norton, who supported the 1571 church attendance bill, was active in drafting this bill, entitled, 'Act to retain the Queen's Majesty's subjects in their due obedience'. But on 7 February, Sir Christopher Hatton informed the Commons that the Lords was considering again the bill on church attendance and receiving communion, and a conference between the houses was arranged. While the Lords' bill had been amended and expanded, it was mild compared with the Commons' bill. Between 8 and 18 February, representatives of both houses met several times and produced a new bill, which in its penalties for non-attendance at church, was even more severe than the first. This bill had thirty-eight provisions, which made saying mass a felony, while hearing mass brought a fine of 200 marks and six months in prison. It excluded Catholics from positions of influence and prescribed penalties for recusant lawyers and schoolmasters. Most interesting for this study were the provisions for non-attendance at church. A fine of 20 pounds a month was imposed on Catholics for non-attendance, increasing to 40 pounds the second, 100 pounds for the third, and the pains of praemunire for the fourth month. Non-Catholic recusants were subject to a scale of 10 pounds, 20 pounds, 40 pounds, and nothing higher. These penalties were not only to be imposed on the head of a household but on his wife as well. Thomas Norton recorded that the dealings with the Lords were not harmonious, and he complained that the bishops involved 'spake most or onely for jurisdiction' and cited one bishop who refused to accept the bill if it meant justices of the peace enforcing

---

[139] Neale, *Parliaments: 1559–1581*, p.349; Edmund Lodge, *Illustrations of British History*, 3 vols. (London, 1791), II, 137–8; *LJ*, i, 731–2, 740; Patrick Collinson, *Archbishop Grindal, 1519–1583* (London, 1979), p.225.

[140] *Parliaments*, Hartley, p.528; Neale, *Parliaments: 1559–1581*, pp.382–5.

religious conformity. While the assertions of Norton and others leave the impression that bishops were reluctant to co-operate, it should be emphasized that Norton was not likely to be sympathetic to the bishops' desire to preserve the jurisdiction of their spiritual courts, and his word should not detract from the essential truth of episcopal support for these measures. In addition, episcopal backing for previous secular legislation further qualifies the significance of Norton's accusation.[141] Elizabeth did not allow this bill to pass into law without moderating its provisions, but the clauses concerning church attendance remained severe: requiring the forfeiture of 20 pounds for every month of absence from church and after twelve months offenders were subject to an additional fine of 200 pounds.[142] While this penalty would have been ruinous for most Elizabethan recusants, Neale noted that there was often a slip between Tudor law making and law enforcement.

While the bills of 1571, 1572, 1576, and 1581 were directed primarily at recusant non-attendance and cannot be identified as purely sabbatarian measures, they illustrate episcopal willingness to promote secular legislation in the enforcement of religious conformity – a point which will be important in the study of later sabbatarian bills. They also demonstrate the intense concern shared by both bishops and more radical protestants. In 1584 Norton declared that bishops had 'neither required their clergy to notify them of all recusants in their parishes, nor have they used the powers vested in them by the High Commission'.[143] But this charge looks ridiculous when faced with evidence from visitation articles, as well as the special measures taken by the bishops in the 1560s and 1570s.[144] Any slackness in this matter was firmly corrected. Parkhurst's failure to take effective action against recusants led to Parker's metropolitical visitation in 1567 and further rebukes in 1571 induced Parkhurst to reprimand prominent recusants personally.[145] When Bishop Downham of Chester

[141] *Parliaments*, Hartley, pp.533–4, 537, 541, 542, 546–7; Neale, *Parliaments: 1559–1581*, pp.386–9; *CJ*, i, 123, 128, 130–1; *LJ*, ii, 29, 44, 46–8; *Archaeologia*, 36 (1855), 111–12.
[142] *Statutes*, Stephens, I, 440. [143] Peel, *Register*, I, 191.
[144] *CSPD: 1547–1580*, pp.559–70; see also William R. Trimble, *The Catholic Laity in Elizabethan England, 1558–1603* (Cambridge, Mass., 1964), pp.24–31, 52, 56, 58; R. M. Fisher, 'Privy Council Coercion and Religious Conformity, at the Inns of Court, 1569–84', *Recusant History*, 15, no.5 (May, 1981), 305–24.
[145] Houlbrooke, *Parkhurst*, pp.93–4, 119, 121–2, 147, 188.

was found lax in this matter in 1570, Grindal ordered the bishop
of Carlisle to make a visitation of Chester on the archbishop's
behalf.[146] The close attention given to recusancy by the High
Commission illustrates the distorted picture provided by disaffected protestants, and emphasizes the danger of accepting without
qualification their critique of the Church.[147] Some bishops were
obviously concerned to preserve the jurisdiction of their spiritual
courts, but tensions over that matter had more to do with attitudes
towards ecclesiastical authority than the enforcement of church
attendance.

The sabbatarian regulations commended to parliament in 1563
as well as the support for later legislation confirms the episcopate's
eagerness for secular legislation on this issue. Indeed the episcopal
promotion of an act which authorized secular officials to enforce
sanctions against excommunicated persons further illustrates the
willingness of bishops to use these officials to maintain spiritual
discipline within their dioceses. There can be little doubt why
Elizabeth suppressed these bills, for, as Professor Collinson has
observed, 'nothing made the queen less Erastian than the Erastia-
nism of the House of Commons'.[148] However, the bishops and
their officials issued many of these regulations through visitation
articles and injunctions. Some dioceses managed better than
others; however, the weaknesses of the Church court system made
enforcement very difficult. Co-operation with local officials in
some areas proved to be the solution. While Professor Collinson
and others have noted this alliance of bishops and local officials,
attention to this subject has been dominated recently by the notion
of a puritan reformation of manners. However, with episcopal
efforts at parliament thwarted by Elizabeth, it seems reasonable
to suggest that the bishops attempted to use the enthusiasm of
local secular officials, who were often eager to pass local orders
and enforce them.

---

[146] Trimble, p.56. For Catholic reactions to this pressure, see Robert Parsons, *A Brief
Discours Contayning Certayne Reasons Why Catholiques Refuse to Goe to Church* (Doway,
1580); John Gerard, *John Gerard: The Autobiography of an Elizabethan*, translated by P.
Caraman (London, 1951), pp.1–6; Fisher, 'Privy Council Coercion', 305–24.
[147] Roland Usher, *The Rise and Fall of the High Commission*, (Oxford, 1913), pp.50, 86.
[148] Collinson, *Religion of Protestants*, p.5.

LOCAL ORDERS

In 1578 the justices at Bury St Edmunds produced a severe penal code which dealt with recusants, non-attendance at church, blasphemy, gaming, sexual offences, and other matters. John Parkhurst's successor, Bishop Edmund Freke, regarded these ordinances as an invasion of his jurisdiction, accusing the justices of meddling in ecclesiastical matters and harassing his commissary. The Bury justices were found guilty of pressuring Dr Day, attempting to coerce him 'to joyne authorities together to the repressing of synne and wickedness'.[149] This argument led to a conflict between the bishop and local magistrates over who had authority to punish moral and spiritual offences. However, the Bury justices were not acting without precedent. In 1572 Parkhurst had agreed to co-operate with Yarmouth bailiffs and commissioned them to suppress sinful behaviour, noting that 'all that I and you with all my officers can do is too little, synne doth so much abound, and punishment thereof is so slack'. He promised to correct any slackness in his officers that they reported, but required that his commissary not be hindered in his duties.[150]

Bishop Freke's concern to preserve ecclesiastical jurisdiction was not unique, for this matter was a source of parliamentary controversies, and was evident in other dioceses as well.[151] Yet it is important to note that Parkhurst's decision was not the desperate action of an administrative failure. Bishop Richard Curtis of Chichester made a similar arrangement with the secular officials of Rye. In 1575 he invested Richard Fletcher, then the preacher of Rye and later bishop of London, with ecclesiastical jurisdiction to punish sin and wickedness. Fletcher was to exercise this authority with the secular officers of the town to secure 'suche a civill and vertuous order to lyvinge as the worde of God dayly taught unto us doth require'.[152] In 1572 the common council of Lincoln issued orders that complimented Bishop Thomas Cooper's 1571 articles and injunctions; and in the twelve years

---

[149] *Ibid.*, p.160.   [150] Houlbrooke, *Parkhurst*, p.215.

[151] Wallace T. MacCaffrey, *Exeter, 1540–1640* (London, 1975), p.98 n.39; Collinson, *Religion of Protestants*, p.171.

[152] Collinson, *Religion of Protestants*, pp.160 n.65, 173–4; Patrick Collinson, 'Cranbrook and the Fletchers: Popular and Unpopular Religion in the Kentish Weald', in *Reformation Principle and Practice: Essays in Honour of Arthur Geoffrey Dickens*, edited by P. N. Brooks (London, 1980), 171–202 (p.195).

that followed local orders were issued requiring church attendance, closing of shops, prohibition of labour, and ordered constables as well as churchwardens to seek out offenders.[153]

Three of the four bishops mentioned above demonstrated a
willingness to share their disciplinary authority with local officials.
Unfortunately, explicit evidence of episcopal and civil co-
operation, as found in Norwich and Chichester, is too rare to allow
a broad generalization. However, it seems evident that there was
more co-operation between local officials and bishops than is
usually acknowledged.[154] The complimentary nature of Bishop
Cooper's regulations and those issued by Lincoln's common
council provide valuable circumstantial evidence; and this pattern
can also be found in York and Chester dioceses.[155] The search for
puritanism in localities has obscured the fact that some bishops
were willing to use secular officials in reforming religion; for these
enquiries have emphasized the conflicts which arose without
clarifying the reasons for strife.

An example of this problem is the Northampton order, issued
in 1571. This order defined the spiritual duties for Sunday,
instituted weekday lectures and established a local court jointly
administered by the bishop and local officials. While this order
was issued 'by the consent of the Bysshop of Peterborough, the
maior and bretherne of the Towne there and others of the Queenes
Majesties Justices of peace', Bishop Scambler is usually portrayed
as an opponent to these measures.[156] Dr Sheils concluded that this
order 'was intended to replace the ecclesiastical courts with a more
regular and vigorous local discipline involving secular officials
also'.[157] No doubt this was the bishop's intention, for the order
established the court so that 'the bisshopes authoritie and the
mayors [being] joyned together', might correct ill living and
'Godds glory sett forth and the people brought in good
obedience'.[158] Unfortunately, Bishop Scambler's experiment in

[153] J. W. F. Hill, *Tudor and Stuart Lincoln* (Cambridge, 1956), pp.99–100.
[154] Professor Collinson's Ford Lectures are a valuable antidote to over-emphasis on 'puritan' activities. However, more work needs to be done on co-operative activities in localities.
[155] Baines, I, 209; Kennedy, II, 115–23; *HMC, Fourteenth Report, Appendix, part IV*, p.587; D. M. Palliser, *Tudor York* (Oxford, 1979), p.255.
[156] *The Records of the Borough of Northampton*, edited by J. C. Cox, 2 vols. (Northampton, 1898), II, 386–90.
[157] William J. Sheils, *The Puritans in the Diocese of Peterborough, 1558–1610* (Northampton, 1979), p.120.   [158] *Borough of Northampton*, J. C. Cox, p.387.

co-operation was thwarted by the efforts of Percival Wiburn, Northampton's preacher, and his followers, who wished to establish presbyterian discipline which excluded episcopal involvement. The bishop soon realized this and six months later suppressed the order and suspended Wiburn. This action led to conflicts that continued well into the 1580s.[159] While one should not neglect the radical protestantism of local leaders in Northampton, it is also important to recognize Bishop Scambler's willingness to share his disciplinary authority. It was the abuse of his good will that created conflict. With this in mind, the identification of sabbatarian regulations with a puritan reformation of manners must be seriously re-examined; for it is reasonable to suggest that local sabbatarian orders were inspired by ecclesiastical injunctions and visitation articles. One can at least conclude that cases of co-operation did exist, and that bishops used local officials to suppress sabbath-breaking and other spiritual and moral offences.

COMPLAINT LITERATURE

Faced with the Church's role in promoting sabbatarian doctrine and discipline, and the bishops' involvement in sabbatarian legislation at the national and local level, little remains to support the received account of Elizabethan sabbatarianism – except the complaint literature of the 1570s. Yet, even this evidence does not detract from the account presented above; for this literature used the Church's teaching on the Sabbath and shared the episcopate's concern that sabbath abuses be suppressed. Humphrey Roberts, in his *Earnest Complaint of Divers Vain, Wicked and Abused Exercises, Practised on the Saboth Day*, published in 1572, justified his concern with a scholastic explanation. He stated that, 'although Christians be delivered from the Ceremonial Law, with all the shadows and ceremonies thereof, yet it is certain that they are bound to keep the Moral precepts'. Roberts included the fourth precept in the moral law, explaining that the Christian Sabbath was moved to the day of Christ's resurrection to put men in mind of their source of salvation. The day was to be dedicated wholly to God's service in public and private exercises of religion and abstinence from all

---

[159] It should be noted that Northampton officials continued to exercise sabbatarian discipline and the bishop did nothing to interfere, unlike Bishop Freke in Norwich. Sheils, pp.25–7, 120–2.

worldly things and ordinary labours. Of particular concern were
the idle pastimes used on the Lord's day, and his list varied little
from that found in the *Homilies*. He condemned drinking,
swearing, brawling, plays, silvergames, bearbaiting, bullbaiting,
dicing, bowling, ales, fencing, carding, and singled out dancing
as one of the most damaging Sunday pastimes. Those who worked
on the Sabbath for gain demonstrated their greed and lack of trust
in God. Roberts explained that sabbath-breakers hindered their
salvation; for man is saved through faith in Christ's merits, and
faith comes by hearing the word of God. Those who did not come
to church, 'both for the preaching and hearing of the word of
God which is commonly used upon the Lord's day, they hinder
their faith, for that they hear not God's word'. He lamented the
neglect of the Lord's day noting that,

So cold is the devotion of a great many, both in the city and in the country:
so little regard Householders and Masters have, to bring up their households
and families in the fear of God: and so little care have Officers and Magistrates
to their charge and office, in punishing of the offenders, that to abuse the Sabbath
day, is counted either no offence at all, or a very light crime.

Roberts stated that while those who steal and murder are punished
with death, idolatry, swearing, and sabbath-breaking incurred no
punishment. Observing that all these sins were condemned in the
decalogue, he asserted that it is necessary 'that some Order of
punishment be had for the abusing of the Sabbath day'.[160]

The works of Thomas White, Abraham Fleming, John Stockwood, Samuel Bird, and others were constructed along a similar
outline.[161] This pattern is significant, for it reveals three basic
themes in sabbatarians' complaints: first, an assimilation of the
sabbatarian doctrine and discipline of the Church; second, anxiety
over sabbath abuses; and third, a belief that ecclesiastical authorities and secular officials were lax in punishing offenders.

---

[160] Roberts, sig.B2v.
[161] Thomas White, *A Sermon* (London, 1578); Northbrooke; Stockwood; Abraham
Fleming, 'The Footpath to Felicitie', in *The Diamond of Devotion* (London, 1581);
[Anthony Gilby], *A Pleasaunt Dialogue betweene a Souldier of Barwicke and an English Chaplaine*
(n.p., 1581); John Field, *A Caveat for Parsons Howlet* (London, [1581]); William Kethe,
A Sermon Made at Blanford Forum (London, 1571); Samuel Bird, *A Friendlie
Communication or Dialogue between Paul and Demas* (London, 1580); Knewstub, pp.73–5;
Stubbes; Christopher Fetherstone, *A Dialogue agaynst Light, Lewde and Lascivious
Dauncing* (London, 1582); Thomas Lovell, *A Dialogue between Custom and Veritie*
(London, 1581); John Field, *A Godly Exhortation* (London, 1583); Bateman; John
Walsall, *A Sermon Preached at Pauls Crosse* (London, [1578]).

While most sabbatarian complaints incorporated doctrine compatible with Church teaching, there were some who took this doctrine beyond its officially established bounds. John Stroud, a preacher at Cranbrook in Kent, preached in 1573 that 'it is no greater a sinne to steale a horse on munday then to sell him in fayre on the sunday. That it is as ill to playe at games as shootinge, bowlinge etc. on Sundaye as to lye with your neygbhors wiffe on munday'.[162] This crude equation of the two tables of the decalogue was condemned by the local preacher, Richard Fletcher. While he would not have denied the morally binding nature of the fourth precept, Fletcher rejected this comparison of the two tables as bad teaching.[163] Fletcher's judgement corresponded with that of Richard Greenham, a noted precisionist and leading Cambridge sabbatarian. He explained in August 1583 that,

When Sathan would not discredit the word by some ordinary shifts, hee would cause men to use reaching and excessive speaches to discredit the same, which do so much the more harm, because they commonly passe in zeale and are afforded for a principal means to credit the truth. As for example, when a man shall say it is as great a sin to boute on the Sabbath as to murther ones father. What is ther reason. The sins of the first table are greater than the sins against the second table. Ans. It is true that when like sins are compared as perjury is a greater sin then murder, but vain speaking is a less sin then murder, and the first is against the first table, and the second against the second table, but it is true of sins equal, whereof ther is an unequal comparison.[164]

Stroud's teaching must be placed at the extreme end of the sabbatarian spectrum, a judaizing tendency condemned both by a moderate like Fletcher and a precisionist like Greenham. None of the published sabbatarian complaints adopted this argument, and remained within the bounds set by the Church, except for a few which rejected holy days.

The complaint literature of the 1570s was primarily concerned with sabbath abuses, and not theological definitions. The items listed varied; but, like Humphrey Roberts, all emphasized the necessity of putting aside worldly labours and pastimes, and devoting the day to God's service. William Kethe observed that 'the Lord God hath commanded, and so do the lawes of the

---

[162] Dr Williams Library, MS Morrice BII, fol. 9v.

[163] In sermons attributed to Fletcher, the morally binding nature of the decalogue is affirmed. (East Sussex Record Office 467/7/9.) It should also be remembered that Stroud's argument was not new, for Erasmus ridiculed the same notion. (Erasmus, *Praise of Folly*, p.155.)

[164] John Rylands Library, Rylands English MS 524, fol. 48r-v.

Realme that the Sabboth day should be kept holy, that the people should cease from labour, to the end they should heare the word of God, and geve themselves to godly exercises'.[165] But Kethe complained that the multitude 'do most shamefully prophane the Sabboth day, and have altered the very name therof, so as where god calleth it his holy sabaoth, the multitude call it there revelying day'.[166] Kethe, Northbrooke, Anthony Gilby, and John Field singled out papists particularly as transgressors of the Sabbath and accused them of inciting others to do likewise.[167] In London much attention was given to theatres, which John Field, John Stockwood, and others claimed were filled while churches stood empty.[168] In the country the chief diversions and sources of complaint were dancing and alehouse disorders.

Like medieval sabbatarians, Elizabethans found God's judgement manifested in sabbath day tragedies. An earthquake occurred on a Sunday in 1580, when many were in theatres watching 'their bawdy Interludes and other trumperies practiced'. Philip Stubbes explained that God 'caused the earth mightily to shake and quaver...wherat the people sore amazed, some leaped down (from the top of the Turrets, Pinnacles, and Towers, where they stood) to the ground, whereof some had their legs broke, some their arms, some their backs...but they went away sore afraid, and wounded in conscience'.[169] Yet he could find no reformation of these abuses.

John Stockwood predicted in his 1578 sermon at St Paul's Cross that God's judgement would fall on sabbath-breakers and singled out Paris Garden, a venue for blood sports, as an example of these abuses.[170] Five years later John Field was able to record the fulfillment of this prophecy. On Sunday afternoon 13 January 1583, during common prayer time an upper gallery at Paris Garden collapsed, 'when the dogs and Bear were in the chiefest battle'. Field reported that seven died and more were injured. He noted that some concluded that the accident was caused by overcrowding and rotten timber, but Field asserted that 'it must needs be considered as an extraordinary judgement of God, both

---

[165] Kethe, fol. 8r.   [166] *Ibid.*, fol. 8v.

[167] Northbrooke, p.12; Field, *Caveat*, sig.D3r; Kethe, fols. 15r-17v; Gilby, *Dialogue*, sig.M3r.

[168] Field, *Exhortation*, sig.A5; Stockwood, pp.23–4.

[169] Stubbes, p.117.   [170] Stockwood, p.50.

for the punishment of these present prophaners of the Lord's day that were there, and also inform and warn us that were abroad'.[171]

The complaints of sabbath abuses and reports of God's judgement did not stop with a condemnation of the people's great neglect, for the authorities were blamed for lax enforcement. Field criticized London magistrates and Mayor William Fleetwood particularly for the Paris Garden tragedy. He pleaded for more diligence in suppressing abuses so that 'no citizen or citizen's servants, have liberty to repair unto any of those abuse places'.[172] Kethe noted in the preface to his 1571 sabbatarian sermon that some thought he had said more than became him, but others took his words to heart, 'for I opened to the Magistrates, how shamefully the Saboth day (which God would have to be kept holy) was prophaned with drunken and ungodly reveling and all kinde of iniquitie'.[173] In 1578 Stockwood commended London officials for orders requiring street cleaning to prevent infection, but cautioned that 'the plague cannot be carried away in a dung carte'. He exhorted magistrates to 'labor for the inward purging and scouring of our Soules'.[174]

Ecclesiastical officials did not escape criticism. Laurence Chaderton, the first master of Emmanuel College, found numerous faults in English society, including 'prophaning of the Lord's Sabbothes', and claimed that the fault rested in lax ecclesiastical discipline, asserting that the disorders of society were caused by the structural disorder of the Church.[175] While Chaderton found the solution in presbyterian structures, twenty years earlier Nicholas Bacon had recommended restructuring diocesan government. In his opening speech to parliament in 1563, Bacon spoke at length on the disciplinary problems of the church and singled out non-attendance as 'a matter of greate momente'. He asked,

How commeth it to passe that the common people in the countrye universallie come so seldome to common prayer and devine service, and when they doe come be there manye tymes so vainely occupied or at the least doe not there as they should doe, but for wante of this discipline? And yet to the helpe of this there was at the last parliamente a lawe made, but hitherto noe man, no, noe man –

---

[171] Field, *Exhortation, passim.*   [172] *Ibid., passim.*
[173] Kethe, sig.A2r-v.   [174] Stockwood, p.25.
[175] Collinson, *Religion of Protestants*, p.151; Laurence Chaderton, *A Fruitful Sermon upon...Romanes* (London, 1584), pp.82–3; Peter Lake, 'Laurence Chaderton and the Cambridge Moderate Puritan Tradition' (unpublished Ph.D. thesis, University of Cambridge, 1978), p.49.

or verye fewe – hathe seene it executed. And playnely to speake, lawes for the furtheraunce of this discipline unexecuted be as roddes for correccion without handes.[176]

Bacon proposed the reorganization of dioceses into smaller deaneries, and 'committeinge of these deaneryes to men well chosen (as I think commonly they be not)'. He recommended that these officers be closely supervised by bishops, with two or three episcopal visitations annually. He charged the bishops assembled to give particular attention to matters of discipline.[177]

One of the results of Bacon's recommendation was the proposed sabbatarian legislation which was approved by the bishops, but never passed through parliament. However, Bacon's criticisms, like those of Chaderton, Field, Stockwood, Kethe, and others, do not present an accurate picture of secular and ecclesiastical efforts at sabbatarian discipline. Clearly, bishops and local officials were making efforts to enforce such discipline. While some were negligent in their duties, many more were thwarted by administrative structures. The examples of Cox and Parkhurst illustrate this problem at two different levels. John Woolton, a canon of Exeter cathedral from 1565 and bishop of the same from 1579, complained in his work, *The Castell of Christians*, that

When they [parishioners] should repayre to the Temple uppon the Sabboth dayes to heare sermons, and be partakers of sacraments: they walke abroade into the fieldes, or into some other place to provide for temporall and worldly thinges: or else doo conteine themselves at home occupied in ydle sportes and pastimes. For they wyll not stycke to saye that they can sowe, and plowe their grounde, know their revell daies, and lyve under lawes in the common wealth, without hearing any Preacher.[178]

Much of the problem lay in the fact that many knew the Church's position, but were unwilling to be governed in this matter. Ann Carter of Maldon, Essex, expressed the sentiments of many when she scolded the constable who presented her for working on Sunday, declaring that 'if he would provide one to do her work she would go to church', and asserted that she 'served God as well as he'.[179]

John Aylmer, bishop of London, used the same warnings commonly associated with John Field and Philip Stubbes. Shortly

[176] *Parliaments*, Hartley, p.82.   [177] *Ibid.*, p.82.
[178] John Woolton, *The Castell of Christians* (London, 1577), sig.E8r.
[179] *The Shirburn Ballads: 1585–1616*, edited by Andrew Clark (Oxford, 1907), p.49.

after the earthquake of 1580, he issued a *Godly Admonition*, which was a special 'Order of Prayer', intended 'to avert and turn God's wrath from us threatened by the terrible earthquake'.[180] Among the many corporate sins cited was the abuse of Sundays and holy days. It was noted that these days were ordained for hearing God's word, receiving the sacraments, and to be used for prayer and godly meditations. This liturgy condemned those who spend those days 'heathenishly, in taverning, tippling, gaming, playing and beholding of Bear-baiting and Stage plays, to the utter dishonour of God, impeachment of all godliness, and unnecessary consuming of men's substances, which ought to be better employed'.[181] Although this special liturgy was heard by many more people than the works of Field and Stockwood, Aylmer's admonition made no discernible difference.

This is the crux of the problem; for while precisionists were assumed to be lonely voices crying in the wilderness, bishops and secular officials were expected to produce results. It is a common fault of those who do not exercise authority to demand the unobtainable from those who do. Even the most fervent of reformers found their efforts thwarted by local self-interest and administrative resistance when they assumed authority – a problem most men could not see until they were in office. When Leicester reprimanded Bishop Scambler in 1578 for the lack of a preacher at Northampton, he reminded the bishop

How often before youe weare Bishoppe you woulde finde faulte with negligence of Bishopps, howe much youe cryed out to have preachers and good ministers increased and carefullye placed and so did youe all almost that be nowe Bishippes: But let me nowe looke into your deedes, and beholde in every Dioces the want of preachers, naye the greate discouragement that preachers finde at your handes. It will make men thinke youe never thoughte as youe speake or have forgotten that ever any suche matter was in your minde to execute those good thinges which I have hard youe bothe teache and professe. For nowe are ye knowen what ye are, and by your fruits shall men judge your doctrine and love indeed to the gospell, and youe are noe more a private man, youe have a greate charge and therefore it behovethe youe to have a greate and marvelouse diligence.[182]

[180] *Liturgical Services...in the Reign of Queen Elizabeth*, edited by William K. Clay (Cambridge, 1847), p.562.
[181] *Ibid.*, p.574; Strype, *Annals*, II pt 2, p.397.
[182] R. M. Serjeantson, *History of the Church of All Saints, Northampton* (Northampton, 1901), p.112. Serjeantson mistakenly attributes this letter to Nicholas Bacon. I am grateful to Professor Collinson for clarifying this point.

This harsh, biting reminder must have caused the bishop to reflect on the naivety of his pre-episcopal complaints. Scambler had been active initially in promoting co-operation with preachers and local authorities, and was one of the first bishops to foster the growth of prophesyings. However, his good intentions had been abused by presbyterians who did not wish to co-operate, but to usurp his authority. His attempts to protect his position resulted in the suspension of preachers and the alienation of local gentry. It was their version of diocesan problems that Leicester heard and believed.[183]

In analysing the complaint literature, it is important to note that there is no reaction from the the the authorities. Indeed the complaints of precisionists, bishops, and secular officials illustrate that frustration over ineffective sabbatarian discipline was not limited to a small group of disaffected 'puritans', but was a concern shared by most responsible and religious Elizabethans. As Professor Collinson has noted, the pessimism of the complaint literature and the apparent neglect in exercising moral and spiritual discipline should not be interpreted without great caution.[184] It seems evident that while bishops and local officers shared the sabbatarian concerns of the famous complainers of the 1570s, they found themselves unable to effect the desired reforms. Bishop Pilkington's criticism of ecclesiastical discipline in 1560 was to be levelled at him and his fellows in the 1570s.[185] Administrative problems, coupled with tensions over the application of Old Testament judicial laws, meant that ecclesiastical officials could never meet expectations.

CONCLUSION

The Church's role in promoting sabbatarian doctrine through the *Homilies*, Nowell's *Catechism*, Bible marginalia, and the works of prominent churchmen establish that the concept of a morally binding Sabbath was not a late Elizabethan innovation, but part of the doctrinal fabric of English religious life. Conflicts over the institution of the Lord's day, holy days, proper use of the Sabbath, and Mosaic judicial laws do not detract from this conclusion. Pilkington, Parker, Grindal, Parkhurst, Cox, Cooper, and many others illustrate that sabbatarian doctrine and discipline were

---

[183] Sheils, *Peterborough*, p.7; Serjeantson, pp.111–12.
[184] Collinson, *Religion of Protestants*, p.199.   [185] Strype, *Annals*, 1 pt 1, pp.270–1.

matters of great interest to many in the episcopate. Episcopal activities demonstrate that the complaint literature provides an incomplete and defective view of sabbatarian discipline in this period; for the ineffective efforts of bishops frustrated them as much as their precisionist critics. It should also be emphasized that their complaints were nothing new – for medieval and Reformation preachers also complained of the ineffectiveness of secular and ecclesiastical discipline. Clearly, the Church's role was crucial in promoting sabbatarian doctrine and discipline in the early Elizabethan period, and it provided the foundation on which later sabbatarians built. The developments in the 1580s and 1590s were not theological *innovations*, but the elaboration of received sabbatarian doctrine. Those who denied the morally binding nature of the Sabbath advocated a novelty, which did not represent the established teaching of the English Church.

4

Late Elizabethan and Jacobean
sabbatarianism: 1583–1617

The previous chapters have examined sabbatarian developments in the medieval Church and Reformation period, and established that the scholastic and analogical interpretations were recognized teaching in the early Elizabethan Church. However, we are now faced with the role of this doctrine in the late Elizabethan and early Jacobean period and must confront the claim of many who assert that the doctrine of a morally binding Sabbath was a puritan innovation. Exploring the causes of regicide and puritan radicalism in the seventeenth century, historians have argued that an intense commitment to sabbatarian principles played an important role. The numerous tracts on the subject in the 1640s and the parliamentary debates in that period emphasize a strength of conviction that had deep roots. Searching for the origins of this commitment, historians have turned to the complaint literature of the 1570s, written by men sympathetic to presbyterian discipline. The debates at the Dedham Classis and the sabbatarian developments at Cambridge in the 1580s provided further points of reference. The suppression of Nicholas Bownde's *Doctrine of the Sabbath* in 1599 and the Book of Sports controversies of 1617, 1618, and 1633 seem to confirm the conclusion that sabbatarianism was indeed a puritan innovation which drove a wedge between precisionists and the established Church. If the case for consensus is to be maintained, these events must be re-examined.

In 1607 Thomas Rogers, a Suffolk minister and chaplain to Archbishop Bancroft, published a revised edition of his *Catholic Doctrine of the Church of England*, with its often cited preface against presbyterians and sabbatarians. This preface provided a history of sound doctrine in the English Church and described the threats to orthodoxy during Elizabeth's reign. Noting the attacks on episcopal government and discipline, Rogers praised Bancroft as one of the first to recognize the presbyterian threat and expose their plot. He reported that 'an army of most valorous and resolute champions and challengers rose up...[and] defended the prelacy, stood for the prince and state...and so battered the new discipline as hitherto they could never, nor hereafter shall ever fortify and repair the decays thereof'.[1]

Rogers explained that the brethren, defeated in their presbyterian scheme, sought to recover some advantage 'by an odd and a new device of theirs, in a special article of their classical instruction'. This ploy was a new doctrine of the Sabbath. Rogers summarized this doctrine in two parts. The first part was that 'the Lord's-day, even as the old sabbath was of the Jews, must necessarily be kept, and solemnized of all and every Christian, under the pain of eternal condemnation both of body and soul'. The other aspect was that 'under the same penalty it must be kept from the highest to the lowest, both of king and people, in sort and manner as these brethren among themselves have devised, decreed, and prescribed'. He asserted that these sabbatarians were judaizers who spread heretical doctrine, teaching that to work on the Lord's day was as great a sin as killing a man or committing adultery. Rogers accused them of encouraging licentiousness and profaneness because they condemned the use of holy days, and observed that 'they set up a new idol, their Saint Sabbath (erst in the days of popish blindness St. Sunday) in the midst and minds of God's people'. Recalling his horror on hearing these notions preached, and reading them in Nicholas Bownde's *Doctrine of the Sabbath*, Rogers explained that he soon recognized this as a presbyterian plot and that the doctrine had made an impression on men's hearts throughout the kingdom. He observed that 'this stratagem of theirs was not observed then, neither, I fear me, is regarded as it should be yet'. He rejoiced in the knowledge that he was the man who exposed these sabbatarian errors and impieties, and achieved the suppression of Bownde's book by both Archbishop Whitgift and Lord Chief Justice Popham in 1599 and 1600. He concluded that these censures confirmed 'that this doctrine of the brethren agreeth neither with the doctrine of our Church, nor with the laws and orders of this kingdom'.[2]

Thomas Rogers' account is crucial, for it is not only the earliest surviving record of this controversy, but also the source of an

[1] Thomas Rogers, *The Catholic Doctrine of the Church of England*, edited by J. J. S. Perowne (Cambridge, 1854), p.17.   [2] *Ibid.*, pp.18–20.

inaccurate and misleading historiographical model. He accused Bownde and others of holding extreme sabbatarian notions. However, the work of these men establish that they did not deviate from the authorized teaching of the Church, and in some cases condemned the notions Rogers ascribed to them. Rogers' claim that the sabbath doctrine was an unauthorized teaching and part of an extreme, crypto-presbyterian plot is demonstrably untrue. Yet his reasons for distorting these events must be discovered before his story can be discounted. Professor Collinson has provided a convincing description of Rogers as a controversialist who wrangled frequently with his clerical neighbours and a careerist in hot pursuit of preferment.[3] The troubles he had with his fellow clergy in Suffolk, of whom Bownde was one, and his dogged pursuit of advancement in the Church would be two good reasons for a 'smear campaign' against Bownde and other precisionist sabbatarians. Indeed his ambitious nature was reflected in the 1607 preface where he included himself among the great men who had defended the Church against presbyterian plots.[4] No doubt he had observed the way Whitgift and Bancroft had used the presbyterian controversies to gain preferment; and it seems plausible to suggest that he attempted to use sabbatarianism for the same purpose – a ploy which did not succeed.

Striking inconsistencies in his account support these suspicions. The most obvious problem is his misrepresentation of Bownde's *Doctrine of the Sabbath*, published in 1595. Although Bownde was a precisionist who favoured presbyterian discipline and opposed holy days, he was circumspect on these issues. His elaboration of the sabbath doctrine did not conflict with the *Homilies* or other authorized works on the subject. The extreme sabbatarian doctrine Rogers ascribed to Bownde was not part of his work. While Bownde claimed that it was more needful for us to be told 'from what things we should rest, then wherin we may labour', nevertheless he condemned judaizing sabbatarians who prohibited necessary labours and acts of mercy, fearing that some through this 'grosse superstition, should fall into the extremity of the Jewes: of whom it is written...that they dresse all their meate the day before: upon that day they kindle no fire, they remove no

[3] Collinson, 'English Sabbatarianism', pp.219–21.
[4] Rogers, *Catholic Doctrine*, pp.3–18.

vessell: *Aluum non purgant*: they doe not ease themselves'.[5] Like his stepfather, Richard Greenham, Bownde would have regarded the crude comparison of the two tables of the decalogue as an over-zealous and misguided attempt to prove the importance of the sabbath precept.[6]

However, even if Rogers' account were accurate, it would not explain why he waited four years before reporting Bownde's 'non-conformity' to the authorities. It also seems unlikely that Whitgift would have allowed such a work to go unmolested until the vicar of a Suffolk parish brought it to his attention, so long after publication. One explanation for this delay could be the political climate of 1599 and 1600. In March 1599, John Chamberlain reported to Dudley Carlton the scandal caused by John Hayward's biography of the usurper, Henry IV, with its dedication to Robert Devereux, the disgraced Earl of Essex. This biography was regarded as a politically subversive work, and so disturbed Elizabeth that she imprisoned Hayward and pressed him to confess that he was shielding the true author with his name. Whitgift issued an order that the dedication be cut out of all remaining copies; and as late as July 1600 Samuel Harsnett sent a letter to Attorney General Coke apologizing for authorizing the book's publication.[7] The suppression of another book associated with Essex in May 1600 emphasizes the concern of the authorities.[8] Elizabeth and her officials were clearly anxious about the possibility of seditious activities from men loyal to Essex.

With this political storm brewing, it is possible that Rogers seized the opportunity to attack Bownde's book, which was also dedicated to Essex. On 10 December 1599, Rogers preached a provocative anti-sabbatarian sermon at the regular Monday exercise at Bury, less than seven miles from Bownde's parish. He declared that it was 'anti-christian and unsound' to teach that Christians are bound to keep the sabbath day. He associated this

---

[5] Nicholas Bownde, *Doctrine of the Sabbath* (London, 1595), sig. A4r.

[6] John Rylands Library, Rylands English MS 524, fol. 48.

[7] *Letters Written by John Chamberlain*, edited by Sarah Williams (London, 1861), pp.47–8; *DNB* for John Hayward; *CSPD: 1598–1601*, pp.165, 450–3.

[8] A letter from Whitgift to Secretary Cecil, dated 10 May 1600, describes the suppression of this book. While the author and title are not known, Dawson, the printer named in the letter, did not print the books of Bownde or Hayward, confirming this as an additional case. (BL, Additional MS 4160, fol. 109.)

observance with Jewish ceremonies and denied that the day was kept before the Mosaic laws. Asserting that no day was established by scripture, he claimed that the Lord's day was enjoined by civil and ecclesiastical constitutions and could be called the Queen's day instead of the Lord's day, Sabbath or Sunday – and used that title in subsequent references to that day. Anyone who objected to his teaching he branded as 'sabatarians and dominicans', and insinuated that their sabbatarianism grew out of papistry or Brownism.[9]

Such a sermon was certain to provoke an outburst from his fellow clergy, particularly Nicholas Bownde. While the evidence is far from conclusive, it seems reasonable to suggest that Bownde may have been manipulated into a politically sensitive position. Rogers' Erastian assertion may have been sharply rebutted with arguments from scripture to deny the authority of the Church and state in this matter. Armed with such a dispute and Bownde's book with its dedication to Essex, Rogers could have presented a convincing account of religious non-conformity and potentially seditious behaviour. He asserted in 1607 that this doctrine 'disturbeth the peace both of the commonweal and church; and tendeth unto schism in the one, and sedition in the other'.[10] Whitgift would have balked at a precisionist's attempt to limit the Church's authority to establish days of observance, and secular authorities would have been suspicious of anyone loyal to Essex. For an ambitious careerist with a troublesome neighbour, it would have been a tempting combination. His effort in 1607 to place himself among the great defenders of the Church lends support to this suggestion; while the Church's teaching and the eight sabbatarian works published by precisionists between 1599 and 1607 illustrate the absurdity of his claim.[11] The appearance of this account in 1607, during a period when Bancroft was harassing

[9] BL, Additional MS 38492, fol. 104.   [10] Rogers, *Catholic Doctrine*, p.20.

[11] Rogers, *Catholic Doctrine*, p.20; Richard Greenham, 'A Treatise of the Sabbath', in *Works* (London, 1599); George Estey, *Exposition upon the Tenne Commandements* (London, 1602); John Dod and Robert Cleaver, *A Treatise or Exposition upon the Ten Commandements* (London, 1603); George Widley, *The Doctrine of the Sabbath* (London, 1604); Bownde, *Sabbathum Veteri*; Burton, *Abstract*; James Balmford, *Three Posicions Concerning the Aucthoritie of the Lordes Daye* (1607); John Sprint, *Propositions Tending to Proove the Necessarie Use of the Christian Sabbaoth or Lords Day* (London, 1607). Robert Loe's *Effigiatio Veri Sabbathismi*, published in 1605, was critical of many points related to the sabbath doctrine. Nevertheless, he did make use of the scholastic interpretation in his own work.

non-conforming clergy, may be further evidence of Rogers' opportunism. Although more evidence is required to confirm this interpretation of the events, it nevertheless seems reasonable to suggest that Rogers' account may not be taken at face value. The suppression of Bownde's book may have had more to do with the political tensions of Elizabeth's last years and Rogers' ambitions than with theological considerations.

THE DOCTRINE OF THE SABBATH

In 1607 John Sprint published his *Propositions Tending to Proove the Necessarie Use of the Christian Sabbaoth or Lord's Day*. This work ended what Bownde's *Doctrine of the Sabbath* began, and serves as a summary of sabbatarian developments in the late Elizabethan and early Jacobean period. Sprint first noted two extreme views of the Sabbath. One view, held by Anabaptists and the Family of Love, was that the Sabbath was abrogated and that no difference should be made between days or times. Advocates of this view asserted that the fourth commandment was merely ceremonial and that Christian liberty put an end to such bondage. At the other extreme were Jews and 'Sabbatary Christians' who claimed that the seventh day Sabbath of the Jews was established from creation and remained as binding on Christians as Jews, because of the perpetuity of the moral law. While Sprint approved of the reasons given by judaizing Christians, he explained that they were mis-applied; for the view of the primitive Church and the position of later purity was that Christians were to observe the first day after the Jewish Sabbath. This was established by the apostles as a memorial of Christ's resurrection, and had been a continual practice from that time.[12] The papistical position stood between primitive and later purity, for they had usurped authority and permitted activities which were prohibited *de jure divino*, like the use of servile labours, markets, and fairs, as well as lawful and unlawful pastimes.[13] The protestant view was that the fourth precept was partly moral and partly ceremonial. The ceremonial side was the rest on the seventh day of the week, the strictness of the rest, and the shadowing of Christ's coming in the ceremonies and sacrifices of the Mosaic laws. The moral side of this precept

---

[12] Sprint, *Propositions*, pp. 2–4.
[13] This point is not historically accurate. See above, Chapter 1. Sprint, *Propositions*, pp. 4–5.

was the public worship of God, which included preaching, receiving the sacraments, prayer, works of mercy, and giving rest to servants and cattle. Sprint explained that this doctrine was a common protestant heritage, citing as proof the works of Calvin, Musculus, Bullinger, Beza, Zanchius, Nowell, Fulke, Perkins, Babington, and other continental and English theologians, as well as the *Homilies*.[14]

However, he noted that there were three 'points of difference among the godly learned'. These concerned whether keeping the seventh day or any other was part of the moral law, whether the first day of the week was established by divine truth and tied the conscience, and whether the Lord's day might be changed again to another day. Sprint confessed a preference for the stricter interpretation, explaining that 'the ground of my persuasion is the evidence of Truth appearing to my conscience, being chayned to the judgement of the present Church of England'. He found support for this view in the *Homilies*, as well as the works of Beza, Zanchius, Nowell, Hooper, Babington, Calvin, Greenham, and many other protestant theologians and medieval scholastics. However, he was not troubled by differences over the issues; for the arguments on both sides put down the opinions of libertines and papists.[15]

Sprint's book is important because it was the last sabbatarian work published before the Book of Sports and it appeared in the same year as Rogers' account. Emphasizing his conformity with the established teaching of the English Church and orthodox protestant theology, he defended the scholastic interpretation with the works of continental and English theologians, as well as the Greek and Latin fathers, the medieval schoolmen, and sixteenth-century Catholic theologians. Tracing various interpretations of the sabbath precept, Sprint's work was a thorough study which explored a long-established tradition. He was not reluctant to criticize Church tradition when it 'conflicted' with scripture, and was severely disciplined in 1602 when he openly denounced the use of holy days.[16] However, Sprint's argument is significant, for he did not rest on scriptural proofs alone, but bolstered his arguments with evidence from Church tradition and canon law. He would not have recognized himself as an innovator or

---

[14] *Ibid.*, pp.5–7. 　　　　[15] *Ibid.*, pp.7–27.
[16] See below, Chapter 4, 'Observance of Holy Days'.

subversive force within the Church; and the fact that no action was taken against him or his book would suggest that ecclesiastical officials were of the same mind.

In the search for an 'official' position which tests the conflicting claims of Rogers and Sprint, the writings of bishops and the Church's chief apologist, Richard Hooker, are essential. While attitudes towards peripheral issues varied, Church leaders used the scholastic interpretation as the basis for their studies on this subject. The anti-sabbatarian position was not a part of their teaching.

In his Easter day sermon before James in 1608, Bishop Lancelot Andrewes preached on the women who went to Christ's tomb to embalm his body, commending them both for their speed and for waiting till the end of the Sabbath. While noting that they were anxious to anoint the body as soon as possible,

> their diligence leapt over none of God's commandments for haste. No, not this commandment, which of all other the world is boldest with; and if they [the world] have haste, somewhat else may, but sure the Sabbath shall never stay them. The Sabbath they stayed, for then God stayed them. But that was no sooner over, but their diligence appeared straight. No other thing could stay them.[17]

These were not the words of the youthful Andrewes 'still in his puritan phase',[18] but those of the bishop of Chichester and a favourite preacher at court. This sermon and others preached before the king illustrate that Andrewes' conclusions concerning the Sabbath had changed little from those found in his catechetical lectures presented at Pembroke Hall, Cambridge in the mid 1580s.[19] His exposition of the fourth commandment used the

---

[17] Lancelot Andrewes, *Ninety-Six Sermons*, 5 vols. (Oxford, 1841), II, 227–8.

[18] Collinson, 'English Sabbatarianism', p.216; M. M. Knappen, 'The Early Puritanism of Lancelot Andrewes', *Church History*, 2 (1933), 95–104.

[19] Andrewes, *Ninety-Six Sermons*, IV 321; Lancelot Andrewes, *XCVI Sermons* (London, 1629), p.526; Lancelot Andrewes, *A Patterne of Catechisticall Doctrine* (London, 1630), pp.232–57; Lancelot Andrewes, *The Moral Law Expounded* (London, 1642), pp.324–62; Lancelot Andrewes, *A Pattern of Catechistical Doctrine* (Oxford, 1846), pp.152–69. In 1656, Heylyn asserted that Andrewes rejected the sabbatarianism of his youth. He claimed that the bishop ordered one of his chaplains 'not to own any thing for his, that was said to have have been taken by notes from his mouth', and that 'in discourse with those about him he would never own it, nor liked to have it mentioned to him, so he abolished (as it seemeth) his own original copy'. Heylyn's reputation as a propagandist, as well as the evidence of Andrewes' later sabbatarian attitudes, give reason to doubt Heylyn's assertion (Peter Heylyn, *Extraneus Vapulans*, London, 1656, p.127).

scholastic interpretation and asserted that the Lord's day was established by apostolic authority, as a memorial of the first day of creation, Christ's resurrection, and the coming of the Holy Spirit at Pentecost.[20] In 1590 his doctoral defence included support of the thesis '*observatio unius diei ex septem est moralis*'.[21] While his close contacts with Greenham, Bownde, Dod, Knewstub, and other Cambridge precisionists in the 1580s have been treated as a 'puritan phase' he outgrew, Andrewes retained the sabbatarian attitudes which they had shared.

Andrewes was not the only sabbatarian among the bishops. Bishop Arthur Lake also affirmed this doctrine in his *Theses de Sabbato*, observing that when the authority of the fourth precept is acknowledged in the liturgy 'we meane not the Jewish Sabbath, but that which analogically to the Originall Sabbath we observe, *The Lords Day*'.[22] Gervase Babington, successively bishop of Llandaff, Exeter, and Worcester, also wrote on the morally binding nature of the Sabbath;[23] and bishops John King and Lewis Bayly presented this interpretation in their writing as well.[24] In 1602 John Howson, then vice-chancellor of Oxford and later bishop of Oxford and Durham, preached a sermon in defence of church festivals. Although he was a staunch opponent of the Oxford precisionists who attacked holy day observance, he explained that the fourth precept was moral in requiring that

Some time should be allowed to the service of God, that we might remember his benefits and magnifie his holy name: to breake this law which is *de jure divino*, that is, to dedicate no time to the service of God, is worse then adultery, worse then murther, but to breake the ceremonies of it, which are *de jure humano*, is not so great a sinne as murther or adultery which are of the second table, and *de jure divino*, against the expresse law of God himselfe.[25]

Howson argued that this observance extended only to the time spent in divine service. While few bishops used such an explicit

---

[20] Andrewes, *Moral Law*, p.33.
[21] British Library, Harleian MS 7038, p.78. I am grateful to Kenneth Fincham for this reference.
[22] Arthur Lake, 'Theses de Sabbato', in *Of the Morality of the Fourth Commandement*, by William Twisse (London, 1641), sig.A3r.
[23] Gervase Babington, *A Very Fruitfull Exposition of the Commandements* (London, 1583), pp.169–78; Gervase Babington, *Workes* (London, 1615), p.10.
[24] John King, *Lectures upon Jonas* (Oxford, 1597), p.96; Lewis Bayly, *The Practice of Piety*, 30th edition (London, 1632), pp.377–482.
[25] John Howson, *A Sermon Preached at St Maries in Oxford* (Oxford, 1602), sig.C1v. For a full account of the events associated with this sermon, see Christopher M. Dent, *Protestant Reformers in Elizabethan Oxford* (Oxford, 1983), pp.201–20.

theological justification, his explanation did allow for the possibility of recreations and other pastimes, which almost all church
authorities permitted – or at least tolerated. Although bishops
Fletcher, Hutton, and Overall did not write specifically on the
sabbath precept, they did accept the binding nature of the moral
law, as summarized in the decalogue.[26]

Richard Hooker also illustrates the unanimity which persisted
on this issue. Although he wrote his *Ecclesiastical Polity* during the
sabbatarian controversy reported by Thomas Rogers, Book v,
published in 1597, contained a scholastic interpretation of the
fourth precept. He observed that 'if it be then demanded whether
we observe these times as being therunto bound by force of divine
law, or else by the only positive ordinances of the Church, I answer
to this, that the very law of nature itself which all men confess
to be God's law requireth in general no less the sanctification of
times, than of places, persons, and things unto God's honour'.[27]
He went on to explain that 'the moral law requireth therefore a
seventh part throughout the age of the whole world to be that
way employed, although with us the day was changed in regard
of a new revolution begun by our Saviour Christ, yet the same
proportion of time continueth which was before... [for] we are
bound to account the sanctification of one day in seven a duty
which God's immutable law doth exact for ever'.[28]

The works of Andrewes, Lake, Babington, Howson, Hooker,
and others confirm that Sprint's position was the authorized
teaching of the English Church. Indeed the strongest case for
consensus on sabbatarianism is the absence of evidence supporting
Rogers' position. Sprint described as 'extremist' Rogers' view
that the sabbath precept was a ceremonial law abrogated by Christ.
This was a fair conclusion, for only the works of the separatist
Henry Barrow support this view. While others must have endorsed Rogers' position, it was clearly not regarded as orthodox
teaching in the Elizabethan Church.[29] While it might be argued

[26] East Sussex Record Office 467/7/9; Strype, *Whitgift*, III, 224–6; John Overall, *The Convocation Book of MDCVI* (Oxford, 1844), pp.87–93. In the Bodleian Library a manuscript on the morality of the fourth commandment is ascribed to John Hayward; however, a contemporary hand attributes many of the ideas to Bishop Overall. (Bodleian Library, Rawlinson MS D.1350, fols. 228–47).
[27] Richard Hooker, *Works*, edited by John Keble, 4 vols. (Oxford, 1836), II, 497.
[28] *Ibid.*, pp.497–8.
[29] Henry Barrow, *The Writings of Henry Barrow*, edited by L. H. Carlson (London, 1962), pp.384–91.

that the evidence above reflects late Elizabethan sabbatarianism
and fails to explore Jacobean evidence, it should be noted that
sabbatarianism did not appear in the published theological debates
of the 1610s; and did not resurface until works against judaizing
Saturday sabbatarians were published after 1617. Although the
1617 and 1618 Book of Sports controversies generated debate over
sabbatarian *discipline*, they were *theological* non-events. It is clear
then that Rogers' account of sabbatarianism in the first years of
James' reign was a highly individualistic departure from the
established orthodoxy presented by Andrewes, Hooker, Sprint,
and others. Working from this perspective, the conventional
account of sabbatarian developments in this period must be
re-examined. We will begin this reappraisal with what has become
the *locus classicus*, the proceedings of the Dedham Classis in the
1580s.

THE DEDHAM CLASSIS

Working from Rogers' account, it is logical to look for the
beginnings of this doctrine in the debates of the Dedham Classis
and the sabbatarian developments at Cambridge during the 1580s.
He explained that while Church leaders were employed in suppressing presbyterian assaults, the brethren devised a 'new fashion'
and 'set upon us afresh again by dispersing in printed books
(which for ten years' space before they had been in hammering
among themselves to make them complete) their sabbath speculations, and presbyterian (that is, more than kingly or popely)
directions for the observation of the Lord's day'.[30] Rogers was
probably referring to Bownde's observation that he had been
solicited to publish the sermons he had preached on this subject
in 1586 and his mention of the unpublished work of Richard
Greenham.[31]

However, the Minute Book of the Dedham Classis has provided
a more tantalizing explanation. The attention given to this subject
over a two-year period and the decision to consult 'some godly
men in Cambridge tutching the question of the Sabbath',[32] seems
to support the conclusion that ministers in the classis and scholars
of Cambridge collaborated in devising a theological innovation.

---

[30] Rogers, *Catholic Doctrine*, p.18.   [31] Bownde, *Sabbath* (1595), sig.A3.
[32] Roland Usher, *The Presbyterian Movement in the Reign of Queen Elizabeth* (London, 1905),
pp.27, 28, 30–5, 47, 75–6.

Yet the debates at the Dedham Classis were not over the morality of the sabbath precept, but over the parts which tied the Christian conscience. The disputations focused on three issues: the existence of a Sabbath, the length of the observance, and the use of ordinary labours on that day. Richard Crick, preacher of East Bergholt, and Henry Sandes, pastor of Boxford, were appointed to present arguments to be discussed in the meetings. Crick did not contest the existence of a Sabbath and apparently argued that the time spent in public worship was commanded by the moral part of this precept, a position also asserted by John Howson. This point was made in Sandes' reply, when he referred to the time of service, 'which you [Crick] thinke to be the morall part of this commandment'.[33] However, Crick argued that the observance of a day and prohibitions on labour were ceremonial aspects which did not bind Christians. Sandes opposed Crick's position, claiming that Sunday observance was a divine institution, and that Christians are morally bound to devote one whole day in seven to spiritual duties and abstinence from ordinary labours.[34] These disputations are easily misinterpreted because the surviving notes are convoluted and fragmented; however, Crick's use of Bullinger and Beza suggest that he argued from a scholastic interpretation, explaining that the Church is free to establish a particular day, the portion of the day used, and the activities to be used in that time. Yet more important, Crick and Sandes were not debating the morality of the fourth precept, but the extent of the ceremonial aspects found in it. Their arguments were built on theological foundations they both understood and accepted.

The same was true of the Cambridge sabbatarians. Greenham's *Treatise on the Sabbath* did not progress beyond the doctrine found in the *Homilies* or Bullinger's *Decades*. Bownde began his defence of the moral side of the sabbath precept by citing Thomas' *Summa*,[35] and devoted only thirty pages out of over three hundred to the theological basis for sabbath observance. The rest of the work was devoted to the divine institution of Sunday, proper use of the day, and pleas for the harsh punishment of sabbath-breakers and strict enforcement of this observance.[36] A similar pattern can be found in his 1606 edition.[37] An examination of works by John

---

[33] John Rylands Library, Rylands English MS 874, fol. 17r.
[34] *Ibid*. fols. 15–25v.   [35] Bownde, *Sabbath* (1595), p.21.
[36] *Ibid*., *passim*.   [37] Bownde, *Sabbathum Veteris*, *passim*.

Dod, George Estye, William Burton, George Widley, William Perkins, and many others reveals little that distinguishes their view from the recognized teaching of the Church. All accepted that there was a ceremonial side to this law, but argued that this did not detract from the morally binding side, to use one day in seven in spiritual duties and rest from ordinary occupations.[38] While their works did not contradict the doctrinal position of the Church, it is important that the conflicts over peripheral issues not be minimized. The obsessive attention given to sabbatarian discipline by Bownde and others no doubt offended many who did not share their zeal, or regard the suppression of Sunday recreations as a matter of great urgency. Disputes over sabbath discipline, as well as several theological issues associated with the Lord's day, contributed to the tensions between precisionists and others within the Elizabethan and Jacobean Church. It is these issues that must now be examined.

THE INSTITUTION OF SUNDAY

At the Dedham Classis in 1584, Henry Sandes confuted Richard Crick's assertion that Sunday was a human institution. He opposed the notion that 'the church is at libertie to change the day', explaining that Sunday was established by the apostles as a memorial of Christ's resurrection and the re-creation of man, transferring the Sabbath to Sunday to mark the special glory of that day. Noting that the first day was specifically mentioned in I Corinthians 16:1 and that this practice had not been broken by

[38] John Dod, *A Plaine and Familiar Exposition of the Ten Commandments* (London, 1604), pp.122–30, 145–6; Dr Williams Library, MS.28.1, 'Dod's Sayings', pp.203–6; George Estye, *Certaine Godly and Learned Exposition* (London, 1603), fols. 48v–52v; W. Burton, *Abstract*, pp.2–10; Widley, pp.1–27; William Perkins, *A Golden Chaine* (Cambridge, 1591), sig.F4v; William Perkins, *Exposition upon the First Five Chapters of the Epistle to the Galatians* (Cambridge, 1604), p.315; William Perkins; 'Cases of Conscience', in *Workes*, 3 vols. (Cambridge, 1609), II, 121–4; see also: Robert Cleaver, *A Declaration of the Christian Sabbath* (London, 1625), p.134; Edward Dering, 'XXVII Lectures, or Readings upon…Hebrues', in *Works* (London, 1625), sigs.S2v–4r, S7v–8v; Edward Elton, *A Forme of Catechizing* (London, 1616), sig.D1r; Dudley Fenner, *Certain Godly and Learned Treatises* (Edinburgh, 1592), pp.111–17; Nicholas Gibbens, *Questions and Disputations* (London, 1601), pp.48–54; George Gifford, *A Catechisme* (London, 1583), sigs.F6v–8r; John Norden, *A Sinfull Mans Solace* (London, 1585), fols. 125v–126v; William Sclater, *The Ministers Portion* (Oxford, 1612), pp.30–1; Robert Some, *A Godly Treatise* (London, 1588), p.1; Christopher Sutton, *Disce vivere. Learne to Live* (London, [1604]), 398–9; William Whitaker, *A Disputation on Holy Scripture against the Papists*, translated and edited by William Fitzgerald (Cambridge, 1849), p.382; Leonard Wright, *A Summons for Sleepers* (n.p., 1589), p.28.

any Church, Sandes concluded that because 'it hath his name, the Lordes day, I thinke it is of his authority in commanding it and severing it from the rest'. He found this conclusion in 'all writers of accompte'.[39] Crick replied that 'to thinke one tyme more holie then another, is to observe tymes although ther be no religious worship given unto them'.[40] While he conceded that Sunday was instituted by the apostles, he denied that these instructions were perpetual or bound the Church. He did not deny the need to remember the resurrection and the re-creation of man, but found no reason for a weekly memorial, noting that 'if any writer affirmeth yt necessarie to have the Resur[rection] of our savyor only remembered by a daie, it is more than I know'. He concluded that this observance was not a commandment of the apostles or Christ, and that the 'church of a nation or province might chandge it if occasion served'.[41] This debate is an instructive microcosm of the different positions found in the Elizabethan and Jacobean Church; for, as John Sprint noted in 1607, this remained a disputed matter among the 'godly learned'.[42] Yet most writers acknowledged at least the apostolic institution of Sunday.[43]

However, there was no consensus on the *divine* institution of Sunday. George Estye observed that 'all learned men are not of one mind', but explained that 'I think they hold the truth that take it to be Christes own changing by expresse appointment, or inspiring his Apostles so to doe'.[44] In contrast, Greenham observed that no particular day was designated by God for the Sabbath; and Babington explained that the apostles changed the day to demonstrate Christian liberty.[45] Yet bishops Andrewes, Bayly, and Lake, as well as Hooker, Bownde, Perkins, and others affirmed the divine institution of Sunday.[46] Indeed Bishop Bayly even claimed that Christ instructed the apostles in this matter on

[39] Rylands Eng. MS 874, fols. 15r-16v.

[40] *Ibid.*, fol. 20r.

[41] *Ibid.*, fols. 20r-22r.

[42] Sprint, *Propositions*, p.7.

[43] Andrewes, *Moral Law*, p.331; Babington, *Workes*, p.10; Babington, *Commandments*, p.169; Bayly, p.394; Howson, *Sermon*, sig.B3r; Lake, 'Theses', sig.A2r; Bownde, *Sabbath* (1595), p.37; Bownde, *Sabbathum Veteris*, p.86; W. Burton, *Abstract*, p.17; Dod, *Ten Commandments* (1604), p.130; Greenham, *Works*, p.356; Widley, p.44; Perkins, *Golden Chaine*, sig.F5r.

[44] Estye, *Learned Expositions*, fol. 50r.

[45] Greenham, *Works*, p.356; Babington, *Commandments*, p.169.

[46] Andrewes, *Ninety-Six Sermons*, II, 426; Bayly, pp.380–1; Lake, 'Theses', sig.A2r; Hooker, *Works*, II, 498; Bownde, *Sabbathum Veteris*, p.86; William Perkins, *Exposition or Commentary upon the Three First Chapters of the Revelation* (London, 1606), pp.42–3; W. Burton, *Abstract*, pp.16–17; Widley, pp.44–5.

the day of his ascension, citing Hebrews 7:11–12 in support of this assertion.[47] But most writers justified this observance as a memorial of Christ's resurrection, man's re-creation, the descent of the Holy Spirit at Pentecost, and the first day of creation.[48]

Rogers' view of Sunday observance as an ecclesiastical convention was just as rare as his position on the sabbath precept. Bownde included additional arguments against this position in the 1606 edition of his work, probably in reaction to Rogers' attack, asserting that this day may not be called the King's day, Queen's day, or Emperor's day, as some divines had done. Although he used the works of medieval schoolmen to prove the morally binding nature of the Sabbath, Bownde condemned their teaching that the Church has authority to appoint the day of observance.[49] Perkins also rejected the notion of Sunday observance as a human convention; and Bishop Lake denied that the *Homilies* left this matter to the Church's authority.[50]

While the institution of Sunday was not a matter of consensus either among Church leaders or precisionists, it was not a divisive issue. The tolerance shown towards Crick's view at Dedham and the observations of Sprint and Estye emphasize that this was not considered a crucial doctrinal difference. The only positions vigorously attacked by contemporaries were the Erastian assertions of Rogers and the rejection of any distinction of days by Anabaptists and the Family of Love.

USE OF THE DAY

Following the two-part command of the fourth precept, almost all sabbatarian writers dealt with the requirement to rest from ordinary occupations and devote the time to spiritual duties. While there were many differences over the strictness of the rest, the spiritual labours required, and the length of the day, there were few who dissented from these basic responsibilities. The works of bishops Andrewes, Babington, and Bayly provided lengthy

---

[47] Bayly, pp.379–80.
[48] Andrewes, *Moral Law*, p.331; Bayly, pp.379–81, 387; Bownde, *Sabbath* (1595), pp.43–6; W. Burton, *Abstract*, pp.12–17; Cleaver, *Christian Sabbath*, pp.131–2; Dod, *Ten Commandments* (1604), p.130; Greenham, *Works*, p.356; King, *Jonas*, p.96; Lake, 'Theses', sig.A2r; Perkins, *Revelation*, pp.42–3; Widley, pp.44–5; Wright, p.28.
[49] Bownde, *Sabbathum Veteris*, pp.100, 117–20.
[50] Perkins, *Galatians*, p.315; Lake, 'Theses', sig.A3v.

statements on the duties of this day.[51] While Babington adhered to Calvin's framework taken from the *Institutes*, the other two used an outline similar to that found in the *Homilies*.[52]

In 1592 William Perkins published his *Cases of Conscience*, containing a description of the rest required on the Sabbath. He explained that there were two extreme views and a middle way. The first bound Christians to keep the outward rest required of the Jews, claiming that the sabbath precept bound Christians as well as Jews and was a sign to God's people. The second view contradicted the first, claiming that after public worship men may use their ordinary labours, as well as honest pleasures and recreations. Perkins dissented from both views. He denied that ceremonial laws of the Old Testament were binding on Christians, and explained that while the Sabbath was a sign for the Jews, Christians had only two signs: baptism and the eucharist. But the other view was equally abhorrent; for it effectively abolished one precept of the decalogue. He explained that 'the fourth Commandment (for substance) is eternal, and requireth (upon pain of the curse) both rest from labour, and a setting apart of the same rest, to the duties of holines and religion'. Perkins advocated a middle way, explaining that 'upon the Sabbath day of the New Testament, men are to rest from the ordinarie labours of their callings'. This rest, required by the moral side of the fourth precept, refreshed the body and provided time to devote to spiritual labours.[53]

While there were disputes over this rest, almost all sabbatarians

[51] Andrewes, *Moral Law*, pp.337–59; Babington, *Commandments*, pp.179–204; Bayly, pp.441–51.

[52] *Homilies*, pp.341–2. See also: Bownde, *Sabbath* (1595), pp.53–7; Bownde, *Sabbathum Veretis*, pp.26–8; Edward Dering, 'A Brief and Necessarie Catechisme', in *Works* (London, 1597), sig.A7v; Dering, 'Hebrues', sig.s3v–4r; Norden, *Solace*, fol. 125r-v; John Norden, *A Pensive Man's Practice* (London, 1584), fols. 41v–42v; Perkins, *Golden Chaine*, sigs.F5r–6r; William Perkins, *The Whole Treatise of the Cases of Conscience* (Cambridge, 1606), pp.453–64; William Ames, *The Marrow of Sacred Divinity* (London, 1642), pp.294–8; W. Burton, *Abstract*, pp.4–5; William Crashawe, *Milke for Babes, or A Northe-Countrie Catechisme*, p.18; Deacon, *Treatise*, sig.G8r; Estye, *Tenne Commandements*, sig.M6r-v; Estye, *Learned Expositions*, fol. 49r; Fenner, *Treatises*, pp.111–12; [Alexander Gee], *The Ground of Christianitie* (London, 1584), p.3; William Harrison, *The Difference of Hearers* (London, 1614), pp.20–1; Adam Hill, *The Crie of England* (London, 1595), pp.19–21; Richard Jones, *A Brief and Necessarie Catechisme* (London, 1583), sigs.B1v-2r; John Terry, *The Triall of Truth* (Oxford, 1600), pp.125–6; William Vaughan, *The Golden-grove* (London, 1608), sig.P4r-v; Widley, pp.120–37.

[53] Perkins, *Whole Treatise*, pp.453–68.

recognized a degree of liberty. They agreed that Christians need not refrain from preparing food, kindling fires, or work in times of great necessity; for this strictness was regarded as superstitious. Bownde cited as an example the story of a Jew from Tewkesbury who fell into a privy in 1257, and refused to be pulled out because of 'the great reverence he had to his holy Sabbath'. The Earl of Gloucester heard of this and would not permit him to be drawn out on Sunday 'for reverence of the holy day: and thus the wretched superstitious Jew remaining there till Monday, was found dead in the dung'.[54] Howson cited a contemporary example from Oxfordshire, of a man 'who lately when his fathers ribbes were broken would not ride for a bone-setter on the Sabboth day'.[55] Most sabbatarian writers, precisionist or otherwise, denounced such superstitious observance and asserted the right of Christians to satisfy basic human needs and perform acts of mercy.

However, the definition of this required rest varied among both Church leaders and precisionists. Babington explained that 'there is required of us this day a resting from our proper labours in our calling', and observed that tradesmen and farmers cannot serve God and work on the Sabbath.[56] Andrewes and Bayly were more explicit, prohibiting all ordinary labours, fairs and markets, recreations, journeys, and even opposing labours in harvest and seed time.[57] Howson opposed this rigour, claiming that to abstain from labour was a ceremony, and was *de jure humano* and not *de jure divino*.[58] While Howson argued that these activities could be permitted by ecclesiastical authorities, Andrewes, Bayly, and Babington came closer to the spirit of the *Homilies*.[59]

The self-conscious application of this practical theology by

---

[54] Bownde, *Sabbath* (1595), p.113. Bownde found this story in Foxe's *Acts and Monuments*.

[55] Howson, *Sermon*, sig.C1r.

[56] Babington, *Commandments*, p.179.

[57] Andrewes, *Moral Law*, pp.337–42; Andrewes, *Ninety-Six Sermons*, II, 227–8; Bayly, pp.440–5.

[58] Howson, *Sermon*, sig.C1r-v.

[59] See also: Bownde, *Sabbath* (1595), pp.63–128; Bownde, *Sabbathum Veteris*, pp.122–241; Dod, *Ten Commandments*, p.152; Ames, *Marrow*, pp.294–6; Richard Bernard, *A Double Cathechisme* (Cambridge, 1607), p.28; Robert Cleaver, *A Godly Form of Householde Governement* (London, 1598), pp.21–5; W. Burton, *Abstract*, pp.19–21; Deacon, *Treatise*, sig.G8r-v; Dering, 'Catechisme', sig.7v; Estye, *Tenne Commandments*, pp.72–119; Estye, *Learned Expositions*, fols. 49v-50v; Fenner, *Treatises*, p.113; Rylands Eng. MS 524, fols. 33v, 39v, 47v; A. Hill, *The Crie*, pp.18–20; Jones, *Catechism*, sigs.B1v-2r; Norden, *Pensive Man's Practice*, fol. 42r; Perkins, *Golden Chaine*, sigs.F5v-6r; Perkins, *Revelation*, p.45; Widley, pp.98–113; Hooker, *Works*, II, 491–8, 514–9.

prominent Englishmen emphasizes the general acceptance of this doctrine. Although the strict observance of a noted puritan like John Bruen has been cited as a model of 'puritan' sabbatarian practice, the conscientious behaviour of great public men also provides striking examples of sabbatarian principles.[60] In a letter to Robert Cecil in February 1599, Attorney General Edward Coke commented that he had been forced by government business to work on the Sabbath, explaining that 'if I were not persuaded, *Quod bonum est benefacere in Sabbate*, I should think that I have broken the whole Sabbath yesterday in speeding of this business'.[61]

Henry Hastings, fifth Earl of Huntingdon, prepared for his son a set of instructions for living, when he feared he might die in 1613.[62] While claiming to have kept the day carefully in his youth, he became more rigorous after God warned him for misusing a Sabbath in 1605. Explaining that he had stayed up all Saturday night playing cards at Harbough, he set out for Ashby early Sunday morning. Six miles out of Harbough his horse threw him 'so as it was a wonder I was not spoiled'. He concluded that 'it pleased God so lovingly to correct me and yet to be so merciful to me, as that I had no hurt. Since that time I have made more conscience of it than even I did before'.[63]

These examples illustrate the prevalence of sabbatarian opinion, and demonstrate that this rigorous observance was taken very seriously by powerful and important laymen. It would be a mistake to claim that Howson, Rogers, and Crick were alone in their lenient view towards sabbath activities; but it would be equally misguided to disregard the many witnesses supporting a strict observance of the Sabbath. It was not simply a 'puritan' obsession or a clerical fixation, for examples of this strict attitude could be found in most levels of English society.

A similar consensus can be found when examining the spiritual duties prescribed for that day. Most sabbatarian writers divided these into public worship, private devotions, and acts of mercy.

---

[60] Nicholas Assheton, *The Journal of Nicholas Assheton*, edited by F. R. Raines (Chetham Society, 1848), pp. 3–4.

[61] *HMC, Salisbury* MSS, Part IX (London, 1902), 9,ix, 74. Also see an account written by Simonds D'Ewes. Simonds D'Ewes, *The Autobiography and Correspondence of Sir Simonds D'Ewes*, edited by J. O. Halliwell, 2 vols. (London, 1845), II, 210.

[62] It was an unwarranted fear, for he lived to be ninety-nine, suffering reprisals for his support of the king in the 1640s. See *DNB*. [63] *HMC, Hastings*, 78, IV, 331.

While the list varied, most writers included corporate prayer, hearing the Word read and preached, and receiving the sacraments, as well as private meditations, giving to the poor, and visiting the sick. But emphases differed; for while Bownde, Dod, Perkins, and others stressed preaching and the use of private devotions, Howson encouraged the use of common prayer and the sacraments, criticizing those who 'gad up and down to heare the word preached'.[64] Howson's criticism, however, should not draw attention away from those Church leaders who emphasized the importance of preaching. Like Humphrey Roberts, Bishop Babington asserted that salvation comes through hearing the word, explaining that 'without knowledge of God there is no love of God, without love no faith, and without faith no salvation by God'. This theme is echoed thoughout sabbatarian works in this period.[65]

PROFANE USES OF THE DAY

John Smith's sabbatarian sermon, preached at Cambridge in 1586 has often been cited as an example of evolving sabbatarian doctrine. But it is more accurately treated as an attempt to clarify the types of activities permitted on the Sabbath; for the scholastic sabbatarian position was assumed in the debate. Smith, who had condemned the use of plays on Saturday and Sunday afternoons as breaches of the Christian Sabbath, was called before Dr Tyndal, the vice-chancellor, William Whitaker, master of St John's, Laurence Chaderton, master of Emmanuel, and the other heads of colleges to account for his position. When asked if the Christian Sabbath was kept *jure divino* from evening to evening, all present answered negatively. But when Smith affirmed that the Sabbath continued for twenty-four hours *jure divino*, his examiners correc-

[64] Howson, *Sermon*, sig.A3v.
[65] Ames, *Marrow*, pp.296–7; Andrewes, *Moral Law*, pp.342–59; Babington, *Commandements*, pp.180–97; Babington, *Workes*, pp.10–11; Bayly, pp.450–60; Bernard, *Catechisme*, p.28; Bownde, *Sabbath* (1595), pp.150–258; Bownde, *Sabbathum Veretis*, pp.285–479; W. Burton, *Abstract*, p.5; Cleaver, *Householde Governement*, pp.25–8; Deacon, *Treatise*, sig.G8v; Dod, *Ten Commandments* (1604), pp.139, 141–3; John Dod, *Old Mr Dod's Sayings* (London, 1678), fol. 14; Estye, *Tenne Commandments*, sigs.N3r–51; Estye, *Learned Expositions*, fols. 51r–52v; Fenner, *Treatises*, pp.114–15; Gee, *Ground of Christianitie*, p.3; Greenham, *Works*, pp.359–69; A. Hill, *The Crie*, pp.19–21; Jones, *Catechisme*, sigs.B1v–2r; Norden, *Solace*, fol. 125v; Norden, *Pensive Man's Practice*, fol. 42r; Perkins, *Golden Chaine*, sig.F5r–v; Perkins, *Revelation*, p.46; Perkins, *Whole Treatise*, pp.462–4; Widley, pp.121–94.

ted him. His assertion that the Lord's day was broken by any action that is not necessary or religious was also rejected. His superiors explained that any action which did not hinder religion or was not an offence to the brethren could be used. Smith was required to preach another sermon, correcting his errors.[66]

In fact, there seemed to be few Sunday pastimes that did not offend. As noted in the last chapter, bishops attempted to suppress many popular pastimes, and Church leaders and precisionists frequently complained of the irreligious use of that day. This pattern was even more evident in the late Elizabethan and early Jacobean period. Bishop Babington condemned more than eighteen pastimes, including drinking, dancing, blood sports, trading, various games, and wakes.[67] Bishop King complained that 'the sabbath is reserved as the unprofitablest day of the seven, for idlenesse, sleeping, walking, rioting, tipling, bowling, [and] daunsing'.[68] In 1592, Bishop Turnbull rebuked those who rejected God's law by their actions, noting that

When the law saith, Remember to keepe holy the Saboth day; yet not regarding that law, to prophane the Lordes day, in banquetting, in surfeting, in dicing, in dancing, in interluding, in play following, in bearbaiting, in bulbaiting, in going and gadding abroad, in sleeping, in idlenesse, in other lewdnesse, or loosenesse of life whatsoever: what is this but to speake evill of the law and condemne it?[69]

Archbishop Abbot, Bishop Bayly, and precisionists like Bownde, Greenham, Dod, Perkins, and many others made similar complaints.[70] Indeed it is not possible to draw a distinction

---

[66] Charles H. Cooper, *Annals of Cambridge*, 5 vols. (Cambridge, 1843), II, 415–16; Strype, *Annals*, III, pt 1, pp.495–7.

[67] Babington, *Commandments*, pp.189–203; Babington, *Workes*, pp.322–3.

[68] King, *Jonas*, p.96.

[69] Richard Turnbull, *An Exposition upon...James* (London, 1594), fol. 249r.

[70] George Abbot, *An Exposition upon the Prophet Jonah* (London, 1600), pp.478–9; Bayly, pp.443–52; Bownde, *Sabbath* (1595), p.263; Bownde, *Sabbathum Veretis*, pp.253–83; Rylands Eng. MS 524, fols. 26v-27r; Dod, *Ten Commandments*, pp.148, 159–67; Perkins, *Revelation*, pp.44–5; Barrow, pp.389, 545; Bernard, *Catechisme*, p.28; Robert Bolton, *Some General Directions for a Comfortable Walking with God*, 5th edition (London, 1638), p.45; Edward Bulkeley, *A Sermon Preached...at Bletsoe* (London, 1586), sig.F6r; W. Burton, *Abstract*, sigs.A3r-6v; William Burton, 'The Anatomie of Belial', in *Works* (London, 1602), pp.139, 185; William Crashawe, *The Sermon Preached at the Cross* (London, 1608), pp.172–4; Arthur Dent, *The Plaine Man's Pathway to Heaven* (London, 1601), pp.138–9, 344, 348; George Gifford, *Catechisme*, sigs.F6v-8r; Harrison, *Difference of Hearers*, pp.140–1, 160–2; A. Hill, *The Crie*, pp.16–17; Norden, *Solace*, fol. 126v; John Norden, *A Progress of Piety* (Cambridge, 1847), pp.177–8; Terry, *Trial of Truth*, p.126; John Udall, *Obedience to the Gospel* (London, 1584), sig.C1r-v; John White, *The Way to the True Church* (London, 1608), pp.210, 317; Wright, p.28.

between episcopal and precisionist attitudes in this matter, for there were few episcopal advocates for toleration of non-religious activities on Sunday. Yet a distinction must be made between the didactic writings of Church leaders and their diocesan discipline, which often tolerated the use of afternoon recreations and other activities. Like the medieval Church, many protestant bishops were obliged to tolerate activities which they did not consider appropriate for Sunday.

OBSERVANCE OF HOLY DAYS

On Accession day in November 1602 John Howson, then vice-chancellor at Oxford, preached a sermon in support of holy day observance in the university church. While acknowledging that the fourth precept bound all Christians to devote some time to worship, he asserted that the Church had authority to appoint times and regulate observance. While the observance of Sunday and the major feast days of Christ were acknowledged to be apostolic institutions, Howson claimed that holy days were used in the early centuries as well. He noted that 'in the times of St. Augustine, which are within the compasse of the pure primitive church these solemnities were multiplied, and not only the feastes of the Apostles celebrated, but of many Martyres, as of St. Cyprian, St. Laurence and Sixtus the Martyr'. These festivals were used with benefit until the calendar was 'overcharged with false and counterfeite popish saints'. Although the reformed calendar included only the most ancient Christian holy days, he observed that some still objected and argued against them.[71]

This opposition was demonstrated four days later when John Sprint, then a student of Christ Church, preached against the ceremonies and discipline of the Church. This sermon rebutted the assertions of Howson, and was the source of great controversy; for the vice-chancellor demanded that Sprint submit a copy for examination and imprisoned him when the order was refused. A commission was appointed and Sprint was forced to read his submission in convocation.[72]

---

[71] Howson, *Sermon*, sig.B3v; also see sig.B4r.
[72] See *DNB* entry for John Sprint; Christopher M. Dent, 'Protestants in Elizabethan Oxford' (unpublished D.Phil. dissertation, University of Oxford, 1980), p.360; Anthony à Wood, *The History and Antiquities of the University of Oxford*, 3 vols. (Oxford, 1796), II, 272–9; C. M. Dent, *Protestant Reformers*, pp.201–20.

This controversy, like the Whitgift–Cartwright conflicts of the 1570s, illustrates the continued tension between precisionists and Church leaders over this issue. Hooker argued that while divine and natural law required one day in seven, the remainder were 'left arbitrary to accept what the Church shall in due consideration consecrate voluntarily unto like religious uses'.[73] Noting that these days were appointed through the authority God gave to the Church, he condemned those that denied this authority and observed that this opinion 'shaketh universally the fabric of government, [and] tendeth to anarchy and mere confusion'.[74] Hooker explained that 'those things which the law of God leaveth arbitrary and at liberty are all subject unto positive laws of men, which laws for the common benefit abridge particular men's liberty in such things as far as the rules of equity will suffer'.[75] Gervase Babington and Christopher Sutton used similar arguments.[76] Greenham and Perkins conceded that days of fasting and solemn days of rejoicing could be appointed by the Church and profitably used by Christians.[77] However, most precisionists opposed the use of feast days. William Ames explained that 'contrary to this ordinance of the Lords day are all feast dayes, ordained by men, they being accounted by holy days as the Lords day ought to be accounted'.[78] Although there is little evidence from the literature explaining objections to holy days, Edward Winslow of New Plymouth spoke for many immigrants when he said 'wee came from thence to avoid...the Hierarchy, the crosses in Baptisme, the holy dayes, [and] the booke of Common Prayer'. In the Plymouth colony only the Sabbath was sanctified and work continued even on Christmas day.[79]

Rogers found this issue quite useful, emphasizing the threat to the established order by noting that 'they ruinate, and at one blow beat down all times and days...besides the Lord's day, saying plainly and in peremptory words, that the church hath none authority, ordinarily, or from year to year perpetually to sanctify any other day to those uses, but only the Lord's day'. He claimed that this teaching had led to 'all licentiousness, liberty and profaneness on the holydays, which is readily and greedily apprehended of all sorte of people everywhere, especially of their

---

[73] Hooker, *Works*, II, 497.　　　[74] *Ibid.*, pp.501, 505.　　　[75] *Ibid.*, p.506.
[76] Babington, *Commandments*, pp.191–2; Sutton, *Disce vivere*, pp.407–12.
[77] Rylands Eng. MS 524, fol. 13v; Perkins, *Golden Chaine*, sig.F3v.
[78] Ames, *Marrow*, p.297.　　　[79] Solberg, pp.113–14.

favourites, to the high dishonour of God...and gross contempt of the necessary and laudable orders of our church'.[80]

While it is doubtful that bishops would have emphasized the use of holy days to the neglect of the Sabbath, few bishops would have supported the abolition of holy days. Indeed Archbishop Whitgift's outspoken support of holy day observance in the 1570s made him a natural champion of that cause during his archepiscopacy. Rogers' use of the holy day issue is important to note, for by confusing Bownde's position on holy days with extreme sabbatarian attitudes and presbyterian tendencies, Rogers' report must have captured Whitgift's attention and spurred him into action.

JUDICIAL LAWS

In 1590 Archbishop Whitgift aggressively suppressed precisionist attempts to establish a rival ecclesiastical discipline. Thomas Cartwright, Humphrey Fen, Edmund Snape, and others were arrested and appeared before the High Commission and Star Chamber to answer for their subversive activities. Richard Bancroft, then a prebendary at St Paul, directed the proceedings against these men, proving himself relentless as a prosecutor. Whitgift prepared a list of charges, recording that they wished to abolish episcopal government, establish rule by synods of ministers, and subordinate the monarch to this clerical body in all matters ecclesiastical.[81] Among other issues, Whitgift noted that these precisionists argued 'that the judicial law of Moses, for the very form of punishing sundry crimes, ought of necessity to be observed', and that 'no prince or law may pardon or save the lives of wilful offenders: as blasphemers of God's name, breakers of his sabbaths, conjurers, soothsayers...and those that conspire against a man's life'.[82]

The previous year Bishop Hutton had conferred with Burghley and Walsingham concerning the matters presbyterians were disputing in Cambridge. He reported to Whitgift that when they discussed the judicial laws of Moses, he divided the Mosaic laws

[80] Rogers, *Catholic Doctrine*, p.18.

[81] This document is attributed to Whitgift by John Strype, who concluded that he was the author or that it was written by his special instruction. Strype, *Whitgift*, II, 12–18.

[82] *Ibid.*, p.17. For a full account see: Collinson, *Puritan Movement*, pp.403–31; Roland Usher, *The Reconstruction of the English Church*, 2 vols. (London, 1910), I, 62–5; John Strype, *John Aylmer* (Oxford, 1821), pp.205–14.

into three categories: the ceremonial, moral, and judicial laws. He explained that the ceremonial laws were shadows and types of Christ and were abrogated; while the moral law concerned the very nature of man and endured for ever. However, the judicial laws concerned the regulation of society and government, and 'may be used or not used, as shal be thought most convenient to the commonwealth'. Noting that these laws were established for Israel only, he explained that 'no nation, no state, is bound to punish sin by judicials of Moses; but may, having always respect to the law of nature and weal public, either encrease the punishment, as of theft in this realm, where it is punished with death; or diminish it, as in adultery, which is not punished with death'. He also approved of the prince wielding authority in ecclesiastical matters.[83]

Presbyterian desires to implement Mosaic judicial laws were rightly regarded as a threat to the established order and peace of the nation; for this position denied the right of secular and ecclesiastical officials to establish religious practices and determine punishments for violations. Whitgift and Hutton could not support the Mosaic prescription of execution for sabbath-breaking, blaspheming, fornicating, or a number of other offences. However, while this notion seemed dangerous to Church leaders, among precisionists it was regarded as good biblical teaching and was actually implemented in Virginia. Encouraged by the sabbatarian William Crashawe to 'let the Sabboth be wholly and holily observed', Lord De La Warr included strict sabbath regulations in the code of law established when he became governor of Virginia in 1610. All were required to attend divine service, preaching, and catechizing on Sunday, and were forbidden to 'violate or breake the Sabboth by any gaming, publique, or private abroad, or at home'. Transgressors suffered the loss of provisions for a whole week. Second offenders lost their allowance and were whipped. Death was the penalty for third time offenders.[84] Virginia was required in 1632 to order religion according to the canons of the Church of England; and the punishment for sabbath-breaking was reduced to a fine.[85]

---

[83] Strype, *Whitgift*, III, 224–5; Strype, *Whitgift*, I, 614–15.
[84] *Tracts and Other Papers*, edited by Peter Force, 4 vols. (New York, 1947), III, 10–11; Solberg, pp.86–9.
[85] There is no evidence that the death penalty was ever used against offenders (Solberg, pp.89–90.)

Whitgift's aggressive assault on presbyterians and their rival ecclesiastical discipline draws attention to two important historiographical problems. If Rogers' sabbatarian conspiracy had been an innovation and part of the presbyterian agenda of the 1580s, it seems doubtful that Whitgift would have overlooked it in 1590. Given the archbishop's vigilance, it also seems unlikely that Bownde's book would have remained unmolested for four years if his sabbatarian doctrine had been offensive. However, more to the point is the problem raised by precisionist desires for harsher punishments; for this dispute has detracted from the basic truth that Church leaders were also concerned about sabbath abuses. As noted in the previous chapter, precisionists criticized Church leaders for slack enforcement of sabbath observance, while ecclesiastical officials asserted their right to regulate observance and determine the punishments inflicted on offenders. Although they championed a common cause, their means to achieve that end conflicted. While precisionist complaints of episcopal negligence have often been accepted at face value, differences over the type of discipline applied seems a more likely explanation of the conflict; for during this period bishops not only demonstrated great interest in suppressing sabbath abuses, but in some regions also achieved greater success in enforcement.

ENFORCEMENT

Thomas Rogers wrote that 'after Elizabeth reigned noble James, who found this our Church, as all the world knoweth, in respect of the grounds of true religion, at unity; and that unity in verity, and that verity by public and regal approbation'. However, he also noted that James was troubled with false information and a petition from a thousand 'ecclesiastical ministers'.[86] This Millenary Petition urged the reform of many liturgical and disciplinary matters, and included a request that 'the Lord's day be not profaned, [and] the rest upon holy-days not so strictly urged'.[87] While Rogers reported that James discerned 'these unstayed and troublesome spirits' and protected the Church, it must be noted that the request for better sabbath observance was received

[86] Rogers, *Catholic Doctrine*, p.21.
[87] *The Stuart Constitution, 1603–1688*, edited by J. P. Kenyon (Cambridge, 1966), p.133.

sympathetically. On 7 May 1603, James issued a proclamation stating that,

We are informed that there hath been heretofore great neglect in the kingdom of keeping the Sabbath day: For better observing of the same, and avoiding all impious prophanation, we do straightly charge and command, that no bear-baiting, Bull baiting, Enterludes, Common Plays, or other like disorders or unlawful Excercises or Pastimes, be frequented, kept, or used at any time, here-after upon the Sabbath-day.[88]

On 23 May 1603 he issued instructions to lieutenants, justices of the peace, and compounders, that they were not to allow 'the Sabbath day to be prophaned with bearbaiting, piping, dancing, bowling, and other unlawful games and exercises'.[89] While these documents seem out of character for the man who issued the Book of Sports, they were consistent with the actions of the king who presided over Scottish assemblies and convocations that issued orders against profanations of the Sabbath in the 1590s.[90] Support for sabbath reforms can also be found at the Hampton Court Conference, which James convened in January 1604 to resolve differences between precisionists and Church leaders. While historians have differed over the effects of the conference, all agree that it was an event filled with controversy, highlighting the differences between the Church leaders and precisionists.[91] Yet when Dr Rainolds, master of Corpus Christi, Oxford, requested a reformation of sabbath abuses he found no opposition. Indeed William Barlow, dean of Chester, reported in his authorized version of the proceedings that this proposal received 'a general and unanimous assent'.[92] This concern was reflected in the Canons approved by the 1604 Convocation, for while Canon 13 used the prescription found in the Queen's Injunctions of 1559, the proviso permitting harvest labours was deleted. In 1605, the newly enthroned Archbishop Bancroft issued sabbatarian visitation articles which were to become the pattern for several decades.

---

[88] E. K. Chambers, *The Elizabethan Stage*, 4 vols. (Oxford, 1923), IV, 335.

[89] *HMC: Twelfth Report, Appendix, Part IV* (London, 1888), I, 391.

[90] J. K. Carter, 'Sunday Observance in Scotland' (unpublished Ph.D. dissertation, University of Edinburgh, 1957), pp.193–215, 288–94.

[91] Usher, *Reconstruction*, I, 310–33; Usher, *Reconstruction*, II, 331–54; Mark H. Curtis, 'Hampton Court Conference and its Aftermath', *History*, 46 (1961), 1–16; Patrick McGrath, *Papists and Puritans under Elizabeth I* (London, 1967), pp.339–63; Collinson, *Puritan Movement*, pp.448–67; Frederick Shriver, 'Hampton Court Re-Visited: James I and the Puritans', *Journal of Ecclesiastical History*, 33, no.1 (January, 1982), 48–71.

[92] Edward Cardwell, *A History of Conferences* (Oxford, 1840), p.187.

His tenth article enquired, 'Whether any persons have lurked and tipled in the taverns or Alehouses, upon Sundayes or other holy dayes, or used his or their manuel craft or trade upon the saide dayes or any of them and especially in time of divine service'. There were other articles enquiring whether the Lord's day was profaned contrary to the orders of the Church and whether churchwardens sought out those who failed to attend church or did not present sabbath-breakers to the Church courts. While no concessions were made on holy day observance, Church leaders issued more detailed sabbatarian articles, using Bancroft's and Grindal's articles as models.

These activities had not been preceded by episcopal neglect, for the concern of early Elizabethan bishops in convocations, parliaments, and diocesan courts had continued throughout the late Elizabethan period. This interest was reflected in twenty-five sets of visitation articles issued between 1583 and 1602.[93] As in earlier articles, church attendance, working, trading, alehouse activities, and popular pastimes remained the principal concerns; with many patterned on the sabbatarian articles issued by Grindal in his 1571 metropolitical visitation articles for York. Bishop Wickham's 1588 visitation articles for Lincoln reprinted Grindal's article against alehouse abuses, farmers and craftsmen working, and the showing of wares before divine service, describing its contents in the marginalia as 'Abuses of the Sabbath day'. Bishop Coldwell of Salisbury enquired in his 1595 visitation articles for Berkshire Archdeaconry,

Whether there hath been great abuses in prophaning the Lordes Sabbaoth consecrated wholie to his service by minstrelsie, dauncing, and drinking, to the great prophanation of that daie and the manifest contempt and dishonour of almightie God under colour thereby to procure some contribution towards the repairing of their church, by the meanes whereof many foule faults have bin and are like thenceforth to be comitted, we have thought good in God his name first to admonish you, and further by mine ordinary authoritie to charge and require you that as well the ministers as parishioners of every place, do carefully endevor themselves by all meanes to shunne and avoide the same, and if any man will be so perverse and obstinate, that he wil this notwithstanding abuse that day in this sort then to present the offenders in that behalfe from time to time that accordingly reformation may be had, as the law and justice shall appertaine.

Coldwell's prohibition of church ales stands in stark contrast to Laud's defence of such events, which resulted in the reissuing of

---

[93] See bibliography.

the Book of Sports in 1633. Richard Bancroft's 1598 London articles, issued the year before Bownde's book was suppressed, enquired about non-attendance, alehouse abuses, and 'whether any do worke or keepe any shoppe open upon Saboth daies, or upon anie holidaies appointed by the lawes of this realme to be holiday, or use any worke or labor, or open shew of their wares in any of those daies'. He also asked whether any had used games or other pastimes during morning or evening prayers.

The interest demonstrated by James in 1603 generated renewed attention to this matter. In his 1603 Injunctions, Bishop Francis Godwin of Llandaff declared that

Notwithstanding the late Proclamation of our Soveraigne Lord the Kings Majestie, straightly commanding a religious sanctification of the Sabbath day, the same is horribly prophaned every where, by using unlawful games even in the time of divine service...especially in the afternoone: I must require you to admonish your parishioners, that heerafter they take heede of prophaning either the Saboth, church or churchyard; and that in repayring unto divine service as well in the afternoone as in the forenoone, they use such diligence as by law they are bound; assuring them otherwise, to finde the uttermost extremity of that punishment which the law will inflict.

Bishop John Thornborough of Bristol, a man noted for his zeal against recusants and service to the crown, enquired in his 1603 visitation articles

Whether the churchwardens or Sidemen, or any of them have suffered any banquets, Feasts, Dinners, Suppers, or any common Drinkings in any of your churches, or whether they have suffered any Faires, Markets, or selling of wares, or any unlawful games to be kept and used in the Church or churchyard; or upon the Sunday or Sabbaoth day, or any other day appointed by the Lawes of this Realme to be kept holy?

While early Jacobean bishops continued to demonstrate an interest in church attendance, greater attention seemed to be focused on working, trading, alehouse activities, and popular pastimes – a pattern consistent with James' proclamations. These articles usually prohibited all pastimes until after evening prayer. Thomas Jegon, archdeacon of Norwich and brother of the bishop, enquired in 1606 whether innkeepers or householders 'suffer any plaies, or games in his house or yard, or doe receive any idle, or lewd persons whatsoever in his house, uppon any Sunday, or Holiday, before evening praier be cleane done in that Parish'. Archbishop Tobias Matthew of York also strictly enforced the king's proclamations in his 1607 metropolitical visitation articles, enquiring whether parishioners used 'Rush-bearings, Bull-baytinge, Beare-baitings, May-games, Morice-dances, Ailes, or such like prophane pastimes or Assemblies on the Sabbath to the hindrance of Prayers, Sermons, or other godly exercises'. William Barlow, who was consecrated bishop of Rochester shortly after publishing his account of the Hampton Court Conference, enquired in his 1605 articles 'whether are there any common haunters of Innes, Tavernes, tipling houses, or victualing houses, or any that doe use gaming upon sundayes and holy dayes, or that does utter and sell their victuails upon those dayes in time of divine service'. These regulations were still evident in the 1610s, when Bishop John King of London asked in 1615 whether parishioners used 'any may-games, Ale-drink, playing with Bowles at a game commonly called Nine-holes, or other game or games...whereby the Sabbaoth or Holy-day is prophaned, and the people led away to much lewdnesse, by those unruly and unlawful assemblies'.

It would be a mistake to emphasize the prohibitions and restrictions established by bishops and their officers without also stressing the intentions of these regulations. Most ecclesiastical officials shared the sabbatarian concerns of precisionists, desiring to see Sundays observed without the distractions of ordinary occupations and frivolous pastimes. Yet while the theological basis for their concern was a common heritage, church officials had the very practical job of maintaining and nurturing the faith in their jurisdictions. Proper observance of the Lord's day was the foundation of their work. Although the verdict on permissible activities did differ, almost all bishops allowed for the use of lawful recreations after evening prayer; a liberty that Bownde and other precisionists found abhorrent and contrary to scripture. Yet precisionist scruples on this point should not detract from the basic truth that sabbatarianism was part of the practical theology used by ecclesiastical officials. Richard Stokes, archdeacon of Norfolk, reflected this concern in his sabbatarian article, issued in 1608. Although he enquired about those who profaned the day in tippling, working, trading, 'or by other disorders', the emphasis in his question was on the religious use of that day. He asked whether parishioners continued 'the whole time of Divine Service: or if any keepe the Lords day or other hollidaies: otherwise then according to God's holy will and the orders of the Church of England, that is in hearing of the word of God, in prayer, in receiving the holy Communion, in visiting the sicke, or other sober and godly conversation'. This attitude, indistinguishable from that of Bownde and other precisionists, illustrates the goals of diligent church officials.

Even if one cynically concluded that ecclesiastical officials were nothing more than a religious branch of the civil service, who were indifferent to religious practices in their jurisdiction, visitation articles would still confirm that sabbatarian discipline was part of official policy, for questions concerning Sunday labours, trading, alehouse activities, and other pastimes were included thoughout this period. Between 1584 and 1617, only 2 documents out of 106 failed to contain an article on one of these issues.[94] Ninety-one contained articles on alehouse activities and eighty-five sought out Sunday traders, while sixty-two enquired about sabbath labours and fifty-nine asked about games, dancing, blood sports, and other pastimes.[95] When studying the place of sabbatarian discipline in the Elizabethan and Jacobean Church, it matters little whether one regards ecclesiastical officials as godly shepherds or apathetic administrators, for sabbatarian discipline was unquestionably part of the Church's definition of an ordered, Christian society.

PARLIAMENT

In parliament, lay leaders and spiritual peers jointly tackled the practical problem of suppressing sabbath abuses. The late Elizabethan and early Jacobean parliaments repeatedly attempted to enact secular regulations against misuse of the Lord's day. Between 1584 and 1614 at least ten sabbatarian bills were debated in parliament. Although none of these measures passed into law, the reports which survive reveal a keen theological awareness in both houses and little conflict over the principle of establishing such regulations. Where such conflicts did arise, the concern was usually over jurisdiction and the severity of punishments. However, the main obstacle to these bills was the royal veto; for Elizabeth and James seemed unwilling to allow parliament to meddle in religious matters. Yet the persistent attempts of parliament throughout the Elizabethan and early Stuart period indicate the importance attached to this issue in both houses.

[94] Exeter VA 1599; St Davids VA 1583.   [95] See bibliography.

While the emphasis in the early Elizabethan parliaments had been on church attendance, the 1584 parliament marked a significant shift in emphasis. The bill for 'the better and more reverent observing of the Sabbath Day' was read on 26 November, and was the first bill of that session. Neale speculated that it was proposed by some bishops who acted through Walter Mildmay, but concluded that 'it was not a Puritan bill'.[96] Although it did not succeed, a new bill was read on 3 December 1584. Cromwell reported in his journal that this draft stipulated that

No market or fayre sholde be kept, ware shewed, or stall buylte upon the Sondaye, and where fayres were befor on the sondaye the same to be kept within iii days befor or after. An exception for heringe bye English mariniers, no unlawfull games, pleyes, bearebaitinges, wakes, ringegames and such lyke hawkinge huntinge or rowinge with bardges uppon the Sundaye for common cawses duringe the tyme of the service or sermon.[97]

This bill was passed two days later by the Commons, but was not approved by both houses until 17 March 1585.[98] This delay was due primarily to disputes over the proper procedure for adding amendments, and had little to do with the contents of the bill.[99] The Speaker, Serjeant John Puckering, gave priority to this bill when presenting acts for royal assent. He explained that,

First beinge persuaded that all good lawes of men ought to be grounded uppon the eternall lawe of God expressed in the second table of his tenne commandmentes, and Callinge to theire remembrance what godlie and Christian Lawes your Majestie hath alreadie published in former parliamentes, both for the worshippinge of the onlie true God, and the worshipping of him aright as himself hath prescribed, and also for your abolishinge and punishment of all devilish [—], popishe Idolatrie, and supersticion, fantasticall prophesieinge, and false hood in forswearinge (offences against the first, second, and third commandments of the first table) Theie have thought it theire partes to goe forwardes, and (by providing for the rest, and right use of the Sabaoth daie) to provoke your majestie to give Lawe, concerning the iiiith and last commandment of the table also.[100]

Elizabeth was not so anxious to provide secular legislation for the

---

[96] J. E. Neale, *Elizabeth I and Her Parliaments, 1584–1601* (London, 1957), p.58.

[97] Trinity College, Dublin, MS 1045, Cromwell's Journal, fol. 74. Many thanks to David Dean for the transcript of this passage.

[98] Simonds D'Ewes, *The Journals of all the Parliaments during the Reign of Queen Elizabeth* (London, 1682), p.369.

[99] *Ibid.*, p.333. This observation is based on David Dean's evaluation of the evidence.

[100] British Library, Lansdowne MS 115, fol. 39r.

fourth precept and vetoed the bill, despite the efforts of Burghley in this matter.[101]

It seems likely that the legislation had been prompted by the Paris Garden tragedy in 1583; and Burghley's distress over that event was significant. Lord Mayor Thomas Blank wrote to him the day after the calamity, noting that it was God's judgement 'for suche abuses of the sabboth daie'. The mayor asked him to 'give order for redresse of suche contempte of gods service', explaining that Surrey justices were willing to punish offenders but lacked a commission to prosecute. Burghley responded swiftly, lamenting that this lesson had been learned by the loss of so many lives. To avoid profane uses of the sabbath, Burghley stated, 'I think it very convenient to have both that [bearbaiting] and other like prophane assemblies prohibited on the Saboth daie'. He promised to encourage the Council to consider a general order against these activities, suggesting that the mayor prohibit all such abuses within his jurisdiction.[102] Burghley kept his promise by backing or perhaps even instigating the 1584 sabbath observance bill. While sincere and vigorous sabbatarian zeal has often been noted in John Field's *Godly Exhortation*, it is much more striking when found in the great statesman Lord Burghley; for he not only could complain about these abuses, but could take action to suppress them as well. Only the queen stood in his way.

In 1589 a private proposal addressed to the queen recommended the restraint of minstrelsy, baiting of wild animals, and other sabbath abuses; but this measure never reached parliament.[103] The 1593 parliament debated a new bill 'to retayne the Queenes Subjects in Obedyence'. Like the 1581 bill, it was aimed at securing conformity by imposing stiff penalties on recusants for non-attendance. Although staunchly supported by Whitgift and Burghley, the bill did not pass.[104]

In 1601 parliament considered four bills relating to the Sabbath. The first bill appeared shortly after the session began and apparently included provisions enforcing attendance and suppressing Sunday trading. On the third reading Edward Glascock, a

[101] Neale, *Parliaments: 1584–1601*, p.60.

[102] Chambers, *Elizabethan Stage*, IV, 292.

[103] SP/12/222, no.70.1. Thanks to David Dean for this reference.

[104] Neale, *Parliaments: 1584–1601*, pp.280–97; Stephens, *Statutes*, pp.463–7; SP/12/244, no.75. Thanks to David Dean for this reference.

young lawyer and opponent of all the sabbath bills in that session, criticized the proviso voiding contracts made at Sunday markets and fairs.[105] The bill was returned to committee and reappeared as two bills. The bill 'prohibiting any fair or market to be held on Sunday' imposed on violators a 10 pound fine and the forfeiture of all goods shown or sold on a Sunday. All markets and fairs licensed for Sunday were to be moved to the following Monday, except the Great Yarmouth free fair. This exception was probably permitted because the chief product sold was herring and delay of sales by a day would endanger the income of many fishermen. The Yarmouth MPs were a powerful lobby, who secured a similar exemption when the 1584 bill was debated.[106] This bill was passed by the Commons on 11 December, and was read twice in the Lords – but disappeared.

The other bill 'against wilful absence from divine service upon the Sunday' was brought into the house on 13 November by Robert Wroth, the last of the Marian exiles in parliament.[107] This bill was to give new vigour to the 12 pence fine for non-attendance established in the first year of Elizabeth's reign. However, the bill proved controversial because a husband would be forced to pay his wife's fine, and a master his servants' penalty. One member objecting to this measure noted that 'every man cann tame a shrewe, but him that hath her'.[108] While Francis Darcy defended this measure, Sir Edward Hoby noted that it also imposed a second fine for an offence already covered by the law, referring to the 20 pound fine imposed on recusants in 1581.[109] Francis Moore responded that this bill was not intended for recusants, but was a punishment for those who 'bee well addicted, yett bee negligent'. Sir William Wraye confirmed that the intention of the committee was that those recusants who could pay the 20 pound fine were not intended to pay the other, which was to 'bee inflicted uppon the poorer sorte of People'.[110] Dr John Bennett, the vicar-general for spirituals and Chancellor of York under archbishops Piers and Hutton, supported this bill as well. Apparently

---

[105] Neale, *Parliaments: 1584–1601*, pp.394–5; Joan Kent, 'Attitudes of Members of the House of Commons to the Regulaton of "Personal Conduct" in the late Elizabethan and Early Stuart England', *Bulletin of the Institute of Historical Research*, 46 (1973), 41–71 (p.69); British Library, Stowe MS 362, fol. 81.
[106] SP/12/283, no.12; Neale, *Parliaments: 1584–1601*, p.395.
[107] *Ibid.*, p.396; BL, Stowe MS 362, fol. 100.
[108] *Ibid.*, fol. 117v.   [109] *Ibid.*, fol. 122r-v.   [110] *Ibid.*, fol. 123r.

dissatisfied with the effectiveness of his own courts, he observed that without execution, the penalty imposed by the Queen's Injunctions 'is lyke a Bell without a Clapper'. He stated that in Yorkshire there were 'at the least xii or xiii hundred recusantes, most of which this lawe, which we nowe have in hande, would constrayne to come to Church...For punishmente will make them doe that by Constrainte, which they ought to doe in Regard of Religion'.[111] Whether he spoke for Archbishop Hutton or not, it is significant that the Chancellor of York promoted the involvement of justices in punishing these offenders, sharing his authority in this matter with secular officials. George Carewe, secretary to the Lord Chancellor, was not satisfied by this arrangement. He disliked the proposal that ' Justices of [the] Peace should have this Authoritye. They have alreadye enoughe to doe, and therefore noe Reason they should meddle in Ecclesiasticall causes. I thinke rather it were fitt to be committed into the handes of the person of the parrish, for it is no pollicie that Justices of the peace should have such power over their neighbours'.[112] Again, one can only speculate whether Carewe spoke for the Lord Chancellor in this matter. However, it is interesting to note the differences displayed by high ranking ecclesiastical and secular representatives; for it would appear that ecclesiastical officials had fewer qualms about secular enforcement of church attendance than has previously been suggested. Townshend reported that after a long dispute the bill was narrowly defeated, 137 to 140.[113]

Yet the issue was far from dead. On 27 November Francis Hastings submitted a new bill, which took into account criticisms of the previous bills. This bill, entitled 'for the more speedie cominge to the Church on Sondaies', dropped the proviso making a householder responsible for the fines on his wife, children, or servants. However, it continued to authorize justices to punish offenders, while not taking 'awaye from the ecclesiasticall or other judges suche jurisdicton and authoritie as they formerlie had, in punishing or censuring of any of the saide offences'.[114] On 2 December Roger Owen, member for Shropshire, opposed the bill on two grounds. First, that it imposed two penalties for the same offence; and second, that it imposed additional labour on already

[111] *Ibid.*, fol. 123v.　　　　　　　　[112] *Ibid.*, fol. 124r.
[113] *Ibid.*, fol. 124; Heywood Townshend, *Historical Collections* (London, 1680), pp.224, 227–9.　　　　　　　[114] SP/12/283, no.16.

overworked justices. He also implied they might not perform this task equitably.[115] Sir Cary Reynoldes, a Privy Councillor and member of the sabbath bill committee, defended Hastings. He explained that the Sabbath was ordained for four causes. 'First, To Meditate on the Omnipotency of God. Secondly, To Assemble our selves together, to give God Thanks. Thirdly, That we might thereby be the better enabled to follow our own Affairs. Fourthly, That we might Hallow that Day, and Sanctifie it'. He noted the precedent set by James VI of Scotland, who ratified laws in 1579 and 1597 against Sunday markets. Recalling God's judgement on the man who gathered sticks on the Sabbath and the Paris Garden tragedy of 1583, he urged that the bill be committed, asserting that 'great Reformation will come if this Bill doth but Pass'.[116] George More, a man favoured by Elizabeth, also refuted Owen's criticism. He supported the bill, explaining that 'without Going to Church, or Doing Christian Duties, we cannot be Religious; [for] by Religion we learn both our Duties to God, and the Queen... Among many Laws which we have, we have none for Constraint of God's service: I say none, though one were made *primo Reginae*; because that Law is no Law, which takes no Force; for *Executio Legis vita Legis*'. He noted that attending church once a month in accordance with this bill 'excuses us from the Danger of the Law, but not from the Commandment of God'. More urged that since the bill agreed with God's law and the 'Rule of Policy' that it should be committed.[117]

Townshend reported a heated debate over the use of justices in enforcing this regulation. John Bond claimed that 'I wish the Sabbath to be sanctified according to the precise Rule of God's Commandment', but urged members to observe St Augustine's Rule: '*Non jubendo, sed docendo, magis monendo quam minando*'. He thought it dangerous to give such authority to justices.[118] Richard Martin, member for Barnstaple, observed that 'I think we all agree upon the Substance, That it is fit the Sabbath should be Sanctified'. He suggested that contentious issues should be settled in a Committee and urged a commitment.[119] Two more members spoke in favour of the bill, one noting that 'every Man agrees, this Bill hath good Matter; and we all consent to the Substance,

---

[115] Townshend, *Historical Collections*, pp.273–4.
[116] *Ibid.*, p.274.   [117] *Ibid.*, pp.274–5.
[118] *Ibid.*, p.275.   [119] *Ibid.*, p.276.

though dissent to the Form'.[120] The question of jurisdiction dominated the debate, with Hastings and Wroth demanding that Bond and others who had criticized justices should answer for their assertions at the bar.[121]

The debate concerning jurisdiction continued at the second reading on 5 December, and became heated again at the third reading.[122] Bond argued that the bill was needless and asserted that 'everie evill in state is not to bee mett with in a Lawe'. He suggested that 'our adversaries [Catholics] may say, this is the fruite of your Labour, to have preached away your audience out of the Church'. He claimed that non-attendance was 'a greater imputation upon our Archbishopps, and other ecclesiasticall governores that they bee eyther remisse in their authoritie, or else that their pereagative hath not soe much power as a xiid Fine'.[123] Hastings came to the defence of the Church. He declared that

there is noe man of Sence and Religion, (pointing at Mr Bond) that made the Speech. First, hee said it would bee an imputation to our Ministeres. That speech was both absurde in Judgement and Slaunderous…The second that it was an imputation to Archbishopps, Bishopps etc. I am so far from blaming their government that I renounce that position. I am verie sorrie that the strength of their authoritie stretcheth not soe farr as I could wishe it in this point. But mee thinkes this Lawe should rather bee a creditt to the ministrie that now wee having gone to Church these 43 yeares ourselves, and are soe fervent in Religion, desire alsoe that others may doe the like.[124]

Dr Bennett also spoke in defence of the Church, noting that 1,300 to 1,500 recusants in Yorkshire were presented both in the Ecclesiastical Court and before the Council of York.[125] Hasting's fervent defence of the Church, supported by the Chancellor of York, further illustrates that this was not a puritan preoccupation, but a matter which concerned every devout protestant. This interest was generated in part by their desire to identify recusants, and may have reflected a particular concern about recusancy in northern England. However, it is also evident that their desire to enforce the use of spiritual exercises grew out of a commonly held perception of proper sabbath practice.

The bill was lost by one vote, 105 to 106, and was followed by wranglings and recriminations. Secretary Cecil finally settled the

---

[120] *Ibid.*, p.277.   [121] *Ibid.*, pp.276–8.
[122] BL, Stowe MS 362, fols. 197r-198r, 236v-242v.
[123] *Ibid.*, fol. 237r.   [124] *Ibid.*, fol. 239r.   [125] *Ibid.*, fol. 240r.

matter, rejecting the points of order raised and attempts to bring
Bond and others before the bar. He stated, 'though I am sorrie
to say it, yett I must needes confesse, lost it is, and Farewell it'.
Townshend reported that 'the house rose confusedly, it being
after 6 of the Clocke'.[126]

The success of the Sunday trading bill in the Commons and the
persistent attempts to establish secular enforcement of church
attendance is significant for several reasons. While divisions
between 'puritans' and Church leaders have been drawn, pointing
to sabbath bills as examples of puritan ploys, no such divisions
can be found in 1601. Indeed Hastings and Bennett illustrated that
'puritans' and Church officials co-operated in parliamentary
efforts to establish more godly sabbath observance. Their common
foes were parliamentary members who opposed the use of secular
officers to enforce this religious observance. While Church leaders
are thought to have jealously protected the authority of their
spiritual courts, the evidence confirms that Bennett and others
were willing to co-operate. The theological assumptions found in
these debates cast further doubts on Rogers' story, and strongly
suggest that Bownde's book would not have been suppressed
unless other factors had complicated matters.

In 1606, the bill 'for the better observing and keeping holy the
Sabbath day or Sunday' provided for the punishment of abuses
condemned in James' 1603 proclamation. The preamble began by
explaining that sanctifying the Sabbath 'is a principall part of the
true service of God', yet 'notwithstanding his Majesties procla-
macion to the contrary' many subjects were found abusing the
Sabbath with 'bear-baytinges, bulbaitinges, Stage playes, morrice
daunces, hunting, coursing, hawking, churchales, dauncing, rushbearing, may games, whitsonales, outhurlings, inhurlings, wakes,
and dyvers other unlawfull games, assemblies, and pastimes'.[127]
These activities were to be prohibited, and violators were to be
fined 10 shillings or put in stocks for three hours on a Sunday.
The bill was introduced on 28 January and passed the Commons
on 17 February, but not without renewed disputes over enforcement by justices.[128] Although the bill remained with the Lords
into the next session, it was not forgotten in the Commons. On

---

[126] *Ibid.*, fols. 241r-242v.
[127] *HMC: The Manuscripts of the House of Lords, Addenda 1514–1714*, edited by Maurice
Bond, new series (London, 1962), XI, 96.   [128] *CJ*, i, 260, 267, 269.

23 November 1610, Nicholas Fuller listed it among other measures passed by the Commons, noting that because the Sabbath 'hath lyen open without any law to unclean feet to come upon it, we have offered it now fenced by a strong law or bar, if it may get passage from [his] sovereign Majesty and the Lords of the higher House'.[129] While it is impossible to know who obstructed the bill, it seems likely that James adopted Elizabeth's position; for evidence from the 1614 session suggests that the initiative did not come from the Lords.

The 1606 bill was reintroduced in 1614 and received strong support in both houses, illustrating the continued consensus on this matter. The 14 May debate primarily concerned additions to the bill. Amendments against football, carriers travelling, and alehouse activities were recommended, and Anthony Cope suggested that provision be made to restrain judges from travelling on the Sabbath.[130] It was also recommended that sheriffs be permitted to arrest sabbath-breakers on Sunday. Edward Mountagu, the brother of Bishop James Mountagu, reported on 13 May that the Committee had prepared the amendments and it was ordered to be engrossed. Yet another debate occurred over justices hearing these cases, with Roger Owen again as protagonist. Angry words followed, but little can be gleaned from the Commons Journal about this dispute.[131] At the third reading on 21 May, Mr Alford observed that provisions regulating Sunday sports had already been established in acts endorsed by Henry VII and Henry VIII, requesting that the bill be reconsidered. Jerome Horsey objected that 'this [is] a trick of old Parliament-men, to give a Bill a Jirk at the last Reading'. However, the tactic did not succeed, for the bill passed that day.[132]

It was introduced to the Lords on 23 May.[133] At the second reading on 26 May, a significant debate was recorded. Lord Saye began by commending the bill, noting that the recreations

---

[129] *Proceedings in Parliament: 1610*, edited by Elizabeth R. Foster, 2 vols. (London, 1966), II, 408. There were two other Sabbath bills in the 1604–10 parliaments: one against arresting on Sunday, and the other against fruit vendors in London selling on the Sabbath. Both failed to pass the Commons (Kent, 'Personal Conduct', p.70; Robert Bowyer, *The Parliamentary Diary of Robert Bowyer*, edited by D. H. Willson (New York, 1971), p.138.)

[130] *CJ*, i, 467,468,476.   [131] *Ibid.*, p.483.

[132] *Ibid.*, p.492; *Commons Debates: 1621*, edited by Wallace Notestein, F. Relf, and H. Simpson, 7 vols. (London, 1935), VII, 643–4.

[133] First reading occurred 24 May. (*LJ*, ii, 706–7.)

specified 'are unlawful sportes and games of themselves, or if they were lawfull unfitt to be used of that day, for the Sabboath is as much broken by recreacions and sportes as the businesses of a mans callinge'. Richard Neile, the future patron and patriarch of the Laudians, observed, 'I think there is noe man that regardes the glory of God and keepinge of the Sabboath day holy but doth like well of this bill'. However, Neile requested two amendments; first, that carriers and packmen be prohibited from travelling that day; and second, that the provision for harvest time labours granted by Edward VI be added.[134]

James Mountagu was the only dissenting voice. While affirming the obligation to sanctify the Lord's day, Mountagu asserted that a moderate use of recreations did not profane the day. He explained that in the fourth commandment '2 principle thinges are required, the one is rest the other is sanctification, the first for our bodies, the latter for our soules...On the Sabboath we may doe that which is *opus necessarium* and those things whereby we breake not rest nor sanctificacion...for their is noe day that we are commaunded to rest but Sunday, and their fore no day else to recreate'. Noting precedents from scripture, Mountagu denied that dancing or other recreations were unlawful, explaining that 'such exercises as are lawfull may be abused with wantonnes and deliciousnes so that the abuse may make that which is lawfull unlawfull'. He claimed that the abuses properly belonged to the spiritual courts and were not within the jurisdiction of secular magistrates, noting that if the bill was passed, a man could be punished in two courts for one offence. He concluded by defending his own observance, stating that 'for my owne part I have alwayes strictly observed and kept the Sabboath day in respect of offendinge eyther in laboure or profaines'.[135]

It is important to identify the roots of Mountagu's dissent. First, it must be emphasized that Mountagu did not deviate from the premises established by the scholastic interpretation; nor was he isolated in his defence of afternoon recreations, for other ecclesiastical and secular leaders were concerned that the people have access to recreations after evening prayer. Indeed even Samuel

---

[134] *HMC: Hastings*, edited by Francis Bickley (London, 1947), vol. 78, pt 4, pp.265–6.

[135] *Ibid.*, pp.266–7. It is unfortunate that the convocation records have not survived; for that source would have provided a more solid basis for evaluating episcopal actions in the Lords.

Ward concurred with Mountagu on this point.[136] At the same time, he was careful to emphasize his own practical orthodoxy in sabbath observance. A secondary, but equally important issue, was episcopal jurisdiction in exercising sabbatarian discipline – which proved to be the focus of Laud's attention in 1633.[137] However, his decision to oppose this bill may well have stemmed from the king. Mountagu was at the time editing James' collected works, and in one of the most important of these, the *Basilicon Doron*, the king defended the use of moderate recreations. In 1599 James explained that the people are often prone to criticize their monarch, 'ever weerying of the present estate, and desirous of Novelties'. To remedy this problem James thought it fit that

Certaine dayes in the yeare would be appoynted for delighting the people with publick spectacls of al honest games and exercise of armes as also for conveening of neighbours for enterteyning friendship and hartlinesse, by honest feasting and merrines...so that alwaies the Sabbothes bee kept holie, and no unlawfull sportes [be used].

He explained that 'this form of alluring the people, hath been used in all well governed Republickes'.[138] In view of the similar phrasing found in the preface of the Book of Sports, and Mountagu's probable involvement in its drafting,[139] it seems likely that Mountagu's role as the sole opponent of the 1614 bill, a measure promoted by his brother in the Commons, was due to his commitments and loyalties at Court.

On 30 May Archbishop Matthew reported that the Lords committee 'did hold the drift and Purpose thereof to be good, and to tend to the Glory of God'. However, because some points needed to be modified, he requested that a conference with the Commons be arranged. The following day twenty-five members of the Lords committee and fifty from the Commons committee met to discuss the bill.[140] Bishop Mountagu reported the points he questioned. His chief concern was that the bill 'takes away all exercises and recreations on the Sabboath day'. He explained that to prohibit all recreations 'is as I conceive it contrary to the divine rule it selfe, and the strictest and reformedest churches, for we

---

[136] Bodleian Library, Tanner MS 279, fol. 352. See Chapter 7, 'Reaction to the Book of Sports'.
[137] See Chapter 7, 'The Book of Sports controversy'.
[138] James I, *Basilicon Doron* (Edinburgh, 1599), pp.63–4.
[139] See Chapter 5, 'The Book of Sports controversy'.   [140] *LJ*, ii, 710,713.

cannot be stricter then the Jewes were in the observacion of the ceremoniall lawe'. Noting that Geneva allowed tennis and other exercises after evening prayer, Mountagu stated that 'in my opinion those recreations that neyther breake rest nor sanctificacion, which are the two partes of performing the due observacion of that day, are lawfull and may be used'. He also objected to putting a man in stocks on Sunday for sabbath abuses, noting that it 'is very unfitt to make the Sabboath a day of punishment'. Observing that it was the poor who would be most frequently punished for this offence, Mountagu asserted that it was 'unjuste that a man should be punished in two places for one and the self same fault'. His last concern was that the bill forced the poor to forgo recreations on their day of rest.

Bishop John Bridges of Oxford displayed very different concerns; for he wished not to delete portions of the bill, but to add to it. He observed that 'as this bill takes away all exercise and recreation upon the Sabboath day soe I thinke fitt it were inserted that their might be noe servile worke done neither buying or selling on that day'. Archbishop Abbot concluded the conference by informing the members from the Commons that 'my Lordes doe comend you for your religious care and give you thankes for the offeringe the same unto them'. He explained that 'the keepinge holy of this day is a duty that much concerns us, none of God his Commandmentes havinge a *Momento* before it but this as a note of the greatnes of this duty'. Abbot noted that in the scriptures 'God punished his people for nothinge more then the neglect of sanctifyinge his Sabboath'. He finished by emphasizing the support for this bill in the Lords, explaining they should not assume that because 'some Lordes spake against partes of this bill [that] they dislike it, for I assure you they are most gladde to imbrace it'.[141] On the morning of 4 June, the committees met again and several amendments were discussed. Archbishop Abbot reported the results to the Lords and the bill was returned to the Commons. However, parliament was dissolved three days later, and the bill died with it.[142]

The parliamentary debates of 1614 are crucial to our understanding of post-Reformation sabbatarianism, for they emphasize the theological consensus found in the Elizabethan and early

141 HMC, *Hastings*, 78, pt 4, pp.278–80.   142 *LJ*, ii, 714.

Jacobean period. The authority justices would exercise in this matter was the chief concern of opponents in the Commons. The arguments of Bishop Mountagu, the only opponent noted from the Lords, concerned practical theology and ecclesiastical jurisdiction. He claimed that moderate use of recreations did not violate the rest or sanctification of Sunday, and were permitted by Scripture. Objecting to religious offences being punished by secular magistrates, he noted the financial problems which could arise for poor laymen caught between two jurisdictions. However, his objections did not conflict with the concept of a morally binding Sabbath. Indeed his argument was founded on that doctrine. Using a scholastic definition of sabbath duties, he denied that divine law prohibited the use of moderate recreations. However, while his fellows in the Lords worked from the same theological foundations, some expressed very different conclusions. Lord Saye explained that all recreations, like labours and trading, violated the rest commanded by God. Bishops Bridges and Neile concurred with Saye and sought to increase restrictions rather than limit the bill's force. Archbishop Abbot praised this rigorous bill, emphasizing the imperative found in the fourth precept and the danger of incurring God's wrath if this commandment was not kept.

A more comprehensive refutation of Rogers' account cannot be found; for in the 1614 debate, bishops were not only promoting a rigorous sabbatarian bill, but also justifying that regulation with the very doctrine Rogers had claimed was unorthodox. The bills presented in 1584, 1601, 1606, and 1614, as well as those found in earlier parliaments, illustrate further the intense sabbatarian concern of many secular and ecclesiastical leaders. However, committed sabbatarians were not just found among the nation's civil and religious leaders, for consistory court evidence indicates that these regulations were supported by parish officials as well.

CONSISTORY COURTS

In the previous chapter, consistory court records for Ely and Norwich illustrated that despite the interest and good intentions of bishops Cox and Parkhurst, many sabbatarian reforms were not implemented because parish officers did not co-operate. This local veto is important to note, for changes in the number or type of presentments over several decades suggest a shift in popular opinion. Such a shift is evident in the court records of Ely and Chichester. These dioceses were initially selected to trace the impact of Andrewes' sabbatarian concerns, for his visitation articles for Chichester in 1606 and 1609, and Ely in 1610 and 1613, enquired about church attendance, working, alehouse activities, trading, and pastimes. While no consistent pattern can be found to establish Andrewes' personal influence on the returns, what does come to light is a significant shift in emphasis away from presentments for non-attendance and greater interest in sabbath labours, trading, alehouse activities, and popular pastimes, with parish officers using language which suggests a theological awareness. The problems of ineffective punishments remained, yet the courts in these dioceses became more effective instruments for sabbatarian discipline in the late Elizabethan and early Jacobean period – a shift which was due directly to the co-operation of parish officials.

Under Cox in the late 1570s, almost half of the 149 sabbatarian offences presented in Wisbech and Ely deaneries concerned non-attendance, with only twenty-seven cases concerning Sunday labours, alehouse activities, and popular pastimes. There were no presentments for trading. By the 1610s this pattern had changed significantly, for as Table 1b column 5 illustrates, non-attendance accounted for only 21 per cent of the cases. Sunday labours made up 37 per cent of the cases, and 19 per cent of the sabbatarian presentments concerned alehouse activities and popular pastimes. Sabbath trading, which received no attention from parish officials in Cox's day, accounted for 9 per cent of the sabbath cases during Andrewes' episcopate. Yet just as significant is the shift in the total number of sabbatarian offences presented; for Table 1a demonstrates that during Cox's episcopate 403 sexual offences were presented, while only 149 sabbatarian offenders were reported. By the 1610s this had changed dramatically. Sunday violations became the most frequently presented offence, accounting for 26 per cent of the total, while sexual offences dropped to 21 per cent of the cases.[143]

A similar pattern can be found in Chichester diocese (see Table 2). Between 1586 and 1589, non-attendance accounted for 71 per

[143] CUL, EDR, D/2/10a; D/2/18; B/2/14; B/2/15; B/2/20; B/2/21; B/2/27; B/2/30; B/2/34; B/2/35.

cent of the sabbatarian cases, while only 17 per cent of the presentments concerned Sunday labours, alehouse activities, or popular pastimes. Sabbath trading also went completely unnoticed in Chichester. However, during Andrewes' episcopate between 1606 and 1609, these previously neglected offences amounted to 63 per cent of the sabbath cases. This pattern continued under Bishop Harsnett, with non-attendance making up 30 per cent of the cases, while these other types accounted for 62 per cent of the sabbatarian presentments.[144]

The evidence from Ely and Chichester provides a very different perspective from that found in complaint literature. No doubt there were many sabbath-breakers who went undetected and unpunished; but the consistory courts were actively pursuing offenders during the late Elizabethan and early Jacobean period, and the number of presentments steadily increased. However, this emphasis on sabbath abuses cannot be attributed directly to Church officials or precisionists. Bishops and their officers had been attempting to enforce this discipline long before large numbers of offenders were presented to the courts.[145] While precisionists preached against these abuses and complained that these practices were not being suppressed, their distaste for diocesan discipline make them an unlikely source of this development. During Richard Greenham's twenty-one years at Dry Drayton, his parish officers presented a total of thirty-seven offenders to the church courts, with only two persons presented for non-attendance.[146] If a notorious sabbatarian precisionist like Greenham failed to induce his officers to present sabbath-breakers, the motivation for this trend must be sought elsewhere. James' early interest might have been an encouragement, but was not the initial motivation; for this shift was evident in Ely by the late 1580s (see Table 1b, column 2), and Elizabeth was hardly a source of inspiration. Perhaps the most plausible answer is a transformation in popular attitudes.

The shift in emphasis from non-attendance to Sunday labours and other Sunday activities suggests that parish officials increasingly perceived their role as something more than the enforcement of conformity in public worship and the detection

---

[144] West Sussex Record Office, Epi/17/6; Epi/17/11; Epi/17/12; Epi/17/13.
[145] See Ely VA 1571, 1573, 1579, 1610, 1613; Chichester VA 1586, 1600, 1606, 1609.
[146] EDR d/2/8; d/2/17a; b/2/11.

of recusants. The 1580s ushered in a new breed of parish officers, who were raised on the *Homilies* and Nowell's *Catechism*. The condemnation of Sunday labours, trading, alehouse activities, and other pastimes found in early Elizabethan teaching must have made an impact on religiously inclined laymen. This being the case, it seems natural that such concerns would be reflected in the presentments made to the Church courts. As Dr Wrightson and Dr Levine have observed, pressure from above does not adequately account for the varying chronology of change in different localities.[147] It seems reasonable to suggest that the greater emphasis on 'moral purity' in post-Reformation religion was crucial in the developments found after 1580; for this new focus replaced the popular piety which was the common heritage of churchwardens during the first two decades of Elizabeth's reign.

In February 1600, Thetford officers presented Humphrey Gaylor for not coming to church 'as he is bound by gods lawes and the Queenes'.[148] Chatteris churchwardens presented William Herd and Thomas Lanam in 1597 for fishing on Sunday, 'havinge no feare to dishonor god by [their] evill example and misdemeanor'.[149] John Ingram appeared at court in 1614 for suffering his wife and son 'to prophane the Sabboth continually by selling of meate'.[150] In Chichester diocese, the alehouse keeper Humphrey Gilbert was presented in 1606 for selling 'victualls and drinks and had a greate number there in his house the most parte of the day and that night where [there] was much disorder to the prophaning of the Lord's daie'.[151] When nine butchers of St Martin's parish, Chichester, were presented in 1609 for selling meat on Sunday, they responded that they did it to accommodate poor people who were unable to buy provisions on Saturday, because they received their wages on Saturday night. They insisted that it was not their intention to profane the Sabbath. Although they were ordered to confess their fault in church and were fined 8 pence, certain theologians were to be consulted to determine 'howe farre furth he may lawfully sell on the Saboth daies'.[152]

However, Sunday labours and trading were not the only matters

---

[147] Keith Wrightson and David Levine, *Poverty and Piety in an English Village* (London, 1979), pp.114–16.   [148] EDR B/2/21, fol. 97r.

[149] EDR B/2/14, fol. 88r-v.   [150] EDR B/2/35, fol. 22v.

[151] WSRO, Ep1/17/12, fol. 37v.   [152] WSRO, Ep1/17/13, fol. 16r.

that attracted the attention of parish officers. Popular pastimes also became a matter of great interest. Thetford officers presented seven parishioners in 1604 for profaning and abusing the Sabbath 'by dauncing of the morrice from towne to towne and so to Wilberton feaste, as well in service tyme as otherwise to the high displeasinge of Almightie God and the offence of manye'.[153] Ten men from Doddington were presented in 1616 for 'profaning of the Sabboth day by playinge at the footeballe in the churchyard being shrove Sunday'. One churchwarden was also presented for joining in the play and failing to present fellow offenders.[154] In Chichester diocese, William Tichenor was presented in 1603 'for playinge upon his fidle pipe or tabler in time of evening prayer upon the Sundaye'.[155] Mr Spencer of Witcham, Ely diocese, was presented in 1601 for piping and drawing 'the youth of Sutton to ill order on the Sabboth dayes and being admonished by the minister [said] he would do yt in spite of him'. The minstrel was ordered to confess his fault in church.[156]

These examples illustrate both the theological awareness of parish officers and other laymen, and their willingness to enforce sabbath observance. While there were some in any community who wilfully disobeyed, there seems little doubt that parishioners understood the Church's teaching, and appreciated the basis for this observance. During Andrewes' episcopate in Ely, 109 of the 856 sabbatarian presentments were prefaced with a reference to offenders profaning the Sabbath or dishonouring God by their actions.[157] The sabbath doctrine was clearly not a theological oddity identified with puritans, but part of the common definition of good Christian practice.

It has become fashionable to talk of the pre-Laudian English Church in terms of consensus rather than conflict; and there is a danger in shifting from one unexamined model to another. Nevertheless, consensus is suggested in the Elizabethan and Jacobean evidence presented above; for the tensions which did arise concerned peripheral issues, not the doctrine of a morally binding Sabbath. The theological works of Church leaders, as well as the sabbatarian discipline promoted by bishops in their dioceses

---

[153] EDR, B/2/21, fol. 151r.   [154] EDR, B/2/35, fols. 49v-52r.
[155] WSRO, Epi/17/11, fol. 17v.
[156] EDR, B/2/21, fol. 52v.   [157] EDR, B/2/27, B/2/30; B/2/34, B/2/35.

and in parliament, confirm the place of this doctrine in the English Church. Unfortunately, Rogers not only succeeded in identifying precisionist sabbatarians with extremes they did not hold, but also managed to associate the Church with a doctrine which conflicted with Elizabethan and Jacobean orthodoxy.

5

The Book of Sports controversy:
1617–18

The Book of Sports controversies of 1617 and 1618 are perhaps
the most compelling events used in support of the received
account of English sabbatarianism. The 1617 Lancashire controversy seems straightforward and the implications obvious: James
returned from Scotland and while passing through Lancashire
quashed an order issued by 'puritan' magistrates which unlawfully
restricted Sunday recreations. His preamble to the declaration
lends support to the common interpretation of this controversy,
for he explained that in his progress through Lancashire he
rebuked 'some puritanes and precise people and took order that
the like unlawfull cariage should not bee used by anie of them
hearafter in the prohibitinge and unlawfull punishinge of our good
people for usinge theire lawfull recreations and honest exercises
upon sondaies and other holidaies after the afternoone sermone
or service'.[1] Roger Richardson in his study of conflicts between
Chester diocesan authorities and puritans stated that 'there is no
doubt...that the *Declaration of Sports* was designed to weaken the
puritan position and to undermine the authority of preachers'.[2]
Dr Richardson's conclusion is quite accurate – but not for the
reasons he gives. The notion that secular and ecclesiastical
authorities were hostile towards sabbatarian discipline which
puritans were using as a ploy for moral reforms is based on a series
of assumptions which have been shown to be untenable. If the
restrictions, which were drafted by Bishop Thomas Morton and
approved by James, are studied without reference to the king's
preface, they differ little from the usual regulations found in
secular and ecclesiastical documents – except for the harsh
prohibition on recusants using Sunday sports. Indeed these

---

[1] Earnest Axon, *Manchester Sessions* (Manchester, 1901), I, p.XXIV.
[2] Roger C. Richardson, 'Puritanism and the Ecclesiastical Authorities: The Case of the
Diocese of Chester', in *Politics, Religion and the English Civil War*, edited by Brian
Manning (London, 1973), 3–33 (p.15).

regulations establish stricter guidelines than most ecclesiastical injunctions and visitation articles.

Yet having said that, it must be added that no document did more to identify strict Sunday observance with puritanism. In the preface James not only condemned recusant Catholics, but also non-conforming protestants, ordering that they either worship according to the Prayer Book and its rubrics or be forced into exile. This was a double blow to many, for while he protected Sunday recreations which many protestants regarded as pro- fanations of the Sabbath, in the same document he threatened those who disliked the established form of worship with exile, causing many to conclude that the king protected the wicked while persecuting the righteous. This action polarized opinion and created much strife in localities and in court. However, this division was not between 'puritans' and Church leaders; for it was the combined efforts of ecclesiastical officials, precisionists, and secular officers which caused James to rescind the order that the Book of Sports be publicly read in 1618. Yet the damage had already been done; for this declaration associated the religious observance of Sunday with rigorous 'puritan' principles – an association which has endured.

CHESTER DIOCESE: 1558–1617

Chester diocese was notoriously atypical. While Chester, Man- chester, and a few other towns were noted centres of reformed religion, whole regions of this vast diocese remained staunchly Catholic, virtually untouched by Protestant teaching and immune to episcopal discipline. With the county of Lancashire divided into only sixty-four parishes, effective pastoral care was impossible. Whalley parish alone covered 180 square miles, contained almost forty townships and had a population of over 10,000.[3] Efforts to convert the population and enforce conformity began in the 1560s and continued up to the Civil War.[4] William Downham, the first Elizabethan bishop of Chester, proved a weak disciplinarian and

[3] Roger Richardson, 'Puritanism in the Diocese of Chester' (unpublished Ph.D. thesis, University of Manchester, 1968), p.2; Christopher Haigh, 'Puritan Evangelism in the Reign of Elizabeth I', *The English Historical Review*, vol. 92, no.362 (January, 1977), 30–58 (p.39).

[4] See: Christopher Haigh, *Reformation and Resistance in Tudor Lancashire* (Cambridge, 1975); Roger Richardson, *Puritanism in North-West England* (Manchester, 1972).

indecisive administrator. His negligence in moving against recusants brought numerous rebukes from archbishops Parker and Grindal, as well as the Privy Council; and in 1571 his authority was inhibited while Bishop Richard Barnes of Carlisle made a visitation of Chester diocese.[5]

William Chaderton was installed as bishop in 1579, two years after Downham's death. Chaderton was a noted scholar, holding the Regius Chair of Divinity at Cambridge after Whitgift's resignation, and was famous for his opposition to Cartwright and his followers. He took up residence in Manchester where he hoped to administer his diocese more effectively, and used the power of the Ecclesiastical Commission in an attempt to improve religious discipline within his diocese.[6] In his first year Chaderton, along with the Earl of Derby, the Earl of Huntingdon, and other commissioners, issued an order against Sunday pastimes, prohibiting piping and minstrelsy, bearbaiting and bullbaiting, wakes and commonfeasts, as well as frequenting alehouses and drunkenness on Sunday.[7] The J.P.s of Salford Hundred joined forces with the Commission to suppress 'those Lewde sportes, tending to no other ende but to stirr opp our freiyle natures to wantonnes'. In a letter to William Farington, Edmund Assheton encouraged him to enforce this discipline in his jurisdiction, explaining that his motivation for suppressing these abuses was the 'prophanation of the Sabbath day...done in some places in contempt of the Gospell and the religion established'. Assheton noted that 'this day is called in Scriptures the Lords day, and [it] was not lawfull under the old lawe to carrye a pitcher of water on the Sabbath... suche regarde was hadde in the tyme of the Lawe to keepinge holy the Sabbath'. Observing that these pastimes were a distraction from good and godly works, he rhetorically asked if Farington could find 'in the presence of the foresaid lewed pastimes good example or profitt to the commonwealth, the defence of the Realme, honor to the Prynce or to the Glory of God'.[8]

---

[5] Haigh, *Reformation and Resistance*, pp.223–4, 247–68.

[6] See *DNB* for William Chaderton.

[7] R. Hollingworth, *Mancuniensis* (Manchester, 1839), pp.88–9; Baines, 1, 183.

[8] *The Farington Papers*, edited by Susan Ffarington (Chetham Society, 1856), p.128. It should be noted that interest in sabbath regulations did not begin with Chaderton's episcopate; for local orders appeared much earlier. In Liverpool orders were issued against Sunday labours in 1558, 1574, 1575, 1576, 1578, and 1579. Lancashire magistrates also issued sabbath regulations in 1574. *Liverpool Town Books*, edited by

The efforts of Bishop Chaderton and the Earl of Derby were commended by the Privy Council in July 1580, and the Council agreed to refer to parliament Chaderton's recommendation that trading at markets and fairs be prohibited till after morning prayer.[9] The bishop must have recognized that it was only through secular officials that religious discipline could be enforced, for his spiritual courts were impotent. Although the population of the diocese was well over 100,000,[10] presentments to the consistory courts were negligible. Between 1580 and 1582, church-wardens in the well-populated deaneries of Blackburn, Chester, Leyland, Manchester, and Warrington made a total of 304 present-ments, with over half relating to sexual offences and only nine cases of recusancy. Despite Chaderton's enquiry about non-attendance and Sunday labours, trading, gaming, and drinking, only nineteen presentments were made in five deaneries.[11]

In a diocese 'infested' with a large recusant population, the enforcement of church attendance and the religious use of Sunday were particularly important. Local secular officials were as com-mitted to this as ecclesiastical officials. The Manchester Court Leet issued alehouse regulations in April 1580 and the Chester Corporation provided a similar order in 1583.[12] In 1584 the Earl of Derby and Sir Francis Walsingham signed a series of suggestions for reforming 'the Enormities of the Saobothe' in this region. The activities to be prohibited were 'wakes, fayres, markettes, bayrbeytes, bullbaytes, ales, maygames, resorting to alle howses in time of divine service, pypinge and dauncinge, huntinge, and all manner of unlawful gaming'. These prohibitions were to be enforced by mayors, bailiffs, constables, 'and other civill offycers', as well as churchwardens 'and other offycers of the Churche, to suppresse, by all meanes lawfull, the said offendours of the Saobothe'. Presentments were to be made to the Quarter Sessions, where offenders were to be dealt with 'so farre as [the]

J. A. Twemlow, 2 vols. (Liverpool, 1918), I, 95; *Liverpool Town Books* (Liverpool, 1935), II, 168–9, 214, 302, 333, 994–5; *HMC, Fourteenth Report, Appendix, pt IV*, p.587.)

[9] Frere, *The English Church*, p.197; *Acts of the Privy Council*, J. R. Dasent (ed.), XII, 125.

[10] Dr Haigh estimates that Lancashire alone had population of 95,000. (Haigh, *Reformation and Resistance*, p.22.)

[11] Kennedy, *Elizabethan Episcopal Administration*, II, 115–22; CRO EDVI/6d. See Table 3.

[12] *The Court Leet Records*, edited by J. P. Earwaker, 2 vols. (Manchester, 1884), I, 210–11; Richardson, 'Puritanism' (Ph.D. thesis), pp.14–15; Gonville and Caius MS 197, fol. 55.

lawe will beare'. They singled out minstrels and bearwardens as the 'chief authores of the said disorders' and recommended that they be apprehended and punished immediately. Churchwardens were to present non-attenders to the Quarter Sessions and alehouses were to be more tightly regulated.[13] This recommendation was enacted verbatim on 17 November 1586, by sixteen Lancashire magistrates.[14] The Quarter Sessions did receive sabbatarian presentments and took action against offenders; however, there is evidence that their efforts were no more successful.[15] In 1590, seventeen Lancashire preachers prepared a report which was sent to the bishop. They complained that recusants went unpunished and observed that 'Wackes, Ales, Greenes, Maigames, Rushbearings, Bearebaities, Doveales, Bonfires, all maner [of] unlawfull Gaming, Pipinge and Daunsinge, and such like, are in all places frely exercised uppon the Sabboth'. Youths refused to attend catechizings and the people did not attend evening service, so that they had no congregations at the appointed times for preaching.[16] The preachers also noted that spiritual courts were generally despised, with citations lightly regarded. Excommunications were not feared and episcopal visitations brought no reformation. But they expressed no more faith in the secular discipline of Lancashire, observing that 'what may be done at the Quarter Sessions and generall Assises for the reformation of these manifold Enormities Knowe we not; what hathe bin done, or rather what hath not bin done heretofore we knowe too well by overlonge experience'.[17] This report was evaluated by Bishop Chaderton, who authorized his secretary to send a summary of it to the High Commission.[18]

Dr Richardson has observed that 'the issue which brought the civil authorities and preachers closest together was that of Sunday observance'.[19] Seventeen Lancashire preachers registered their dissatisfaction with the performance of both ecclesiastical and

[13] *HMC, Fourteenth Report, Appendix, part* IV, p.590.

[14] British Library, Harleian MS 1926, fols. 80r-81r. John Harland's transcription of this document is given the approximate date of March 1588/9. His dating is either incorrect, or he confused it with a reissuing of the 1586 order in that year. John Harland, *The Lancashire Lieutenancy*, pt II (Chetham Society, 1859), 217-21.

[15] James Tait, *Lancashire Quarter Session Records* (Manchester, 1917), I, 8, 11, 14, 51, 60.

[16] *Chetham Miscellanies*, edited by F. R. Raines (Chetham Society, 1875), V, 2.

[17] *Ibid.*, pp.12-13.   [18] PRO, SP/12/235, no.134.

[19] Richardson, *Puritanism in North-West England*, p.147.

secular officials – and it was the bishop who forwarded the information to higher authorities. What must be grasped is that in Lancashire, as elsewhere, concern and co-operation in this matter was demonstrated by 'puritans', secular officials, and ecclesiastical authorities alike. The complaints of the preachers were directed at *all* in authority, and provide yet another example of those without power demanding more of officials than they could accomplish.

It is also important to clarify the motivations for the sabbatarian articles sent out by Chaderton and the secular orders issued by magistrates. G. H. Tupling in his 'Causes of the Civil War in Lancashire' claimed that 'none of all these regulations can be ascribed to Sabbatarianism, which as a movement originated only towards the end of the sixteenth century'. Yet he went on to suggest that while 'the enactments of the legislature and the injunctions of the bishops were not based on Sabbatarian principles, it is not improbable that the attitude of the local magistrates was influenced by Puritan teaching'.[20] Dr Haigh has observed that 'strict sabbatarianism was enforced in Lancashire not because the Lord's Day had to be kept pure but because otherwise the preaching of protestantism would be fruitless'.[21] Doubtless there were pragmatic motives, and the conversion of papists was a great concern; however, there was a theological justification for this observance which must not be ignored. While there is no direct evidence of Chaderton's sabbatarian views, his actions in Chester diocese can leave little doubt that he accepted and attempted to enforce the Church's teaching on the Sabbath. The Lord President and Council of the Marches of Wales prohibited Sunday markets and fairs in 1595 because such activities brought 'the displeasure of Almighty God by prophaning His Sabaoth'.[22]

By the end of Chaderton's episcopate, Chester consistory courts were making greater efforts to improve sabbatarian discipline. In the early 1590s, these courts were receiving three times the number of cases presented in the early 1580s, with 1,050 cases appearing between 1592 and 1593 in the five deaneries mentioned above. As can be seen in Table 3, 21 per cent of the cases concerned sabbath abuses, compared with 6 per cent in the earlier period. Yet complaints that the consistory courts were ineffective were quite

---

[20] Tupling, pp.8–9.   [21] Haigh, 'Puritan Evangelism', p.54.
[22] *Acts of the Privy Council*, J. R. Dasent (ed.), xxv, 63–4.

accurate, for 71 per cent of the cases disappeared with no resolution or with the offender 'standing excommunicated'. It should also be noted that while 215 cases of sabbath abuses appeared, fifty came from Manchester parish alone. Although it might be suggested that strong puritan influences were the cause, it is also possible that this emphasis was due to the personal influence of the bishop in that township. This suggestion seems quite plausible, for between 1598 and 1599, over three years after Chaderton was translated to Lincoln, churchwardens for Manchester parish and its dependent chapels presented only fifteen cases for sabbath abuses, ten of which concerned a single incident of excessive Sunday drinking.[23] Indeed after Chaderton's episcopate, sabbatarian presentments declined to a much smaller proportion of cases, although the total number increased. In Bishop Richard Vaughan's 1604 visitation, only 5 per cent of the cases concerned sabbath abuses.[24] In 1606 sabbatarian cases amounted to 8 per cent of the presentments. In 1611 they comprised 12 per cent of the total, and in 1614 11 per cent.[25] As we have noted previously, this pattern does not necessarily imply that bishops Hugh Bellot, Richard Vaughan, or George Lloyd were negligent. Given the size of the jurisdiction and the unmanageable administrative structure of the diocese, as well as the large recusant population, it would have been surprising if they had exercised effective religious discipline.

The sabbatarian orders of 1579 and 1586 continued in force during the Elizabethan and early Jacobean period, with new episcopal and secular orders appearing from time to time, refocusing attention on that issue. In Liverpool an order against piping and dancing was issued in June 1598. Seven years later Bishop Lloyd ordered churchwardens to present those who 'prophane the Sabboth day by unlawfull games, by piping, dauncing, [and] Stage playes', as well as those who spent their

[23] See Table 3. CRO, EDV1/10; EDV1/12a, for drinking case, see fol. 87v.

[24] This was a period of great turmoil; for with the new king came a vigorous suppression of recusants in Chester diocese. In the 1604 visitation, 2,058 recusant related cases appeared, and 664 persons were presented for 'revolting'. (CRO EDV1/13.) This evidence contradicts James Tait's claim that 'during the last years of Elizabeth and the first years of her successor the authorities seem to have been content to let sleeping dogs lie'. (James Tait, 'The Declaration of Sports for Lancashire', *English Historical Review*, vol. XXXII (1917), 561–8 (p.568).

[25] See Table 3. CRO, EDV1/14; EDV1/17; EDV1/19.

Sunday drinking or working. In 1611 Manchester magistrates issued an order against street vendors, who sold their goods on Sunday.[26] Yet an important point which must be stressed here is that most of these orders stipulated or implied that these activities were prohibited until after evening prayer, conforming to the pattern found in other regions of the country. This will be a crucial point to remember when examining the Lancashire controversy of 1617.

Despite these provisions, sabbath abuses were not successfully reformed. Dr Haigh has provided numerous examples of piping, dancing, drinking, and gaming during this period; and there is little doubt that consistory court evidence and quarter session records provide only a glimpse of the problems faced by ecclesiastical and secular officials.[27] The frustration of the preachers in 1590 was echoed in 1614 by William Harrison, who noted that 'for one person which we have in Church to hear divine service, sermon and catechism, every piper (there be many in one parish) should at the same instant have many hundreds on the greens'.[28] These complaints were not expressions of unfounded paranoia. In 1596 Nicholas Hargreaves of Newchurch in Pendle was presented 'for playing upon organs in the house and drawing people from evening prayer upon the sabbath'.[29] In 1611 Eccles parish officials presented John Foxe, Thurston Robinson, Thomas Luigard, and William Grundien's wife for 'haveinge Ales on the Sabboth daie and thereby drawinge people from churche';[30] although it should be noted that when Mrs Grundien confirmed that her ale had occurred after evening prayer the charges were dismissed.

Catholics were accused of inciting these disorders. John White, the brother of Bishop Francis White and minister of Eccles, complained in 1608 that recusants encouraged profanations of the

[26] Twemlow, *Liverpool Town Books*, II, 753; Chester VA 1605; Earwaker, *Court Leet Records*, II, 264.

[27] Haigh, 'Puritan Evangelism', pp. 52–3. For some of the cases concerning these abuses found in Chester consistory court records, see: CRO EDVI/10, fols. 141r, 147v, 170r, 171v, 115v; EDVI/12a, fols. 23v, 128v, 138r; EDVI/14, fols. 22v, 118v, 121r–122r; EDVI/17, fols. 115v, 124r, 175r, 180r, 190r, 194v, 196; EDVI/19, fols. 68v, 71r. Also see EDC 1591–1600 Miscellaneous (I am grateful to Dr Michael Moody for this reference.)

[28] Raines, *Chetham Miscellanies*, V, 2–3; Harrison, *Difference of Hearers*, Epistle Dedicatory, sig. A8r.   [29] Haigh, 'Puritan Evangelism', p. 53.

[30] CRO EDVI/17, fol. 102. For other examples see: EDVI/17, fols. 98v, 110r, 112r; EDVI/19, fol. 92v.

Sabbath, explaining that 'in all excesse of sinne Papists have been the ringleaders'.[31] Bishop Chaderton, Lancashire preachers, local officials, and Privy Councillors agreed that recusants used these activities as a ploy to keep the people in ignorance of the reformed religion.[32] However, these transgressions were not simply a part of recusant opposition to protestantism; for popular religious customs persisted in spite of efforts made by priests to introduce a counter-reformation activist emphasis, which was hostile to traditional, community centred religious practices. Like many protestant activists, these priests emphasized individual responsibility and moral purity; and strict sabbath observance was a natural part of their teaching.[33] Post-Tridentine catechisms illustrate the similarities between the sabbatarian concerns of the Jesuit priest and the protestant preacher.

Laurence Vaux, the Lancashire born priest who was a curate at Manchester during the Marian period,[34] presented a strict interpretation of the sabbath precept in his catechism, first published at Louvain in 1568. He explained that on the Christian Sabbath

we ought to search our conscience, and purge it from sinne. We should crye and call unto God for mercie and grace, thanking him for his manyfold benefites bestowed upon us. We ought to have in memorie Christes passion, paradise, and hel and Purgatorie, so to absteine from sinne, and exercise our selves in thinges that be Godly for our soules health: as in going to the Churche, to pray devoutly, [and] reverently to heare Masse and other Divine service.

He stated that the Sabbath was broken by servile work, although he allowed for the provision of human needs and works of mercy or necessity. Failure to attend mass or divine service was also a breach of Sunday observance, and he condemned those who demonstrated a lack of reverence for holy places by talking, walking, gazing, or occupying themselves idly in church. He also noted that the Sabbath was profaned by 'unthrifty games, as cardes and dise, for covetousnes, or when we should be at Divine

---

[31] J. White, *True Church*, p.210.

[32] Haigh, 'Puritan Evangelism', pp.53–6; Raines, *Chetham Miscellanies*, v, 1–13; *Acts of the Privy Council*, J. R. Dasent (ed.), XXII, 549.

[33] Christopher Haigh, 'The Continuity of Catholicism in the English Reformation', *Past and Present*, 93 (1981), 37–69 (p.63, *passim*.); John Bossy, 'The Counter-Reformation and the People of Europe', *Past and Present*, 47 (1970), 51–70.

[34] He carried the pope's message to English Catholics in 1566, forbidding them to attend protestant services. See *DNB* for Laurence Vaux.

service: or if we use daunsing for wantonnes, or if we idely straie about... or if we frequent tavernes or bowling alleyes, or if we use any unhonest place or company. By these wayes and such like we breake the holy-day, and so offende God'.[35]

The continued use of these Sunday activities in the face of both protestant and counter-reformation Catholic teaching emphasizes the strength of popular religion in northwest England and other parts of the country. However, it should also be noted that their use in the post-Reformation period must have acquired a new significance for some Catholics as a badge of dissent and opposition to the established religious and political order. This suggestion seems plausible, given the reports from religious and political officials in the Elizabethan and Jacobean period, and would explain why these disorders, which were not treated as sectarian disorders elsewhere, came to be identified with Catholics in Lancashire.

Given this background, the sabbatarian order issued by Lancashire magistrates on 8 August 1616, was not an unusual event – except in one important point; for the magistrates included a provision prohibiting 'piping, dancinge (bowling, beare or bullbaitinge) or any other profanacion upon any Saboth day in *any parte of that day*: or upon any festivall day in tyme of devyne service'.[36] This regulation was supported by the local officials of Warrington Hundred in March 1617, with an order that 'no person uppon *anie parte of the Sabboth day* shall upon the heath, in the streetes or in the houses, use anie shuteinge, bowleinge, diceinge, cardinge, ball playinge, drinking, or anie other unlawfull games or exercyses tendinge to the breach of the lawe'.[37] In 1617, the newly consecrated bishop, Thomas Morton, copied an article issued by his metropolitan, Tobias Matthew, asking whether 'any Rush bearings, Bul-baitings, Beare-baitings, Maygames, Morrice-dances, Als, or such like prophane Passetimes, or Assemblies on the Sabbath be used on the Sabbath to the hindrance of Praiers, Sermons, or other godly exercises?'[38]

---

[35] Laurence Vaux, *A Catechisme* (Antwerp, 1574), fols. 34r-37r.
[36] Manchester Central Library, MS 347.96.M2, fol. 25. Italics are mine.
[37] *A Lancashire Miscellany*, edited by R. Sharpe France (Blackpool, 1965), pp.29–30. Italics are mine.
[38] Chester VA 1617. For Toby Matthew's article, see York VA 1607.

The secular orders and episcopal article were complementary, except in one important respect. While the local regulations established an absolute prohibition of Sunday recreations, Morton's article allowed the possible use of pastimes as long as religious duties were properly performed. These local orders went beyond the bounds commonly accepted in England and no doubt frustrated many who were accustomed to using these pastimes after evening prayer. Yet there was no apparent conflict between the bishop and secular officials over this issue. Indeed despite the bishop's well-known opposition to puritan extremes, his friend and biographer, John Barwick, emphasized Morton's sabbatarian concerns and determination to suppress this 'grosse abuse' in his primary visitation.[39] However, there was clearly opposition from some quarters and this dissatisfaction generated the setting for the Lancashire controversy in 1617.

THE LANCASHIRE CONTROVERSY

On 11 August 1617, James entered Lancashire on his return from Scotland. Two days into his journey the king met a group of laymen at Myerscough, who presented him with a petition, complaining that the people of Lancashire were debarred from lawful recreations on Sunday, by recent orders issued by the county magistrates. The petitioners requested that he nullify the orders of 1616.[40] Barwick claimed that this request was the ploy of recusant leaders, who hoped to play on the king's 'readiness to hear any complaint against a thing that carried but the name of publick grievance'. Having wrangled recently with Scottish presbyterians over the Five Articles of Perth and having quarrelled over the use of a version of the Prayer Book in Scotland, it is little wonder that James reacted against local orders that imposed the rigorous restrictions which had not passed parliament in 1614.[41] With encouragement from members of the court, James received the petition and made a speech on the liberty of Christians to pipe, dance, and engage in lawful recreations on Sundays. The following

[39] J. E. B. Mayor, 'Materials for the Life of Thomas Morton, Bishop of Durham', in *Cambridge Antiquarian Communications* (Cambridge, 1879), III, 15–18; John Barwick, *A Summarie Account of the Holy Life...of...Thomas Late Bishop of Dureseme* (London, 1660), pp.78–80.   [40] Assheton, *Journal of Nicholas Assheton*, p.41.
[41] Gordon Donaldson, 'The Scottish Church 1567–1625', in *The Reign of James VI and I*, edited by Alan Smith (London, 1973), 40–56 (p.55).

Sunday a group misused this liberty, piping and dancing outside a parish church near Houghton Tower during service time. This led to new protests. When the king heard of these abuses from Bishop Morton, he 'utterly disavowed any thoughts or intention of encouraging such prophaneness'. James turned over the offenders to Morton, who singled out the leader for punishment – a piper whom Morton had formerly 'laid by the heeles' for a similar offence. He prescribed the usual penalty, ordering the man to make a 'publick acknowledgement of the fault, and penance for it'. Yet there were some in the king's company who complained that the bishop's action was 'rigorous and tyranicall', observing that these people only desired 'some Innocent Recreation for servants and other inferiour people on the Lords day and Holy dayes, whose laborious callings deprived them of it at all other times'. Desiring the king's favour in this matter, they also noted that it was 'the generall desire of most of that country'. James conferred with Morton to determine how he might satisfy their desires without running the risk of turning liberty into licence.[42]

The bishop retired to his Preston lodgings and drafted six restrictions and conditions which bound those who used Sunday recreations. He presented this draft to James the next day. Barwick noted that the 'King did very well approve of [them], and added a seventh; saying only, he would "alter them from the words of a Bishop, to the words of a King."' This declaration prohibited bearbaiting, bullbaiting, interludes, and bowling, which were all forbidden by law. He also debarred recusants who abstained from attending church and ordered parish officials to present any who used lawful recreations 'before the endinge of all Devine service for that day'. All those who used Sunday sports were required to hear divine service first, were forbidden to wear offensive weapons while playing, and could only use those recreations within their own parish.[43]

---

[42] Barwick, pp.80–3. See also: Assheton, *Journal of Nicholas Assheton*, pp.41–2; Tait, 'The Declaration of Sports in Lancashire'; Lionel A. Govett, *The King's Book of Sports* (London, 1890); Baines, I, 209–10; Tupling, 'Causes of the Civil War in Lancashire'; Robert Halley, *Lancashire: Its Puritanism and Non-Conformity*, 2 vols. (Manchester, 1869), I, 225–35; John Nichols, *The Progresses, Processions and Magnificent Festivities of King James the First*, 4 vols. (London, 1828), III, 397. The account above is based principally on John Barwick's work, who observed at the end of his account that 'all I can positively say in it, is what I have here said, and this I can positively say because I have often heard it from this reverend Bishops own mouth'. (Barwick, p.81.)

[43] Axon, *Manchester Sessions*, pp.xxv–xxvi; MCL MS 347.16.M2, fols. 14–15.

The paradox of the Book of Sports is that the restrictions prescribed mark it out as a sabbatarian document; for it was far more restrictive than most visitation articles and secular orders. The reprinting of James' *Basilicon Doron* in 1616, with its endorsement of moderate recreations, may well have influenced those who approached the king; for it provided a regal precedent against the total prohibition of Sunday recreations enforced by the 1616 Lancashire orders. In any case, James Mountagu was there and supported their request. William Prynne reported that Mountagu and Neile were the instigators of the Lancashire declaration; an alliance which at first seems improbable. However, it should be noted that the issue on which they combined, that of afternoon recreations, was a policy which was incorporated into all visitation articles examined. The Lancashire orders *were* innovatory. Yet their innovation was indicative of a trend found even among the episcopate; for not even Neile showed any inclination to resist the moves to prohibit recreations in the debates of 1614. The action of Mountagu and Neile in 1617 suggest a 'rear-guard' action, and a timid one at that. They seem to have been joined in this action by another courtier who favoured recreations, John Williams. Yet what is most striking about this combination is the modest effect they seem to have achieved. The provisions of the declaration leave the unmistakable impression that it was a sabbatarian document; for it restricted recreations to those living within the parish and penalized recusants and others who refused to attend church. The anti-sabbatarian impact of the declaration is derived not from the actual provisions, but from the preamble James subsequently added to it.[44]

James departed from Houghton Tower on 18 August, but did not issue the declaration until 27 August, nine days later at Gerard's Bromley. This document contained a lengthy preface in addition to Morton's restrictions, which explained how 'we did justlie in our progres throughe Lancashire rebuke some puritanes and precise people and tooke order that the like unlawfull cariage should not be used by anie of them hearafter'.[45] However, noting

---

[44] Barwick indicated that Andrewes was also consulted. His involvement, as well as Morton's role in drafting the restrictions seem to account for the conservative nature of the restrictions. James I, *Workes* (London, 1616), p.164; William Prynne, *The Antipathie of the English Lordly Prelacie* (London, 1641), pp.223, 290. Thanks to Dr Andrew Foster for this reference. Barwick, pp.80–3.

[45] Axon, *Manchester Sessions*, pp.xxiv.

that the county was 'infested' with 'Papists and Puritans', and not wishing for his actions to be misinterpreted as a victory for one and defeat for the other, he thought it best to 'make our pleasure to be manifested to all our good people in those partes'. While gratified that the judges and bishop were able to report some progress in bringing recusants to conformity, he was sorry to hear 'the generall complainte of the people that they weare barred from all lawfull recreacion and excersise upon the sondaie...after the endinge of all Devine service'. He noted that this prohibition would hinder the conversion of recusants, would leave men unfit if needed for war, and might cause men to 'sette upp filthie Typlinge and Drunkennes' which could lead to 'idle and discontented speeches in theire Alehowses'. Requiring that the laws of the realm and canons of the Church be respected in Lancashire, he declared that all lawful recreations might be used after evening prayer. However, he also demanded that all 'puritans and precisions' conform to the Prayer Book or be forced to leave the country, thus striking equally at those who were 'the Condemners of our authoritie and adversaries of our Church'. He encouraged the use of piping, dancing, archery, vaulting, and rushbearing. In addition to this preface, James directed Morton to append an order requiring all preachers to 'instruct the people concerninge the lawfulnes of recreacion upon Sondaies accordinge to the Limitts and restraints set downe in his majesties Declaracion'. Those who refused to prepare food on Sunday and would not permit others to do so were to be reported for their error. In addition, ministers were to conduct divine service according to the Prayer Book and afternoon sermons were not to exceed 'the compass of an howre least that his majesties former favourable In-tenddement and Indulgencie to his people may seeme to bee Deluded thearby'.[46]

James' preface and postscript altered the implications of this declaration dramatically, for while the provisions remained within the accepted norms, he associated strict sabbath observance with 'puritanism' in three ways. First, he rebuked the magistrates for establishing and enforcing regulations which prohibited lawful recreations, and stigmatized their rigorism by labelling them 'puritans'. Second, his requirement that ministers conform to the Prayer Book or face exile, seemed to imply that a strict attitude towards Sunday recreations was another characteristic of non-conformity. Finally, his order that judaizing sabbatarians be reported further associated the prohibition of recreations with protestant extremists.

While it is understandable that these issues have been confused with the commonly accepted sabbatarian attitudes of the period, the cause of each concern stemmed from recent events and peripheral issues. The Lancashire magistrates had overstepped the bounds of their powers and jurisdiction, an issue which Bishop Mountagu had raised in the 1614 debates, and James' rebuke seems to be a warning to those who sought to establish at the local level a regulation which had not passed in parliament. His preoccupation with the Prayer Book must have stemmed from the disputes he had with presbyterians in Scotland, for the relative calm in the English Church during this period did not warrant such harsh measures. The action against judaizing sabbatarians may have been a local issue which was brought to James' attention.

It is difficult to determine why the Book of Sports became a national declaration in 1618, for nothing is known about the events leading up to its reissuing. The trial of John Traske, a judaizing Saturday-sabbatarian, may have been one cause.[47] It should also be noted that the activities permitted were revised, and more closely resemble those allowed in *Basilicon Doron*.[48] However, this declaration did overturn his instructions issued on 23 May 1603, which not only prohibited bearbaiting, bowling, and other unlawful games, but also Sunday piping and dancing.[49] The most significant amendment was the requirement that the 'Declaration shall be published by order from the bishop of the diocese through all the parish churches, and that both our judges of our circuit and our justices of the peace be informed thereof'.[50] James and his advisors must have hoped that this declaration would define the proper use of Sunday recreations, thus preventing possible tensions caused by over-zealous local orders. In

[47] See Chapter 6, 'Saturday sabbatarians'.
[48] James I, *Workes* (1616), p.164.
[49] *HMC: 12th Report, Appendix, Part* IV, vol. 1, 391.
[50] J. R. Tanner, *Constitutional Documents of the Reign of James I, 1603–1625* (Cambridge, 1961), p.56. It seems likely that Bishop Mountagu was involved, for he was at Greenwich when the national declaration was issued. He died two months later of jaundice and dropsy. (See *DNB*.)

fact, the Book of Sports complicated matters and created new tensions.

REACTION TO THE BOOK OF SPORTS

James did not intend to associate the religious observance of Sunday with puritanism; for his hostility was directed against what he took to be an English recurrence of the 'extremism' he had found so exasperating in Scotland. But his actions were seized upon by irreligious laymen, and in many communities divine service was disturbed by rowdy behaviour. In November 1618 the parishioners of Allbriton, Staffordshire, were disturbed while at evening prayer by 'a company with a drum and guns, and, striking up in the churchyard and under the church wall and windows, shot off their pieces, and cried, "Come out, ye Puritans, come out."' In the same month at Lea Marston, a group came 'into the church in the fools' coats, they sat awhile ridiculously, and ere the second lesson was read, impatient of delay, they rose up and went into the churchyard...and at an alehouse [close] by, they tabred and danced the whole sermon time'.[51] Sir Arthur Throckmorton reported a similar example in September 1618.[52] However, confusion was not limited to the common laity, for J.P.s and clergy acted on conflicting interpretations of the declaration.

The most striking example of discord was the dispute between Sir Edward Mountagu, who had promoted the 1614 sabbath bill, and John Williams, a favourite at court, who rapidly rose to power between 1618 and 1621. Two months after the national declaration was issued, constables reported to Mountagu and his fellow J.P., Thomas Brooke, that a wake was being planned at Williams' parish, Grafton-under-Wood, on Sunday, 18 July 1618. Wakes were traditional celebrations, usually held on the Sunday before or after the feast day of the saint to whom the parish was dedicated. These occasions had long been associated with excessive drinking, dancing, and often the use of pastimes prohibited on Sunday. These festivals were frequently condemned by ecclesiastical and secular officials as abuses of the Sabbath. Bishops Babington, Coldwell, and Chaderton, and Archbishop Matthew had prohibited wakes in their jurisdictions; and parliamentary bills in

---

[51] HMC: *Report on the Manuscripts of the Duke of Buccleuch and Queensberry, Mountagu House* (London, 1926), III, 213–4.
[52] *Ibid.*, p.212.

1584, 1606, and 1614 included these festivals among the forbidden Sunday activities.

Warned 'that there are likely to grow many abuses and disorders at the Feast' and that 'some have set up brewing without license…contrary to the law', Mountagu and Brooke issued a warrant giving strict orders for regulating the event. They began by forbidding unsolicited fiddlers to enter the town. Summarizing 'the King's Majesty's pleasure', they ordered that those who used lawful recreations before the end of all divine services, or used those recreations outside their parish were to be 'sharply punished'. These regulations were to be strictly enforced and any who refused to co-operate were to be reported.[53]

The result was a sharp clash with John Williams, who had recently been appointed J.P. for that jurisdiction. When the constables attempted to enforce the warrant, Williams demanded to see it, read it publicly and then told the alewives to sell the brew provided for the occasion. Warned that the ale had been prepared without a licence, Williams told the constables that 'that is another matter, yet I say they shall sell their ale notwithstanding any warrant', and said, 'am not I Justice of the peace and Justice of the quorum, Doctor and parson of the town? therefore never a precise Justice of them all shall have anything to do in my town without me'. He ordered the fiddlers to play despite the constables and told the strangers there that day, 'You honest men that are come to the town, you shall use your pastimes and your sports, for I will have no such precise doings in this town'. Cudgels were used after evening prayer and one man reported being beaten when he entered an alehouse where fiddling and drinking had continued after 9 o'clock that evening. Edward Mountagu noted in his report that 'the people in other towns have since taken encouragement to use disorderly courses'.[54]

Williams sent a letter to Edward Mountagu on 25 July. He explained that he knew of the reports taken, and attacked the 'tumultuous and schismatical constable', who was 'false in his suggestions to procure his warrant and most boisterously indiscreet in the execution of the same'. The rector claimed that he had only advised the constable 'to forbear the raising of those tumults until he found some occasion offered to put his warrants in practice'. He noted that while the warrant seemed 'somewhat

[53] *Ibid.*, p.207. [54] *Ibid.*, pp.207–9.

opposite to the meaning of his Majesty's declaration', he had been scrupulous in his efforts to avoid false accusations, preaching both in the morning and afternoon. Yet having said that, he found it intolerable for a constable to accuse him of 'abusing authority entrusted unto him' as a justice. Williams concluded by reporting that the constable maintained 'saucily':

1. that the King's declaration was a bolstering up of sin and breach of the sabbath. 2. That his Majesty therefore ought to be prayed for, that God would give him an understanding heart. 3. That the observation of the sabbath in religious worship must be continued for twenty-four hours. 4. That he and such as he can keep the sabbath thus, when they are fast asleep; and the like.[55]

Williams used his influence at court to protect himself. An unidentified source informed Edward Mountagu 'that your opposite hath acquainted the King with the business, hath made the whole Council, man by man for him, and that it shall be brought to the Council Board'. The informant also reported that 'Lord Spencer, Sir Arthur Throckmorton and all the great ones on that side of the country are wholly his'. Mountagu was being accused of meddling in Williams' jurisdiction. It was argued that 'if other Justices had intermeddled at a feast at Barnwell to send a warrant of like nature thether, where Sir Edward Mountague did reside, would it not have been an indignity unto him, and taxation of his discretion'. It was also argued that the intention of the declaration was abused, for it required that all must attend divine services where they are on Sunday, meaning that a visitor 'is for that day...of that parish, [and] to take his recreation there. *Ergo*, no offense [is] committed by them of out towns'. His informer finished by stating that 'I doubt not but you have expected the onset, and therefore accordingly prepared yourself for the combat, wherein I wish you all good success'.[56]

Mountagu had done exactly that. On 3 August he solicited the aid of his brother, Lord Chief Justice Henry Mountagu. After commiserating over the recent death of their brother, Bishop Mountagu, Edward related his problem. Regretting that misinterpretations of the king's declaration had 'begotten many disorders and great assemblies', he expressed his approval of the principle, noting that magistrates had never before had 'so much power of restraining public assemblies, which commonly breed disorders'.

[55] *HMC: Report on the Manuscripts of Lord Montagu of Beaulieu* (London, 1900), pp.94–5.
[56] *Ibid.*, p.95.

He observed that 'if that may be held which I take it to be plain in his Majesty's Declaration, that each parish by itself should use their recreation, there never was so good a device to keep the people in order, especially upon Sundays'. Describing the disorder at Grafton and public dispute with Williams, Edward Mountagu stated that 'it were good that it were called into question, to settle diversity of opinions, and that magistrates may run all in one course'. He sought his brother's advice and requested that Attorney General Henry Yelverton be acquainted with the particulars. Perhaps troubled by Williams' charge that he was a precisionist, he added in a postscript that 'it is not mine own cause, for I have executed justice, notwithstanding what was said'.[57]

Henry Mountagu sided with his brother, observing in a letter to him that 'it is not the King's intention to have the liberty he allows turned into abuse; neither is such a boldness to be borne with one Justice to expose others in such a fashion'. He explained that the Attorney General had been acquainted with the details and that after Dr Williams had been questioned, 'if I find ground enough, at the King's returning we mean to acquaint the King with it, and have order given to Mr. Attorney to prosecute it'.[58]

News of the scandal spread. Edward Mountagu's informant was mistaken about the views of Arthur Throckmorton, who wrote to Edward on 23 August and condemned Williams' behaviour, explaining that 'although he may begin his new office [as Justice] with his diligence to see his Majesty's Declaration in so pleasant a matter...It had been meeter for his ministry rather to have suffered than to oppose, yet I think he will have small credit or content thereby'. He promised to make his view known.[59] A jubilant Throckmorton wrote again on 17 September 1618 and stated that the 'great Judges' ruled in Mountagu's favour, noting that 'example cannot be better made than on a man of his [Dr Williams'] coat, who should have been furthest from such fault', and continued, 'it will be a means I hope to restrain such abuses'.[60]

[57] *HMC: MSS of Buccleuch and Queensbury*, III, 209–10.
[58] *HMC: Report on the Manuscripts of the Duke of Buccleuch and Queensbury* (London, 1899), I, 253–4.
[59] *HMC: MSS of Buccleuch and Queensbury*, III, 210. Throckmorton sent another letter two days later, explaining the sources of his information and some particulars he had heard. *HMC: MSS of Buccleuch and Queensbury*, III, 211.
[60] *Ibid.*, pp.211–12.

The disorders at Allbriton and Lea Marston and the heated dispute between Mountagu and Williams are examples of the abuses and conflicts which arose in various parts of the country. The 1621 parliament registered the concern of lay and spiritual leaders by reintroducing the 1614 bill, with Edward Mountagu leading the Commons committee. James Chudleigh of Devonshire stated that 'when his majesty shall be informed by the experience of the justices of peace in the country that it [the Book of Sports] hathe done more harm than it hath done good in converting papists, I doubt not but he will be pleased to call it in again'.[61]

Professor Collinson has observed that 'modern historians could have spared much of their effort to arrive at a "correct" definition of puritanism if it had been more clearly understood that we are dealing with a term of art and stigmatization which became a weapon of some verbal finesse but no philosophical precision'.[62] In the study of sabbatarianism, it is more important, and more accurate, to determine when this doctrine became identified with puritanism rather than searching for the 'puritan' origins of this concept.

While it would be incorrect to claim that the Declaration of Sports established sabbatarianism as a puritan characteristic, there is little doubt that it reinforced the prejudice of those who associated strict attitudes towards Sunday recreations with puritanism. However, the equation of religious uses of Sunday with puritanism not only resulted in the derision of religiously minded Englishmen, but also led to a disregard and contempt of the established religious order. The high spirited group at Allbriton, Staffordshire, derided as 'Puritans' a congregation gathered for evening prayer, disrupting a service which by statute they were bound to attend. The men who entered an evening prayer service at Lea Marston parish in fools' coats were ridiculing the authorized worship of the Church by their actions. While John Williams described Edward Mountagu as a 'precise Justice' for his attempt to regulate strictly the parish wake at Grafton, the same label could be applied to generations of bishops and secular officials who prohibited such festivals in their jurisdictions and supported

---

[61] *Commons Debates, 1621*, edited by W. Notestein, F. H. Relf, and H. Simpson, 7 vols. (London, 1935), II, 104–5.

[62] Patrick Collinson, *English Puritanism* (The Historical Association, London, 1983), p.10.

sabbatarian legislation in parliament. The examples above illustrate both a disregard for strict Sunday observance and the violation of long-established secular and ecclesiastical regulations. It is not necessary to turn to puritan literature in search of reproofs for such behaviour, for the *Homilies* condemned those who used Sunday in this manner as the worst type of sabbath-breakers.[63]

While Williams may be regarded by some as a 'typical' Anglican in his attitudes, many disapproved. The fact that the censure on Williams was not hindered by the court suggests that the king himself may have been among them. Arthur Throckmorton, who was by no means a 'puritan', observed to Edward Mountagu that James was willing to countenance 'many things in the remote places of his Realm which he will not do in the centre of his Kingdom'.[64] Throckmorton was delighted by the decision, observing that Williams' vocation required 'rather a restraining of sin, especially upon the Sabbath day than suffering a soiling of the same'.[65]

It seems, then, that rather than reducing local tensions over this issue, James' declaration incited disorders, increased friction in communities, and caused some to regard him as a maintainer of wickedness. The constable at Grafton-under-Wood charged that the king's declaration 'was a bolstering up of sin and breach of the sabbath'.[66] Mr Turnell, vicar of Horninghold, was reported for quoting 'passages of Scripture, in opposition to the King's Book of Recreation on the Lord's Day'.[67] Gerard Prior, vicar of Eldersfield, Worcestershire, publicly prayed for 'God to turn the King's heart from profaneness, vanity, or Popery'.[68] On 1 August 1619, William Clough preached against the declaration at Bramham. Reading the fourth commandment, he observed that

The king of Heaven doth bid you keepe his Sabboath and reverence his sanctuarie. Now the king of England is a mortall man and he bids you breake it. Chuse whether of them you will followe... I will tell you the reason why the king of England made Lawes against gods Lawes... the reason is because he durst doe noe other for plaine feare for the saftie of his owne body in his progresse.[69]

While these sentiments have always been attributed to 'puritans', bishops and other Church officials also opposed the declaration.

[63] *Homilies*, pp.343-4.
[64] *HMC: MSS of Buccleuch and Queensbury*, III, 210.
[65] *Ibid.*, p.210.
[66] *HMC: MSS of Lord Montagu of Beaulieu*, pp.94-5.
[67] *CSPD: 1611-1618*, p.608.
[68] *CSPD: 1619-1623*, pp.72-3.
[69] PRO, SP/14/113, no.13.

Although Bishop Mountagu defended the use of Sunday recreations in the 1614 parliamentary debates, the comments made by Bishop Bridges and Archbishop Abbot indicate that Mountagu's views were not shared by his fellow bishops. Indeed, an examination of fifteen sets of visitation articles issued between 1618 and 1620 failed to produce one example of ecclesiastical officials enforcing the reading of this declaration; and Dr Robert Pearson of Suffolk archdeaconry actually banned on Sunday the use of 'cards, tables, footbal, dauncing, bowling, excessive ringing, or immoderate drinking, or other foolish delight or vaine pleasure'.[70] Archbishop Abbot forbad that the Book of Sports be read from the pulpit in his presence on the Sunday appointed, and persuaded the king to rescind the order that it be read in church. Apparently recognizing the problems created by misunderstandings and misinterpretations of his declaration, James accepted the archbishop's reaction, although others in the court were not so acquiescent. One report observed that 'the King was pleased to wink at [Abbot's response], not withstanding the daily endeavours that were used to irritate the King against him'.[71]

The failure of the 1618 Declaration of Sports had less to do with the dissent of precisionists than with the lobbying of influential secular and ecclesiastical officials. The disorders that resulted were clearly not intended by the king, who had attempted to preserve moderate use of recreations after all the religious exercises of Sunday were finished. However, the declaration polarized opinion on this issue and contributed to the identification of strict attitudes towards Sunday recreations with puritanism – an association which was to be exploited in the 1630s.

[70] See bibliography. Suffolk Archdeaconry VA 1618. Articles relating to the enforcement of the Declaration of Sports can be found in the episcopal register of Bishop Francis Godwin of Hereford (Hertfordshire Record Office, AL 19/16, p.449). I am grateful to Dr Fincham for this reference.

[71] Nichols, *Progresses*, III, 397.

6

The 1620s: continued consensus

After the great attention given to the sabbath doctrine at the turn of the century, the 1610s were notable for the relative neglect of this issue. The reappearance of lengthy sabbatarian studies after 1618 would seem to be the logical outcome of the Book of Sports controversy. However, while the declaration did prove controversial in the parliament of 1621, the attention of theologians was drawn towards a more pressing concern – the appearance of Saturday sabbatarians in 1617. These judaizing Christians denied the divine institution of Sunday and observed Saturday according to the Jewish sabbath laws. While a few theologians attacked the scholastic interpretation as the source of this misunderstanding, all but two of the published works on the Sabbath defended the morally binding nature of the fourth precept. Indeed the scholastic interpretation remained the generally accepted view as late as 1633.

SATURDAY SABBATARIANS

Saturday sabbatarians first appeared in the late 1610s as the result of a rather unusual 'revelation'. During 1616 or 1617 Hamlet Jackson, a disciple of the judaizing preacher John Traske, was sent out to preach obedience to the Jewish ceremonial laws and to propagate Traske's own brand of latter day gnosticism. While Traske's sect strictly observed the Old Testament sabbath regulations, they observed Sunday and not Saturday – a practice which troubled Jackson. His apprehensions were 'verified' by a 'Damascus road' experience, as he travelled on a Saturday. Struck by a shining light, Jackson took this as a sign that the light of the Law was more fully understood by him than any other since the apostles. Traske and his followers, convinced that this revelation was authentic, began observing a Saturday Sabbath instead of the Lord's day.[1]

Hamlet Jackson's 'revelation' was another logical, though extraordinary, step in the evolving rigorism of judaizing Christians in Elizabethan and Jacobean England.[2] Like continental judaizers, this development stemmed from a fixation on Levitical laws and the prophetic books of the Old and New Testaments. Little is known about these judaizers except that which comes from the anathemas hurled against them. The most frequent criticism concerned their sabbatarian rigorism. As noted in earlier chapters, their refusal to prepare food, kindle fires, or perform acts of mercy and necessity were scorned as Jewish superstition by Richard Fletcher, Richard Greenham, Nicholas Bownde, John Howson, and others.

However, these practices persisted and in the 1610s found a persuasive advocate in the itinerant preacher, John Traske. Born in 1585, Traske worked as a schoolmaster in his native county of Somerset and was ordained in September 1611 by James Mountagu, though he boasted that he had 'never byn more than a guest in any University'.[3] While he claimed to have been preacher for a time at Axminster in Devon, he became notorious as a travelling preacher, spreading heterodox and judaical teaching. Traske did not limit his circuit to the diocese of Bath and Wells, but preached in many parts of the country. In 1614 twenty-three persons were presented to the Ely consistory courts for abandoning their parish churches to hear 'a strange preacher beinge called Mr. Traske'.[4] He also had a following in London.[5] While there is no positive evidence that Traske worked in Chester, Bishop Morton's articles appended to the Lancashire Book of Sports suggest that he may have influenced some in that diocese as well.[6] In 1615 Traske was

---

[1] E. Pagitt, *Heresiography* (London, 1661), pp.190–1; *The History of King-Killers* (London, 1719), p.40.

[2] John Sprint refers to 'Sabbatary Christians'; but if he had any contemporary English examples in mind, he failed to note them. Sprint, *Propositions*, pp.2–3.

[3] Somerset Record Office, D/D/VC 74, fol. 23r (thanks to Kenneth Fincham for this reference); B. R. White, 'John Traske (1585–1636) and London Puritanism', in *Transactions of the Congregational Historical Society*, vol. xx, no.7 (1968), 223–33 (p.223); D. B. [J. Falconer], *A Briefe Refutation* (n.p., 1618), p.8.

[4] EDR B/2/35, fols. 3r, 76v–77v, 113v, 190r-v.   [5] Falconer, *Refutation*, pp.7–8.

[6] The article ordered the presentment of those who 'encline to a kind of Judaisme by neither eatinge meate themselves nor sufferinge others to dress it upon the Lords day'. (Axon, *Manchester Sessions*, p.xxvi.)

imprisoned in Newgate 'for goinge upp and downe as a wanderinge minister'.[7]

However, it was not until 1618 that the extreme judaizing tendencies of the Traskites were dealt with by the authorities. Nathanial Brent in a letter written on 28 February 1618 reported to Carleton that

Here is now a new sect called Thraschits, so named from theyr leader Thrasce who is now in prison here in London. Theyr opinions made his majestie exceeding merrie on sunday at dinner, and were almost the sole subject of his discourse. Amongst other things which they foolishly maintein, they hould it absolutely unlawful to eate any swines fleshe or blacke puddings. The ecclesiastical power hath them in chase: but what will be don with them, no man, I thinke, can tell yet.[8]

Traske was initially tried before High Commission and sentenced to imprisonment to prevent him from 'infecting' others. However, after writing 'a most scandalous letter' to the king, he was tried in Star Chamber and, at his sentencing on 19 June 1618, Lancelot Andrewes defended the institution of the Lord's day.[9] The prescribed punishment was severe. He was to be kept close prisoner in the Fleet for the rest of his life, degraded from the ministry, and fined 1,000 pounds. In addition, he was to be whipped from the Fleet to Westminster, wearing a paper inscribed with the words, 'For writing presumptuous lettres to the Kinge, wherein he much slandered his Majesty, And for slandering the proceedings of the Lord Bishopps in the high Commision, And for maintayninge Jewish opinions'. He was then to have one ear nailed to the pillory and his forehead burnt with the letter 'J'. This was to be repeated at Cheapside.[10]

Eighteen months later Traske recanted of his errors and in 1620 published a work entitled *A Treatise of Libertie from Judaism*. Displaying his new-found orthodoxy, Traske affirmed the morality of the fourth commandment and asserted the divine institution of Sunday.[11] He was released from prison and permitted to preach,

[7] David S. Katz, *Philo-Semitism and the Readmission of the Jews to England: 1603–1655* (Oxford, 1982), p.19.

[8] SP/14/96, no. 38. John Chamberlain also sent a report on the Traskites to Carleton. (McClure, II, 65.)

[9] Andrewes, *Miscellaneous Works* (Oxford, 1854), pp.83–94.

[10] *Transactions of the Baptist Historical Society*, vol. 5 (1916–17), 8–11, 114; Bodleian Library, MS C.303, fol. 38. I am grateful to Mr J. R. Spencer and Dr J. Morrill for this account.

[11] Katz, p.26; John Traske, *A Treatise of Liberty from Judaism* (London, 1620), *passim*.

though he persisted in his itinerant pattern. Fuller described him as a man 'as unsetled in judgment as place'.[12]

His unfortunate followers, including his wife, proved more faithful to their cause. Returne Hebdon, the son of a Sussex gentleman, died in 1625 after eight years in prison. Dorothy Traske also remained in prison until her death.[13] Hamlet Jackson and another Traskite, Christopher Sandes, escaped to Amsterdam and became Jewish proselytes.[14]

Traskites were to become important as examples of the extremes that could result from precisionist attitudes. The king himself voiced this concern in 1619, warning his subjects not to trust

that private spirit or holy ghost which our Puritanes glory in; for then a little fierie zeale will make thee turne Separatist, and then proceed stil on from Brownist to some one Sect or other of Anabaptist, and from one of these to another, then to become a Judaized Traskite, and in the ende a profane Familist.[15]

It seems quite likely that Traske's trial was an important factor in the decision to issue the national Declaration of Sports in 1618. Yet it was the stimulus he provided for theologians which is clearly evident and interests us here.

THEOLOGICAL REACTIONS: 1619-33

The earliest account of these reactions appeared in Chester. In August 1619 John Ley, a Cheshire minister, wrote to Bishop James Ussher for advice on the sabbath doctrine. He explained that Chester had recently experienced 'a great Contraversie about the Saboth', and reported that he had '3 manuscripts against the morality of one day in 7, and of late theise positions...were preached by a prebend of Chester, there which occasioned mee to ayr the pulpit there with sounder doctrine'.[16] Bishop Bridgeman ordered both men to submit copies of their sermons and 'for peace sake were both injoyned to forbeare preaching of the matter untill

---

[12] Katz, p.26; Fuller, *Church History of Britain*, III, 307.

[13] Katz, p.28; Henry Phillips, 'An Early Stuart Judaising Sect', *Transactions of the Jewish Historical Society of England*, vol. xv (1939-45), 63-72 (p.68). For a more complete account of her troubles, see Pagitt, *Heresiography*, pp.164-83, 190-4, 209-14.

[14] Katz, pp.28-30. For more complete accounts see Katz, pp.18-34; Pagitt, pp.161-222; Phillips, 'Judaising Sect', *passim*; White, 'John Traske', *passim*.

[15] Katz, p.25.

[16] Bodleian Library, Rawlinson MSS Letters 89, fol. 30. Thanks to Peter Lake and Kenneth Fincham for this reference.

the Bishoppe mighte have time to peruse and Judge of what wee had taught'. Ley was content, noting that the bishop 'gave mee many evidences of such love of the truth, and respect of mee that I doubt not when hee hath taken full notice of the cause, he will conclude the matter to my full contentment'. Yet desiring to improve his argument, Ley wished to tap Ussher's knowledge of the Greek and Latin Fathers to clarify confusing statements and to refute evidence used against the morality of observing one day in seven.[17]

This account of anti-sabbatarian teaching in 1619 is the first example I have found since Rogers' 1607 preface. It can hardly be coincidental that this argument reappeared after the notoriety of the Traskite trials and the order issued by Morton against sabbatarian extremists in 1617. No doubt those who shared Rogers' views found in Traskite teaching the logical extreme of the scholastic interpretation, and used the opportunity for a public airing of their position. Yet a survey of literature on the Sabbath published in the 1620s and early 1630s reveals a surprisingly one-sided argument – for only two works, both written by the Oxonian, Thomas Broad, defended the anti-sabbatarian position. Little is known about Broad, except that he became rector of Rendcombe, Gloucester, on the death of his father in 1611. His works were the focus for repeated attacks in the 1620s and 1630s, and George Abbot, an M.P. in the 1640s, published and rebutted two more treatises by Broad in 1641.[18] Robert Cleaver, in his 1625 *Declaration of the Christian Sabbath*, refuted Thomas Broad's assertions that the sabbath precept was an abrogated ceremonial law. Quoting the *Homilies*, he explained that the English Church had always taught that the fourth commandment was a moral and perpetual law.[19] Henry Burton presented a similar argument in *The Law and Gospel Reconciled*, published in 1631.

However, refuting anti-sabbatarian assertions was a minor concern compared with the attention given to judaizing sabbatarians. The first work to appear on this subject was written by the Jesuit, John Falconer. In his *Briefe Refutation of John Traske's*

---

[17] *Ibid.*, fol. 30.
[18] Thomas Broad, *Three Questions Concerning the Obligations of the Fourth Commandment* (Oxford, 1621), *passim.*; Broad, *Tractatus de Sabbato* (London, 1627), *passim.*; George Abbot, *Vindiciae Sabbathi* (London, 1641), *passim.*
[19] Robert Cleaver, *A Declaration of the Christian Sabbath* (London, 1625), *passim.*

Judaical and Novel Fancyes, published in 1618, Falconer recognized the propaganda value of exposing inconsistencies in the protestant defences of the Lord's day. With specific reference to William Crashawe, the Jesuit noted that while he railed 'against Catholikes for admitting traditions and pointes of faith not contayned in Scripture, he supposeth without further proofe, that Christ in conversation with his Apostles after his ressurrection taught our keeping of the Sunday in place of the Sabaoth'. Falconer noted that Traske had identified these inconsistencies, rejecting 'arguments deduced from the authority and universall practise of Christs Church in all ages before him', and accusing them of fighting 'against him with the Catholikes borrowed weapons'.[20] However, after this jab at his protestant adversaries, the Jesuit joined them in defence of the scholastic interpretation, explaining that 'the substance and chief intention' of the fourth precept was to keep one day in seven holy.[21] He observed that 'John Traske and other Puritans in their ceremonial and precise manner of observing the Sabaoth, are rather superstitious imitators of the Jews, our Saviours adversaries, then humble and faithfull members of Christs Catholic Church, ever knowne to have practised a morall, and not the Jewish and ceremonial observance of the Sunday'.[22] Falconer observed that 'one day of seaven is still as a morall precept to be holily observed by all Christians'; but noted that 'that day of the weeke is chiefly to be observed by Christians, which our Lord was pleased to make, and have called his own day'.[23]

Falconer's position is not surprising; nor is it a revelation that leading English churchmen used similar arguments. In 1622 the Calvinist John Prideaux, Regius Professor of divinity at Oxford, defended the morality of the fourth precept, citing Aquinas in defence of his position. While dubious about the current arguments in support of the Lord's day as a divine institution, he nevertheless assented to the idea that Sunday observance was founded on divine authority. Like Falconer, he rebuked 'the sabbatarians of this Age, who by their Sabbath speculations would bring all to Judaisme'. Prideaux's lecture against judaizing sabbatarians was to prove important in the controversies of the

[20] Falconer, *Refutation*, pp.11–12.   [21] *Ibid.*, pp.27–9.
[22] *Ibid.*, p.31.   [23] *Ibid.*, pp.45–6.

1630s, when it was misapplied by Heylyn to attack critics of the Book of Sports.[24]

Griffith Williams, the Arminian prebendary of Westminster and later bishop of Ossary, also defended the scholastic interpretation in his work, *The True Church*, published in 1629. In an effort to describe the significance of this day, Williams rather eccentrically explained that 'as the blessed Virgin Mary is the chiefest among all women; so the Sabbath is the chiefest, and as it were the mother of all the daies of the weeke'.[25] Describing the place of the sabbath precept in the moral law, Williams noted that it 'is an usuall thereme in theologie, to say, "The observation of all precepts depends upon the observance of this fourth Precept."'[26] Borrowing a phrase used by Greenham, Bownde, Dod, and others, Williams observed that 'The Sabbath day is, as it were, God's market day', and explained that

Notwithstanding all the strictnesse of lawes to observe his day, and all the preaching of the most painful men, to teach us our duties toward God and man; we see how carelesse and cold we are in God's service, void of heavenly zeale, and full of all worldly cares. It is most certaine, that if there were no Sabbath, the whole service of God would be soone forgotten, and quite rooted out from man.[27]

Williams stated that this practice was part of natural law, citing Bownde in defence of this assertion,[28] and explained that 'it is of the morality of the Precept to have a seventh day perpetually sanctified unto the Lord; and therefore, that it pertaineth not unto the pontifical or canon law, to determine what day that day of rest shall be, as the Schoolmen and Canonists doe affirme'.[29] He noted that 'Junius, Peter Martyr, Zanchius, Master Perkins, Doctor Bound, and all the Divines of soundest judgement are of the same minde, that the Sabbath ought to be upon the seventh Day and upon none other'.[30] Citing the works of Wolphius, Junius, Beza, and Lewis Bayly, Williams explained that the Christian observance of the Lord's day had been established by Christ and could never

[24] John Prideaux, *The Doctrine of the Sabbath* (1634), pp.12, 19.
[25] Griffith Williams, *The True Church* (London, 1629), p.293.
[26] *Ibid.*, p.295.   [27] *Ibid.*, p.298.
[28] *Ibid.*, p.297.
[29] This is a reference to the scholastic position that Sunday was not a divine institution, but established by the Church. See Chapter 2, 'Medieval Sabbatarian Doctrine'.
[30] G. Williams, *True Church*, p.300.

be changed.[31] He condemned those who were too precise, refusing to do works of necessity, such as preparing food, easing themselves, kindling fires, or even scratching where it itches. However, he noted that 'these precise men [be] but few, like the grapes of vintage, here and there one'.[32]

Even John Cosin supported this doctrine, preaching three sermons on the morally binding nature of the fourth precept in 1633. He stated that 'we should be sure to remember and regard this as one of his special commandments', and observed that 'this precept is the very life of all the Decalogue'.[33] Noting that this commandment called for rest from idleness and common affairs so that spiritual exercises could be used, Cosin concluded that 'every festival, lawfully appointed, and made sacred, is a Sabbath', and explained that 'we are bound to keep them [holy days], every one'.[34] However, Cosin drew a distinction between the Lord's day and holy days established by the Church. Observing that the Jewish Sabbath was 'buried with Christ in His grave', he stated that with the resurrection 'arose the beginning of a new day, which now we call the Lord's day, to remain for ever, and not to be altered'.[35] He noted that Calvin and 'some other new writers' disagreed, saying that 'neither one day in seven, nor yet that this day of the Lord, is commanded or established but still alterable by the Church'. Cosin stated confidently that 'both Scripture and the Fathers' supported his belief in the divine institution of Sunday.[36]

An examination of works by Peter Barker, John Mayer, Edward Brerewood, Bishop Joseph Hall, and others yields no surprises; for all used the scholastic interpretation in their studies of the Sabbath.[37] There was also a notable consensus on the divine institution of the Lord's day; no doubt inspired by the challenges presented by Saturday sabbatarians on the one hand and anti-

---

[31] *Ibid.*, p.302.
[32] *Ibid.*, p.311.
[33] John Cosin, *Works*, 5 vols. (Oxford, 1843), I, 153–5.
[34] *Ibid.*, pp.157–8.
[35] *Ibid.*, p.171.
[36] *Ibid.*, pp.171–2.
[37] Peter Barker, *A Judicious and Painefull Exposition upon the Ten Commandments* (London, 1624), pp.172–91; John Mayer, *The English Catechisme Explained* (London, 1623), pp.261–8; Edward Brerewood and Nicholas Byfield, *A Learned Treatise of the Sabbath* (Oxford, 1630), pp.39–43; Edward Brerewood, *A Second Treatise of the Sabbath* (Oxford, 1632), pp.1–6; Joseph Hall, *Works*, 7 vols. (London, 1808), VII, 254–6; Richard Byfield, *The Doctrine of the Sabbath Vindicated* (London, 1631), pp.70–95; T. Adams, *The Happiness of the Church* (London, 1618), pp.226–7; Alexander Leighton, *Speculum Belli sacri* (n.p., 1624), pp.267–9.

sabbatarians on the other.[38] Only Thomas Broad and Edward Brerewood asserted that the institution of Sunday was a human convention, established and maintained by the Church.[39] The work of English theologians found affirmation and support in the resolutions of the Synod of Dort and the strict regulations established by the United Provinces; for the English representatives, George Carleton, John Davenant, Samuel Ward, and Joseph Hall, endorsed the Synod's conclusions, which included a defence of the scholastic interpretation.[40]

These defenders of the scholastic interpretation and the divine institution of Sunday produced nothing new and appear commonplace and repetitive. Their condemnations of 'puritans' and 'sabbatarians' were directed at judaizing Christians who practised an extremely rigorous Sunday observance or reverenced Saturday instead of Sunday. The works of Bownde and other precisionists were cited by leading Calvinists and Arminians in defence of the Church's teaching; for the scholastic interpretation remained the acknowledged orthodoxy as late as 1633, when new and forceful voices challenged this position and altered the meaning of the terms 'puritan' and 'sabbatarian'.

PARLIAMENT: 1621–29

Parliamentary debates in the 1620s illustrate further the broad support for religious uses of the Lord's day, and a desire to regulate tightly the recreations used after evening prayer. In seeking a definition of 'puritan activities' in the late Jacobean parliaments, Professor Conrad Russell observed that 'if we take a wider definition [of puritanism] involving such things as a desire for further reformation and cult of the Sabbath, then "puritanism"

---

[38] Henry Burton, *The Law and Gospel Reconciled* (London, 1631), pp.48–59; Richard Byfield, *Sabbath Vindicated*, pp.124–40; Mayer, *Catechisme Explained*, pp.266–7; Hall, *Works*, VII, 254–6.

[39] Broad, *Three Questions*, pp.21–2; Broad, *Tractatus de Sabbato*, p.14; Brerewood, *Treatise of the Sabbath*, pp.37–9, 62–74; Brerewood, *Second Treatise*, pp.6, 18–40. Brerewood was the first professor of astronomy at Gresham College. His writings on the Sabbath concerned the question of servants obeying orders on the Lord's day; and were stimulated by an over-scrupulous nephew, who lost his apprenticeship for refusing to run errands on Sunday. Although published in 1630 and 1632, these works were written in the 1610s.

[40] Hessey, pp.233–4, 444–7; Henry Burton, *A Brief Answer to a Late Treatise of the Sabbath Day* (London, 1635), p.31.

was an official creed, and George Abbot was, as Richard Montagu would have him, a "puritan archbishop"'.[41] The persistent reappearance of sabbath bills and their repeated and swift passage through both houses illustrate the common concern of lay politicians and spiritual peers. The failure to gain James' assent had more to do with personal conflicts than the clash of ideologies. The bill which was passed in 1621, 1624, and 1625 was clearly intended to modify and tighten some aspects of the king's declaration. If this is taken on its own, James' veto appears to be simply a stubborn resistance to such alterations. However, the activities of Edward Mountagu in the Commons committee of 1621, and the newly acquired power of John Williams as Lord Keeper in the same year complicate the matter. The fate of the bill in 1621, 1624, and 1625 may well have been determined by Williams' ability to influence policy.

The 1621 parliament was the first opportunity for lay and spiritual leaders to react to the king's Book of Sports. Little time was lost. Early in the second week, Walter Earle delivered a bill 'for the Punishment of divers Abuses on the Sabaoth-day, called Sunday'.[42] This bill, which had been passed by the Commons in 1614, prescribed that 'all assemblyes at Church Ales, Danceing, May-games, etc., were made unlawfull'. John Pym reported that all offenders, on the proof of two witnesses, were 'to forfeit at the discretion of the Justices before whome it should be brought, not exceedinge 5s. nor under 12d.' This penalty was to be levied by distress and sale of goods or, if payment was not possible, offenders were to sit in the stocks for three hours. At the first reading, provisos were added that offenders should be brought to court within three months after committing the offence, and that ecclesiastical jurisdiction must not be impeached.[43]

The second reading on 15 February occasioned a speech by Thomas Shepard, a suspected papist, which produced an angry response; for he described the bill as 'very inconvenient and indiscreete'. He objected to the word 'Sabbath' in the title, arguing that it referred to the Saturday observance of Jews; and complained that dancing and other exercises had been condemned, noting that 'the Kinge by his edict hath given leave to his subjects to daunce'. Suggesting that they should 'let Divines first resolve

[41] Conrad Russell, *Parliaments and English Politics 1621–1629* (Oxford, 1979), p.28.
[42] *CJ*, i, 511, 514.   [43] *Commons Debates, 1621*, IV, 33.

what is lawfull and unlawfull', Shepard wondered whether
parliament should 'make a lawe in the face of the Kinge, against
that which proceeded from his owne witt and judgment'. He
asserted that 'the occasion of the Bill growes from a kind of Cattle
that will not submitt themselves to the Ceremonyes of the Church.
It savours of the spirit of a Puritan.' Complaining that many snares
were set for papists, but 'not a Mouse-trappe to catch a Puritan',
he noted that 'noe sooner is any Complaynt made against this kind
of people but some Justice of Peace or other is ready to protect
them'. He concluded by stating that 'this was the humor that gave
occasion to the Bill and he that preferr'd it is an perturbator of
the Peace'.[44]

It is understandable that Shepard's speech was vigorously
attacked, for he combined a defence of the declaration with an
assertion that the bill's supporters were non-conformists, stigma-
tizing them with the label of 'puritan'. Pym observed that Shepard
spoke 'with a greate deale of scorne and Malepeirt gesture; and
though the mislike and muttering of the House troubled him
often, yet he protested he would speake and if he did offend, his
bodye and his Fortune should answere it'.[45] He was ordered to
leave the house, and Thomas Wentworth, Edward Gyles, George
Moore, and Walter Earle spoke against Shepard, demanding that
he be brought before the bar. Edward Coke defended the bill,
stating that 'whatever hindereth the sanctifying of the Sabbaoth,
is against the Law of God'.[46]

The following day, Pym made his maiden speech in the
Commons. Taking great pains to point out the divisive nature of
Shepard's speech, he explained that Shepard had slandered Walter
Earle who presented the bill, had spoken slightingly of J.P.s, and
had offended the Commons. Pym noted that Shepard sought 'to
bring us into the ill opinion of the Kinge...[by] sayinge that we
went about to make a law in the face of his Majestie, opposite to
his Royall judgment declared in printe'.[47] Other members
attacked Shepard for his abuse of God's word, and the Commons
passed a resolution that he should be 'cast out of the House as
an unworthy member'.[48]

---

[44] *Ibid.*, pp.52–3; Wilfrid Prest, *The Inns of Court under Elizabeth I and the Early Stuarts: 1590–1640* (London, 1972), p.184.   [45] *Commons Debates, 1621*, IV, 53.

[46] *CJ*, i, 521–2.   [47] *Commons Debates, 1621*, IV, 62–5.

[48] *Commons Debates, 1621*, II, 96; Also see: pp.82, 95–6, 104; V, 11–12, 467–8, 472, 499–503, 513; VI, 361–2.

On 19 February, it was reported to the Commons that 'his Majesty thought the censure just but withal wished that as we had stricken the papists in the right hand so we could strike the puritans on the left'. He went on to caution the Commons to 'take care how we passed a bill that was opposite to the edict which he had set forth'. Sir James Perrod requested that the bill be amended to conform with the king's declaration; and James Chudleigh indicated that 'if I had thought the main intent of the bill had been to oppose his Majesty's edict, I would not have given my consent so freely to it'. Noting the good intentions of James, Chudleigh nevertheless hoped that 'when his majesty shall be informed by the experience of the justices of peace in the country that it hathe done more harm by increasing profaneness than it hath done good in converting papists, I doubt not but he will be pleased to call it in again'.[49]

Edward Mountagu reported on the committee's progress on 1 March, observing: 'I am not ashamed for any nick[name] to further the observance of any of God's commandments.' He explained that the committee had 'been careful to pen it agreeable to the laws of this realm, his Majesty's proclamation and Declaration, and if it forbid that which is forbidden in those, I hope no man will be against it'.[50] Clearly bearing the marks of Mountagu's influence, the bill prescribed that 'Bulbaytinge and bearebaytinge, interludes and concourse of people to any sportes out of the parishe [be] prohibited'. The penalty was reduced to 3 shillings 4 pence and punishments were moved from the Sabbath to weekdays.[51] At the third reading on 5 March, the bill passed 'without one negative', and was sent to the Lords.[52]

When members of the Lords and Commons met on 24 May, Archbishop Abbot requested one alteration – that 'the title may be altered to the Lords day'. He explained that 'we desyere the word Saboth showld be left oute, because many of late times have runne to Judaisme, as some have written for the very day...For the suppresing of this we desyre this name to be taken away.' Edward Coke accepted this point, observing that 'we found the title of Sabbath in the Morall Law, which signifies a rest. Ther

---

[49] *Commons Debates, 1621*, II, 104–5 Sir Charles Howard's account indicates that James' reaction was more hostile. (VI, 361–2.)
[50] *Commons Debates, 1621*, II, 150.
[51] *Commons Debates, 1621*, V, 16; *CJ*, i, 533.   [52] *CJ*, i, 538.

are diverse Saboths. In the New Testament ther are but two things attributed to the Lord, the Lords day and the Lords supper.'[53] With concord on this revision, the bill passed in the Lords on 28 May and was approved by the Commons the following day.[54] Six days later parliament adjourned for a recess, with the 'Lord's day bill' awaiting royal assent – which James refused to give.[55]

Responsible men of the realm could not have sent a clearer signal of their reaction to the king's declaration. While couched in the language of loyal obedience, parliament rejected the declaration because it resulted in the misuse of Sunday and disturbed the peace of the commonwealth. While some historians might wish to divorce religious concerns from the practical matter of maintaining social order, on this issue the two were interrelated. Shepard's outburst was an aberration. Although he may have hoped to gain royal favour, his actions earned a swift expulsion from the Commons instead; for he stood against the over-whelming consensus of the Commons. Indeed concern for re-ligious observance of Sunday and the strict regulation of afternoon pastimes was evident in the actions of both houses. The king's long-standing interest in protecting Sunday afternoon recreations seems the most plausible reason for his veto. It also seems unlikely that James would have approved of parliament imposing a stricter interpretation of his declaration than he intended.

Yet John Williams' presence as Lord Keeper must have been an important factor as well. After the heated dispute with Edward Mountagu in 1618 and his embarrassing censure in the courts, Williams was in a position to get even. Mountagu had clearly drafted the legislation to combat the problems which arose at Grafton and included his own conservative interpretation that the use of recreations within parishes should be strictly regulated. Williams could only have regarded this as a further affront. Although this suggestion is difficult to substantiate from evidence in 1621, the king's reasons for vetoing the bill again in 1624 bear the marks of Williams' influence.

While many were distressed by James' action, some were more vocal than others. On 14 July 1621, John Chamberlain reported to Carleton that 'Bishop Baylie, bishop of Bangor was committed to the fleet for disputing (they say) some what malapertly with the

---

[53] *Commons Debates, 1621*, III, 299; also see: IV, 377–8.
[54] *LJ*, iii, 137,138.   [55] *Commons Debates, 1621*, III, 374; VII, 300.

king about the Sabbath'.[56] John Davenant, newly consecrated bishop of Salisbury, registered his opinions by his actions, refusing to travel on the Lord's day to attend the king at Newmarket. Thomas Fuller reported that he was treated more kindly than Bayly; for although he arrived a day late, Davenant was 'no less welcome to the king, not only accepting his excuse, but also commending his seasonable forbearance'.[57]

When parliament convened in 1624, Robert Snelling of Ipswich delivered the sabbath bill to the Commons again, noting that this bill had passed the last parliament 'and hath ever, sithence 27 Elizabeth passed this House'. It gained speedy passage, with the Commons approving the bill in eleven days. When Archbishop Abbot reported on the bill on 9 March, the only question raised concerned whether the exercise of arms after evening prayer was forbidden by the act. The Lord Chief Justice of King's Bench and several other leading judges conferred and reported that because the exercise of arms was not a sport forbidden by the law, it was not hindered by this legislation. The bill passed the same day.[58]

James vetoed the bill on 28 May 1624, explaining that he 'did not love to doe contradictory things'. Noting that in 1617 he had found differences over this matter, James observed that he had 'thereuppon published a declaration in print for the allowance of some exercises after evening prayers'. He indicated that the bill violated both the letter and spirit of his declaration – an assertion which is not substantiated by the evidence. First, he condemned the bill for prohibiting activities allowed in his declaration, describing, as lawfull recreations 'Bullbayting, Bear-beating, Wakes, and bowles'.[59] This assertion is puzzling, for bearbaiting, bullbaiting, and bowls were specifically condemned by James' 1603 proclamation and his 1617 and 1618 declaration.[60] While wakes were not specifically prohibited or permitted in James' edicts, precedents for their suppression can be found in Henrician injunctions, Elizabethan statutes, and in many local orders.[61] The

---

[56] sp/14/122, no.23.

[57] Thomas Fuller, *Worthies of England*, II, 360. While the exact date is unknown, this event occurred sometime during the summer of 1621.

[58] *CJ*, i, 671, 673, 678; *LJ*, iii, 248, 249, 252.   [59] sp/14/165, no. 61.

[60] Chambers, *Elizabethan Stage*, IV, 335; *HMC: Twelfth Report, Appendix*, pt IV, I 391; Axon, *Manchester Sessions*, p.xxvi; *Declaration of Sports* (1618), pp.7–8.

[61] William Prynne, *Canterburie's Doome* (London, 1646), p.128; Hollingworth, p.88; sp/16/255, no. 39i-ii.

second part of James' complaint referred to Mountagu's provision that people would be prevented from 'going to other parishes to make merry'. He saw no reason to forbid such movement and observed that if he let it pass 'no man might walke into another parish'. Here again James objected to a point he had stipulated in the Book of Sports; for he had specified that 'every person shall resort to his own Parish by it selfe to use the said Recreation after divine service'.[62] James concluded by stating that 'churches themselves have been abused. So perchaunce have these sportes bene. But let the abuses be taken away but not the churches'. He refused to agree to a bill 'which is but to give the puritans their will, who thinke all consistes in two sermons a day and will allow noe recreacon to poor men that labour hard all the weeke long to ease themselves on the Sunday'. The bill was pronounced 'le roy advisera'.[63]

A more permissive attitude in his latter years may explain the contradictory reasons given for the veto; yet his stand was consistent, for, like Elizabeth, he had been reluctant throughout his reign to allow parliament to legislate on this issue. James' interest in wakes and the restriction of recreations within parish boundaries also recalls the Grafton-under-Wood conflict. The particulars of the bill and Mountagu's role in drafting it suggest that the Lord Keeper would have opposed its passage, and encouraged James to use his veto. However, given Prince Charles' own support for the bill in the Lords, it is not surprising that the next parliament brought success.

At the opening of Charles' first parliament in 1625, the Lord's day bill appeared at the beginning of the session. On 23 June the committee reported that it was thought best not to alter the bill, because both houses had already passed it and 'the Kinge then a Member of the Upper House gave his voice to it, and therefore is not like to denye his assent now, unless it receive alteration'. It was also noted that the bill was a probationer and could be altered by the next parliament. The Commons passed the bill and sent it to the Lords, which passed it on the same day it appeared. With the king's assent, it became law.[64]

In the 1626 parliament a new bill appeared for 'the further

---

[62] *Declaration of Sports* (1618), p.9.   [63] SP/14/165, no. 61.
[64] *CJ*, i, 799, 800; *Debates in the House of Commons in 1625*, edited by S. R. Gardiner (Camden Society, 1873), new series VI, 14, 18; *LJ*, iii, 451.

Reformation of sundry Abuses commited on the Lord's Day, commonly called Sunday'. The bill passed both the Commons and the Lords, and received royal assent in the next parliament.[65] This act prohibited Sunday travelling and butchering, noting that 'the Lord's day...is much broken and profaned by carriers, waggoners, carters, wain-men, butchers, and drovers of cattle, to the great dishonour of God and reproach of religion'.[66]

Until further evidence comes to light, Charles' decision to alter the pattern established by Elizabeth and James, by approving sabbatarian legislation, will remain a matter of speculation. However, it seems fairly safe to assume that his actions stemmed from political rather than religious considerations. He must have noted that 'the lower house was much discontented' by his father's veto in 1624, and may have attempted to use these bills to his advantage.[67] The easy passage of this previously hindered bill in 1625 suggests that Charles hoped his co-operation in this and other matters would be repaid with measures to provide the increased revenues he required. If this was Charles' hope, he was to be deeply disappointed.[68]

While James resisted and Charles' motives may have been less than pure, the 1620s parliaments leave us in no doubt that secular and religious leaders were in general agreement on this issue. The 1621 bill, which grew out of concern over the problems caused by the 1618 Book of Sports, was repeatedly presented and passed by both houses of parliament. The additional bill, approved in 1627, emphasizes the consistent attention and support given to tighten sabbath regulations. Most striking is the deference shown towards ecclesiastical jurisdiction; for in both measures it was stipulated that 'this act shall not in any sort abridge or take away the authority of the courts ecclesiastical'.[69] While there was a small group of lay and religious leaders who did not approve of these restrictions, a point which is evident from events in the 1630s, they do not detract from the basic consensus found in the 1620s. If anything, this period should be regarded as a triumph for lay

---

[65] The delay of royal approval is a curiosity; however, there was no apparent dispute over this measure. See: Russell, pp.276–7.

[66] *CJ*, i, 825,827,839,842,846; *LJ*, iii, 567,569. For 1627–8 proceedings see: *CJ*, i, 877,894,903; *LJ*, iii, 788,794. For the text see: Stephens, *Statutes*, pp.537–8.

[67] Walter Yonge, *Diary of Walter Yonge* (1848), p.75.

[68] See Russell, *passim*.   [69] Stephens, *Statutes*, pp.538–9.

leaders and spiritual peers, who after decades of persistent attempts finally saw their efforts bear fruit. While not denying that anti-sabbatarians may be found, it is nevertheless evident that sabbatarian doctrine and discipline remained part of the Church's teaching and practice. Indeed given the general agreement in the 1620s, the divisive nature of the sabbatarian issue in the 1630s is puzzling. It is to that controversy that we must now address ourselves.

7
The sabbatarian controversy

Given the open conflict between Calvinists and Arminians in parliament, court, and the Church during the early years of Charles' reign, to argue that there was general agreement on the sabbath doctrine would seem to stretch the case for consensus too far. However, the evidence calls for such a conclusion. Arminian and Calvinist defences of the scholastic interpretation illustrate that while these men clashed over the weighty matters of predestination and the limits of God's grace, the morally binding nature of the Sabbath was a commonly acknowledged point of orthodoxy.[1] Visitation articles from the 1620s and 1630s demonstrate that sabbatarian discipline continued to be a priority, despite the controversies after 1633. To understand the conflicts of the 1630s, we must first pursue several personal clashes, which initially focused on episcopal and secular jurisdiction. These disputes, which resulted in the reissuing of the Book of Sports, broadened into a theological debate, as Laud's supporters defended the reissuing of the Book of Sports against sabbatarian attacks. Although Laud's apologists were unified in their support of episcopal authority and the use of recreations on Sunday, they did not present a consistent position on the sabbath doctrine. Indeed while Heylyn, Pocklington, and others claimed that the scholastic interpretation was a puritan innovation, Christopher Dow declared that the Church had always acknowledged the morally binding nature of the sabbath precept. The sabbath doctrine was being used as a theological football once again, and was to become the war-cry of those who opposed the Laudian innovations of the 1630s.

[1] For a detailed account of the Arminian-Calvinist struggles in the late 1620s and 1630s see Nicholas Tyacke, 'Puritanism, Arminianism and the Counter-Revolution', in *The Origins of the English Civil War*, edited by Conrad Russell (London, 1973), 119–43; Nicholas Tyacke, 'Arminianism in England' (unpublished D.Phil. thesis, University of Oxford, 1968), *passim*.

SABBATARIAN DISCIPLINE: 1618–40

Visitation articles and injunctions issued during the 1620s and 1630s provide striking evidence that sabbatarian discipline continued to concern bishops throughout this period. Of the eighty-six documents examined, which were issued between 1618 and 1632, all enquired about alehouse disorders on Sunday, seventy-eight contained questions on the use of labours, and seventy-five asked about Sunday trading. The only ominous gap concerned the use of recreations and pastimes, with nineteen documents failing to raise this question and thirteen of this group appearing after 1625.

While this seems to suggest an Arminian shift towards a more 'liberal' position on Sunday recreations, the evidence does not support this conclusion. Although Bishop William Piers and a few others can be identified with the new and rising powers in the Church, Archbishop Abbot was among those who issued the delinquent documents.[2] Matters are further complicated by William Laud's questions concerning the misuse of recreations in 1628 and 1631, and Richard Montagu's 1628 article for Chichester, which enquired whether 'any in your Parish prophane the Sunday by unlawfull gaming, drinking, or tipling in the tyme of common prayer or Sermon; and by working and doing the ordinary workes of their vocation and trades'.[3] Bishop Francis White, the anti-sabbatarian writer of the 1630s, issued similar articles.[4]

Articles issued between 1633 and 1640 continued this pattern. Of the seventy-nine documents examined, all contained questions on Sunday alehouse activities; seventy-two enquired about Sunday labours and seventy-one about trading on that day. Again, nineteen failed to contain questions on the use of pastimes and recreations.

It is evident that no discernible shift in diocesan discipline can be found in the visitation articles and injunctions issued during this period; for they varied little from those issued during the Elizabethan and early Jacobean period. Given the contentious nature of the sabbath doctrine in the 1630s, such a conclusion seems a paradox. However, events in 1633 reveal that while

[2] Peterborough VA 1631; Coventry and Lichfield VA 1632; Exeter VA 1627.
[3] This was a common form for this period.
[4] Carlisle VA 1627; Norwich VA 1629. Also see Neile's Winchester VA for 1628.

sabbatarian *discipline* remained part of a consistent pattern, the sabbath *doctrine* became a weapon used in disputes over episcopal jurisdiction.

WILLIAM LAUD

Buckingham's efforts to advance Laud in 1621 were finally rewarded with Laud's nomination to St David's. The king was reluctant to co-operate, for he had misgivings about Laud's suitability. James is reported to have told Buckingham,

The plain Truth is, that I keep Laud back from all Place of Rule and Authority, because I find he hath a restless Spirit, and cannot see when Matters are well, but loves to toss and change, and to bring Things to a pitch of Reformation floating in his own Brain, which may endanger the stead fastness of that which is in a good pass, God be praised.[5]

Whether those are James' words, or Hacket's commentary on Laud's personality viewed in retrospect, they serve as an apt description of Laud's role in the Book of Sports controversy of the 1630s. Laud was a man of strong convictions who did not hesitate to defend principles he valued. Prominent among these were ecclesiastical jurisdiction and episcopal authority. It was these issues that were the source of the conflict in 1633 – not sabbatarianism. The anti-sabbatarian literature which appeared after 1633 was written in reaction to attacks on the archbishop's part in the reissuing of the Book of Sports, and his vigorous suppression of ministers who refused to read it from the pulpit. While Laud acted in defence of ecclesiastical jurisdiction and episcopal authority, his opponents were driven by the sabbatarian principles which had been defended by theologians and parliament throughout the Elizabethan and early Stuart period. It was this clash of priorities and principles that made sabbatarianism such a volatile issue in the 1630s.

The London court of aldermen shared the concern of so many secular leaders in the 1620s over sabbath abuses. In 1620 and 1621, they sent delegations to Bishop John King to co-ordinate lay and clerical actions against sabbath-breakers. Similar action was taken in 1623 during George Montaigne's episcopate. Despite the theological differences between King and Montaigne, both co-

---

[5] John Hacket, *Scrinia reserata* (London, 1693), p.64.

operated with these efforts.[6] This policy of co-operation changed when William Laud became bishop of London.

On 20 April 1629 Richard Deane, mayor of London, issued a strict order against sabbath abuses. He observed that 'notwithstanding divers good Lawes provided for the keeping of the Saboth day holy according to the expresse comandment of Almightly god, divers Inhabitants... of this Citty and other places have noe respect of duty towards god, his Majestie or his Lawes'. He prohibited Sunday labours, trading, carting, and alehouse disorders, and required that this order be enforced by all local officials. Laud regarded this order as a transgression of his authority, annotating the back of his copy with the observation: 'The Ld Maior of London's warrant against breakers of the Saboth – Mye jurisdiction interessed'.[7] Early in 1633 Sir Nicholas Rainton, the new mayor of London, provided Laud with an opportunity to defend episcopal jurisdiction, when he prohibited a poor woman from selling apples within St Paul's churchyard on the Lord's day. Laud rebuked the mayor for meddling within his jurisdiction, threatened to complain to the king and council about this interference, and asserted that she could continue to sell apples there 'notwithstanding his [Rainton's] Command to the contrary'. While Prynne and Heylyn rarely agreed on anything, they both concurred that Laud's concern was the protection of his authority – not the question of selling on Sundays.[8]

Yet Laud was defending a principle which had long since been abandoned by the episcopate. The architects of the Elizabethan settlement had sought the co-operation of secular officials in suppressing sabbath abuses and other moral offences. Although some bishops had expressed concern over confusion of jurisdiction, the evidence presented in previous chapters demonstrates episcopal willingness to promote such co-operation so long as their authority was not impugned. The protection of ecclesiastical jurisdiction in the 1625 and 1628 sabbath bills emphasized this spirit of co-operation. Laud's efforts to reverse this long-

---

[6] Corporation of London Record Office, Repertory 34, fol. 324; Repertory 36, fol. 4; Repertory 38, fols. 9v, 33; D. A. Williams, 'Puritanism in the City Government: 1610–1640', *Guildhall Miscellany*, vol. 1, no. 4 (London, 1955), 3–14 (p.9).

[7] Lambeth Palace Library, MS 943, p.129; Rushworth, II, 22–3; William Prynne, *Canterburies Doome* (London, 1646), p.132; D. A. Williams, 'City Government', p.9; Peter Heylyn, *Cyrianus Anglicus* (London, 1671), p.242.

[8] Prynne, *Doome*, p.132; Heylyn, *Cyprianus Anglicus*, p.242.

established practice must therefore have caused consternation and concern to both secular and religious officials. Yet this dispute was only the beginning of Laud's efforts in this cause; for his attention soon turned to the prohibition of wakes by secular officials in Somerset. If Laud's primary interest in the Somerset controversy was indeed episcopal authority, rather than sabbatarian discipline, the vigour of his intervention over the issue of wakes requires explanation. In the standard account of this *cause célèbre*, Professor Barnes has offered an interpretation in terms of court/county opposition, complicated by local electoral friction. It seems more precise to conclude that Laud's sensitivity about episcopal jurisdiction was exploited in a county quarrel. The events in Somerset suggest that sabbatarian discipline was a convenient ploy, and was only by chance the point on which the conflict over jurisdiction was to turn.

THE 1633 BOOK OF SPORTS CONTROVERSY

For decades west country justices had issued orders against wakes and punished offenders. Regulations issued in 1594, 1600, 1607, 1615, 1624, 1628, and 1631 reflected concern over the irreligious nature of these events as well as their attendant disorders. The 1594 regulation ordered that 'no Church ale be admitted to be kept within any part of this sheire', and was signed by Chief Justice John Popham and ten other justices. Serjeant Henry Mountagu and other justices in 1615 were spurred into action by reports of 'severall manslaughters committed at two churchales' and the 'continuall prophanaton of gods Sabboth at these and other such like unlawfull meetings'. In July 1628, the month Laud was translated to London, Baron Denham issued yet another order against 'the infinite number of inconveniences dayly arising by meanes of Revells, Church ales, Clerkes Ales and publike Ales'. This order was not only to be circulated by secular officials; every minister was required to 'publish it yearely in his parish Church the first Sunday in February'.[9]

Though the repeated issuing of these orders suggest that they were not adequately enforced, offenders who were presented often

---

[9] PRO, sp/16/96, no. 7,7i; sp/16/155, no. 39i-iii; Somerset Record Office, Session Rolls, 2, no. 77; Quarter Session Minute Book 1620–7, fol. 394; Session Rolls, 61, i; PRO, Assize 24/20, fol. 35v.

received harsh punishments. In 1617, Nicholas Ruddock and Katheren Canker were convicted of conceiving a child after a dance held on Sunday. The judges ordered Ruddock to pay 8 pence weekly for the child's maintenance, and both were to be 'whipped through the high streete of Glaston... until there bodyes shalbe both bloody and that there shalbe during the tyme of there whippinge two fiddles playing before them in regard to make knowne their lewdnes in begettinge the said-base child upon the Sabboth day cominge from Danceinge'.[10]

In 1632, disturbed by reports of persons murdering 'Bastard children begotten at Wakes and Revels' and 'sundry other grand disorders occasioned by these intemperate meetings', Baron Denham and Lord Chief Justice Richardson issued an amended version of the 1628 order, requiring that ministers 'shall publish it yeerely in his parish church upon the first sonday in February and two sondayes before Easter yeerely'.[11] The first reading of this order in Somerset pulpits occurred in February 1633, coinciding with Laud's conflict with Sir Nicholas Rainton. Laud used this event to further his cause, complaining to the king that the judges' order was an invasion of Bishop Piers' jurisdiction and that they had unlawfully prohibited church festivals. The Lord Keeper informed Chief Justice Richardson that the king charged him to revoke all orders prohibiting wakes in his Lent circuit. Richardson fulfilled only a part of the order, for while he revoked the prohibitions at the Dorset assizes, he did not make the required repeal at Somerset as well.[12]

This was an extraordinary act of wilfullness from a man who had demonstrated dedication to the crown both in parliament, as Speaker, and as a judge. However, Laud's initiative in this matter was important, for the two men had recently quarrelled. Lord Dacre has commented on Laud's loathing of lawyers, and the bishop had good reasons for disliking Richardson in particular.[13] In February 1633, Henry Sherfield, the recorder of Salisbury, appeared in Star Chamber accused of destroying a stained glass window. The judges were unanimous in their condemnation but

[10] SRO, Minute Book 1613–20. fol. 511; Marchant, *Church under the Law*, p.225.

[11] Prynne, *Doome*, p.132; Heylyn, *Cyprianus Anglicus*, p.242; Barnes, 'Puritan Cause Célèbre', pp.110–11; PRO Assizes 24/20, fols. 49v-50r; SRO, DD/PH 222 fols. 118–19.

[12] SRO, DD/PH 222, fols. 120r, 137.

[13] H. R. Trevor-Roper, *Archbishop Laud* (London, 1962), p.103.

disagreed over the sentence. Laud urged that he be fined 1,000 pounds, dismissed from his office as recorder, and ordered to make a public confession. While Archbishop Neile concurred, the chief justices Heath and Richardson, and Lord Keeper Coventry voted for a milder sentence. Sherfield escaped with a 500 pound fine, acknowledgement of his fault, and the costs of repairing the window. Shortly after this event, Laud was intriguing against the Lord Keeper.[14] Richardson was no less a target, and must have known it. The reading of the Somerset order coincided with this dispute and provided Laud with an opportunity to humiliate Richardson as well as further the cause of episcopal jurisdiction raised by his conflict with Rainton. This seems the most plausible explanation for Laud's actions, for he had shown no interest in Denham's 1628 order while bishop of Bath and Wells.

However, this does not explain why Richardson revoked the prohibitions in Dorset, but not in Somerset. The solution to that problem may be found in a separate conflict, with the parliamentarian and Somerset justice, Sir Robert Phelips. Discord had been sparked by Richardson's dismissal of a case pressed by Phelips. The offender, John Boyse, had contemptuously refused to comply with a magisterial order made by Phelips; and though a minor gentleman, had boasted that he was as good as Phelips, and called him a liar. Phelips described Boyse as 'so impudent, so proud, and so insufferable a piece of humanity did I never know in these or any other parts'.[15] Richardson dismissed charges against Boyse without even the requirement of an apology to Phelips. For a man who was out of favour at court and found his leadership in Somerset threatened by the newly created Baron Poulett, Richardson's action was not only insulting, but a challenge to Phelips' position in the county as well. Phelips accused Richardson of concealing the truth and displaying partiality. The subsequent conviction and punishment of Boyse by the Council vindicated Phelips, but heightened the tensions between him and the Chief Justice.[16] It seems reasonable to suggest that upon hearing of Laud's disputes with Rainton and Richardson, Phelips found in the Somerset order an opportunity to advance himself at court, while also striking a blow at Richardson. This seems the only

[14] *Ibid.*, p.111.
[15] Barnes, 'Puritan Cause Célèbre', p.113; SRO, DD/PH 222, fol. 145.
[16] Barnes, 'Puritan Cause Célèbre', *passim.*, p.113.

plausible interpretation of Phelips' actions; for few other reasons could have motivated a man of Phelips' precisionist reputation to collaborate with William Laud. Yet, just as important, it explains why Richardson chose to omit the revocation at the Somerset assizes, rebuking a constable who raised the issue, apparently on Phelips' instigation.[17]

While Richardson may have wished to demonstrate that a man of his stature could not be bullied, Laud had the ear of the king. On 2 May 1633, Charles sent a letter to Phelips, Sir Henry Berkeley, and the Rev. Dr Paul Godwin, requesting a report on the Chief Justice's actions at the Somerset assizes 'for the recalling of any such former order made against the said feastes, as our expresse command twice signified unto him by the Lord Keeper ... was he shold doe'. Charles balanced this request with a caution to the justices, emphasizing his concern that the Sabbath not be profaned. He explained that

> Our intention in this Busines is no way to give a liberty to the breache or prophanacon of the Lordes day, which we will to be kepte with that solemnity and reverence that is due to it, but that the people after evening prayer may use such decent and sober recreations as are fitt. And to that end we do heerby require you and all other the Justices of peace in your severall divisions to take speciall care, that all excesses in those feastes and disorders in those recreations be prevented.[18]

The report which the justices returned could not have been more damaging. They first noted the precedent established by Denham in 1628, though they asserted that the requirement to read the order in the pulpit had only recently been enforced.[19] The amended order issued by Richardson and Denham in March 1632 was executed 'without any warrant from the then Lord Bishop of this diocese [William Piers]...who told one of us that he did not knowe, nor had heard of any such direccons before the order itself was by the clergie in sundry churches of this County read and divulged'.[20] This negligence was a breach of episcopal jurisdiction protected by the 1625 statute and was crucial in Laud's case against Richardson.

In dealing with Richardson's conduct at the Lent assizes, the three justices hung the Chief Justice on his own rope, presenting the evidence with little commentary. They confessed that

---

[17] SRO, DD/PH 222, fol. 136r.   [18] *Ibid.*, fol. 120r.
[19] *Ibid.*, fol. 124v.   [20] *Ibid.*, fol. 125v.

Neither by our owne observacon, who were there present att the Assizes, nor by the informacon of others, of whome we have with diligence enquired, doth it appeare unto us that he did make or publishe any order, for the revokinge and annullinge the former orders and direccons given against the said feast daies and Revells, neither did he in any sort at that time declare it to be your majesties pleasure that those feasts in this countye, should be againe restored to theire accustomed and orderly use and practice.[21]

They went on to commend the use of 'feast daies and Revells', observing that they 'serve to nourishe acquaintance and affeccon amongst them, eache parishe at those times, mutually entertayninge one another, with arguments of love, freedome and hospitality'. While noting that no festival is free of disorderly people or unpleasant incidents,

we have not knowne in our divisions (for which we praise God) any such bad encounter to have happened, neither hath the conversacon at such times bene soe irregular, profane, or excessive, as that it hath ministred matter of severe reprehension, or hath given...cause of scandall to men soberly minded and not too much addicted to the waies of an overstrict singularitie.

They concluded with assurances that these liberties would not be misused and agreed with the king that 'the Lordes daye, under color and pretence of sober and decent recreacion should not be irreligiously prophaned, nor the fitt and religious duties thereof should be in any sort neglected or contemned'.[22]

Richardson had played into the hands of Laud and Phelips; for while his actions were apparently calculated to snub both men, Phelips assumed the role of loyal subject by reporting the Chief Justice's insubordination, and Laud pressed a legitimate grievance against Richardson for violating episcopal jurisdiction. The Chief Justice had no grounds for defence and his enemies seized the advantage. Charles personally ordered Richardson to revoke the orders on the next circuit.[23]

However, Richardson was not yet subdued, for his loathing of Phelips and Laud was manifest at the Somerset assizes in early August. Labouring under a strong conviction that he had been unjustly treated, Richardson presented the history of churchale suppressions before those gathered at the assize. Explaining that he and Denham had issued the recent order against wakes at the request of the justices of Somerset and Devon, Richardson

---

[21] *Ibid.*, fols. 125v–126r, 136r.
[22] *Ibid.*, fol. 126.   [23] Barnes, 'Puritan Cause Célèbre', p.115.

reported that 'some ill affected persons had misinformed his Majestie concerning this Order, who had given him [Richardson] an expresse command to reverse it'. The Chief Justice expressed doubts that this was in his power 'because it was no order made by himselfe, but by the joynt consent of the whole Bench, and a meere confirmation and enlargment of diverse Orders made by the Judges and Justices in that Circuit, in Queen Elizabeths, King James, and King Charles their reignes'. In reading through the precedents, Richardson noted in the 1594 order the name of Phelips' uncle, Thomas Phelips, vexing his adversary with an enquiry about the man's identity.[24] The Chief Justice then revoked all orders against churchales promulgated at quarter sessions and assizes, declaring that 'all former Orders heretofore made by any Judges or Justices for the suppressing of Church ales, Clerkes Ales, Wakes and Revells be revoked (as much as in him lyeth) and made utterly void'.[25]

Richardson did not leave things there. Inviting the justices into his chambers after assizes, they were asked to sign a petition to the king for the suppression of wakes. The petition requested that Charles restore the prohibition, noting that these assemblies had 'for a long time beene forborne and not used, to the great good and quiet of the said County'. It was claimed that rumours concerning the revocation of prohibitions had spread since the Lent Assizes, resulting in the 'Prophanation of the Lords Day, riotous tipling, contempt of Authoritie, Quarrells, Murthers, etc.'[26] This was apparently a reference to the churchale riot at Coleford on Holy Thursday that year. Reminiscent of the 1618 and 1619 reaction, some parishioners celebrated a wake with excessive drinking, which ended in a riot. Many were injured and there were rumours of one death.[27] Twenty-five justices signed, most notably Lord Poulett, Phelips' rival in the county. However, twenty-four abstained, much to the disgust of Richardson.[28]

Richardson was in a precarious position, and Phelips knew it. While he had incited the justices to express their disapproval of royal policy, an action out of keeping with his role as the king's

---

[24] Prynne, *Doome*, pp.152, 153, 154.   [25] SP/16/255, no. 39iv.
[26] SP/16/255, no. 39; Prynne, *Doome*, pp.147–8.
[27] SRO Session Rolls, 70, no. 121; Barnes, 'Puritan Cause Célèbre', p.116.
[28] For an account of the county politics which motivated this split, see: Barnes, 'Puritan Cause Célèbre', pp.113–14, *passim*.

representative, he had failed to gain the support needed to justify his actions. On 18 August Phelips wrote to the king, reporting the Chief Justice's actions, and noting that 'it pleased him [Richardson] to laye publique aspercons uppon myselfe and others who were by your Majestie imployed in that occasion [the revoking of wake orders]'. Phelips also stated that 'hee menconed the office of the Bishop slightlie if not with scorne', and went on to report the invitation to sign his petition and Richardson's insinuation that the revocation was not valid. Phelips observed that the Chief Justice's actions 'laid an aspercon upon your Majesties direccons for there revocacon', and concluded with the suggestion that the matter be turned over to the Lord Privy Seal and the bishop of London – which Charles did on 25 August.[29]

On 12 November, the king ordered that Richardson be examined by the newly enthroned Archbishop Laud, Lord Keeper Coventry, the Earl Marshall, and the Lord Privy Seal. Phelips was required to give evidence.[30] At the examination, Phelips not only attacked Richardson for casting aspersions on Charles' order and directing insults at himself, but also insinuated that Richardson favoured precisionists, noting that the Chief Justice 'mentioned the puritans in a favourable distinction'.[31] While there are no records of Laud's words, he was undoubtedly harsh. Prynne reported that Richardson 'was so shaken up by the Archbishop, that comming very dejectedly with tears in his eyes out of the Councel Chamber, the Earle of Derset seeing him in such a sad condition, and demanding him how he did? he answered "Very ill my Lord, for I am like to bee choaked with the Archbishops Lawn-sleeves"'.[32] The punishment dealt out was humiliating, for while he retained the office of Chief Justice, he was assigned to the Essex circuit, reputedly the most demanding and difficult of the six assize circuits, and usually assigned to the inferior ranks of the legal profession. Richardson died fifteen months later, a broken man. One news writer, reporting his poorly attended funeral observed, 'never sat there a judge in that court that was less respected'.[33] Laud and Phelips had triumphed over their foe.

While the Richardson case bears all the marks of a personal vendetta, we must not forget that Laud was also defending a

[29] SRO, DD/PH 222, fol. 131r.
[30] *Ibid.*, fol. 133.
[31] *Ibid.*, fols. 137–8.
[32] Prynne, *Doome*, p.148.
[33] Barnes, 'Puritan Cause Célèbre', p.118; Trevor-Roper, p.157.

principle. The Chief Justice had not only crossed the archbishop in the Sherfield case, but had issued orders against church festivals without consulting Bishop Piers, had obstinately defied Laud's wishes (expressed through the king's command) at the Lent and mid-summer assizes, and had spoken slightingly of bishops. When viewed from this perspective, the 1633 Book of Sports controversy emerges as a 'Laudian *cause célèbre*'.

With Richardson's ruin all but certain by September 1633, Archbishop Laud turned his attention to the issue which had sparked the conflict. He suggested Charles reissue the *Declaration of Sports* with an amendment protecting wakes. While Laud was not fond of frivolities and was critical of self-indulgence, his efforts to end the Scottish use of Sunday as a fast day suggest that he had a long-standing concern to protect the traditional concept of the Lord's day as a feast day.[34] While Laud's defence of wakes might seem an attempt to protect Church practices from the overstrict regulations of the 'preciser sort', it should be remembered that bishops Babington, Chaderton, and Coldwell and Archbishop Matthew had prohibited these festivals within their jurisdictions; and parliamentary bills in 1584, 1606, 1614, and 1621 had included wakes among the activities to be prohibited.

Yet much more evident in the Somerset controversy was Laud's determination to protect episcopal jurisdiction. The Book of Sports uniquely served his purposes; for while it reasserted the right to use recreations after evening prayer, justifying his actions in Somerset, it also provided a basis for enforcing 'conformity'. James' 1618 declaration ordered that the bishop was to 'take the like straight order with all the Puritans and Precisians within the same, either constraining them to conforme themselves, or to leave the Countrey according to the Lawes of Our Kingdome, and Canons of Our Church'.[35] Concepts of orthodoxy and the definition of 'puritanism' had shifted over the intervening fifteen years, and Laud was to use this clause to his advantage in events that followed.

Charles was not easily persuaded that reissuing the declaration was necessary, and asked Laud to collect more information from ministers in Somerset. On 4 October, Laud wrote to Bishop Piers,

[34] Trevor-Roper, p.156; William Laud, *Works*, 7 vols. (Oxford, 1853), III, 307–10.
[35] *Declaration of Sports* (1618), p.6.

stating that Charles required Piers 'to send for some of the gravest of your Clergy, and such as stand best affected to the Church and government in the several Partes of your Diocess, and by them to enforme your selfe how these Feasts have been ordered for this last yeare, and how free they have been from Disorders'.[36] Bishop Piers received the letter on 12 October and in the following weeks interviewed seventy-two ministers who produced the desired answers. They all agreed that these events had long been used in their parishes, provided neighbourliness, had been used without abuses, and that the people desired their continuance. The bishop reported that 'if I had sent for an hundred more of the clergy within my Diocesse, I should have received the same answer from them all'. He then extolled the value of these feasts as a civilizing influence and a means of recreation for those who laboured throughout the year. He also noted that they proved useful in raising funds for church repairs and providing income for the parish clerk. Paraphrasing the 1618 Book of Sports, he noted that the 'chiefest cause of the dislike of these Feasts amongst the Preciser sort is, because they are kept upon Sundayes', and observed that if the people did not have recourse to these festivals, that they would 'goe either into tipling houses, and there upon their ale-benches talk of matters of the Church or State, or els into conventicles'.[37] However, having said that, Piers paradoxically confessed that wakes were very rare in Somerset. He stated that 'concerning church-ales, I find that in some places the people have bin persuaded to leave them off, in other places they have bin put downe by Judges and Justices, so that now there are very few of them left'. This confession lends further support to the suggestion that the controversy was generated by Laud, and had little or nothing to do with local concerns.[38] Piers' survey and lengthy report was prepared in four weeks and sent on 5 November.

However, Piers' diligence had not proven swift enough for the archbishop. By the third week of October Laud had convinced Charles to reissue the declaration, which he did on 18 October 1633. Attached to the original Book of Sports was a short preface

---

[36] SP/16/247, no. 24.
[37] It should be noted that Lord Dacre misquotes Bishop Piers, citing him as saying that 'the true cause of the outcry against them [wakes]...was sabbatarianism'. This interpretive summary of Piers' words alters significantly the meaning of the passage. (Trevor-Roper, p.157.)　　[38] SP/16/250, no. 20.

by Charles, with an order protecting wakes appended at the end. It stipulated that J.P.s 'in their several divisions, shall look to it, both that all disorders there may be prevented or punished, and that all neighbourhood and freedom, with manlike and lawful exercises be used'. Justices of assize were required to see that 'no man do trouble or molest any of our loyal and dutiful people, in or for their lawful recreations, having first done their duty to God'. It was also ordered that 'publication of this our command be made by order from the Bishops, throughout all the parish churches of their several dioceses respectively'.[39]

REACTION TO THE BOOK OF SPORTS

What followed was a disturbing clash of priorities and principles. For Laud, the primary issue was episcopal jurisdiction and the protection of a traditional church feast. Reading the Book of Sports became a test of obedience for clergy around the country. Yet there were many ministers and laymen who found very different issues at stake. The 1618 declaration had been unpopular among secular and church leaders because of the disorders that ensued and profane abuses of the Lord's day. The parliamentary bills and theological works of the 1620s reflected a widespread concern that crossed theological divides. Many would have concurred with Lord Saye's 1614 parliamentary speech that even lawful recreations were 'unfitt to be used on that day, for the Sabboath is as much broken by recreacions and sportes as the businesses of a mans callinge'.[40] The Book of Sports troubled the consciences of many good men, who interpreted the Church's teaching very strictly, and believed the dire warnings found in the *Homilies*. Yet many ministers wished to obey their bishop while not violating their conscience. The difficulty of striking this delicate balance is revealed by an exchange of letters, written shortly after the declaration was issued.

In January 1634, Nicholas Estwick, rector at Warkton, Northamptonshire, sought the advice of Samuel Ward, master of Sidney Sussex, Cambridge. He reported that the Book of Sports had 'caused much distraction and griefe in many honest mens hearts

---

[39] S. R. Gardiner, *Constitutional Documents of the Puritan Revolution* (Oxford, 1906), pp.99–103. [40] *HMC: Hastings*, vol. 78, pt 4, 265.

in our Diocese whiche have reade it; and many there be to the
number at the most of three score... which have refused to publish
it'. Noting that these men were 'orthodoxal, diligent preachers
and conscionable practisors of what they preach', Estwick expressed concern that 'if they should be deprived (which God
forbid) what a losse that would be amongst us and what a blowe
it would give to the power of religion your worship apprehen-
deth'. He explained that 'I do not question the morality of the
Christian Sabbath', observing that 'I dare not dissent from those
famous Protestants... which do hold a necessity that one day of
seaven should be kept holy.' However, he confessed that 'albeit
I have laboured in the point: yet I am not satisfied, but do hange
in suspense whether recreations on the Lords day be lawful or
not'. He expressed particular concern about dancing, rushbearing,
Whitsun ales, and May games, explaining that 'I do vehemently
suspect that some of theis in our countrie townes are seldome or
never used on that day, if at any time, without sin and many times
with great disorder, and I can scarcely believe that they and the
sanctification of the Sabbath are compatible in our villages'. Yet
because he was uncertain that God's moral law prohibited these
activities, he was not willing to join those who refused to read
the declaration, stating that 'I would be loath to suffer for
disobedience to mans law as in point of Ceremonie'.[41] He
expressed regret at the manner of its publication, noting that 'it
might have been done by Proclamations published by Cryers at
the Market Crosses and not by Gods Ministers in our holy
Churches'. Yet Estwick asserted that 'sithence it hath pleased his
Majestie to take this latter way, I have caused the booke to be
published in my church, not looking at the Contents but at his
authority which commands the publication thereof, and I hold this
position to be true'. Estwick reluctantly obeyed the authorities in
order to preserve his ministry, and asked Ward to help him
convince others to do the same. He cited several precedents,
observing, 'what minister makes scruple, to reade the Canon
Command viz lowly reverence to be given to the Lord Jesus albeit
may be he will alledge the practice is a will worship!' He also noted
that 'many an unconformable minister can endure a conformable
Curate to baptize with the sign of the crosse'. Estwick regarded
the Book of Sports as a similar case. He was distressed by those

---

[41] This attitude distanced him from Elizabethan precisionists!

who refused to read the king's declaration for conscience's sake, observing that 'this scrupulosity would lay the foundation of disorder and confusion both in the Church and the Comonwealth'.[42]

Although a man respected by precisionists,[43] Estwick was not confident that his opinion alone would convince, and sought Ward's support. He hoped to save the ministry of many by persuading them that 'they ought, [or] at least may with a good conscience publish the book' and stated that 'the most likely way to this end would be if a man famous for learning and of high estimation with them for his soundnes of faith and integritie of conversation would declare his judgment that my ground was good'. Estwick regarded Samuel Ward as the most suitable man to aid him and requested that Ward respond to his questions and lend support to his cause.[44]

Ward wrote back 'to signify my concurence'. He explained that 'a minister with safety of conscience, may publish in his church, being commanded by sovereign authority such edicts, the contents whereof he doth not approve in his owne conscience as you rightly show by sundry instances'. Ward also affirmed that recreations on the Lord's day were lawful and denied that all sports violated the 'law of the Sabbath'. Noting that 'every minister is not bound to examyne the justice of the princes action', Ward stated that 'though a minister hath a speculative doubt...yet he knoweth it is his duty to publish it, who by lawfull authority, he is commanded'. Ward noted the good intentions of James, who had published the declaration to curb popery and maintain men in fitness for time of war. Ward saw no harm in 'honest Recreations, as pitching of the bar, ringing a pole, shooting at butts, playing at stool ball, [or] setting up a maypole', and observed that 'our Saviour was present att a feast on the Sabbath day'.[45]

The correspondence between Estwick and Ward is a significant illustration of the dilemma faced by the English clergy. Fifteen years before, Archbishop Abbot had been in the forefront of those opposing the declaration's promulgation from the pulpit. However, the tables were now turned, with the king endorsing the rigorous enforcement of this requirement upon the insistence

---

[42] Bodleian Library, Tanner MS 71, fols. 186–7.
[43] Estwick had preached the funeral sermon of Robert Bolton.
[44] Bod. Lib., Tanner MS 71, fols. 186–7.   [45] Bod. Lib., Tanner MS 279, fol. 352.

of Archbishop Laud. Many ministers were faced with the problem of reconciling their firm belief in the divine imperative found in the sabbath precept, with the necessity to obey those in authority over them. While Estwick, Ward, and others were able to bend their conscience and obey despite their disapproval, many found this impossible. These clergy may have been inflexible, but Archbishop Laud proved equally rigid.

Prynne's assertion that Laud desired 'to insnare, silence and root out all conscientious, preaching Ministers' overstates the case. Many ministers recognized the challenge and read the declaration, or had someone else read it in their parish church. The noted sabbatarian Richard Bernard, rector of Batcombe, continued to preach undisturbed, having complied with the authorities in this matter.[46] T. H. Peake, in his study of the clergy in Somerset, notes nine other precisionist ministers from Bath and Wells archdeaconries who passed the test.[47] However, many could not stretch their conscience that far, and were suspended for refusing to read the Book of Sports, or for preaching against its contents. While it has long been assumed that these ministers were precisionists, there is reason to suggest that many were not. Indeed in Somerset, Peake found only nine 'puritans' among the twenty-four ministers suspended by Bishop Piers.[48]

For those who could not in conscience comply, only two options remained: either go into voluntary exile or stand firm and face persecution. Hugh Peter and others chose exile. Peter recorded that 'many of my Acquaintances going for New England, had engaged me to come to them when they sent, which accordingly I did. And truly, my reason for myself and others to go, was meerly not to offend Authority in that difference of Judgment; and had not the Book for Encouragement of Sports on the Sabbath come forth, many had staid'.[49]

However, many did stay to defend the divine command they found in the decalogue. George Garrard, writing to Thomas Wentworth on 6 December 1633, reported

much Difference in opinion about the Book; for, though it be the same verbatum that was published in King James's Time, yet it is commanded to be read in al

---

[46] T. H. Peake, 'The Somerset Clergy and the Church Courts in the Diocese of Bath and Wells: 1625–1640' (unpublished M.Litt. thesis, University of Bristol, 1978), p.456.

[47] *Ibid.*, p.463.

[48] *Ibid.*, pp.458–63. It is difficult to determine Mr Peake's criteria for these classifications.

[49] Hugh Peter, *A Dying Fathers Last Legacy to an Onely Child* (London, 1660), p.101.

the Churches here, and in the country. In some Churches in London it hath been read. One Dr. Denison [Stephen Denison?] read it, and presently after read the Ten Commandments, then said, "Dearly Beloved, you have heard now the Commandments of God and Man, obey which you please." Another in St. Giles in the Fields read it, and the same Day preached upon the Fourth Commandment; and I hear...Mr. Holdsworth and Dr Gouge have refused to read it.[50]

On Easter Monday of 1634, Mr Edward Williams of Shaftesbury, Dorset, delivered a sermon in support of strict Sunday observance. Repeating the words of the declaration which demanded 'the observation of the lawes of the kingdome, and Canons of the church', he read portions of the 1625 Lord's day observance act which forbad 'certayne recreations or sportes to be used' and set out 'pointes of doctrine as well out of some of the fathers, as also out of holie Scripture, to move the people to the strict observation of the Saboth day'. The following Sunday he continued this discourse, reading 'the 13th Canon for the due celebration of the Sunday', as well as passages from the Homily 'Of the Place and Time of Prayer'. He went on to observe that if the Sabbath should be free of ordinary labours, it should not be profaned by recreations, declaring that St Augustine said, 'better it was to goe to plowe then daunce on the Saboth'. Those who reported his actions noted that he concluded his sermon with the dire warning that 'it were a most dreadfull thinge and neere damnable, if not absolutely damnation to use any recreations on the Saboth or Lordes day'.[51] Many other ministers preached against the Book of Sports and were suppressed for their defiance of the authorities.[52]

Although the reaction of parishioners is very difficult to ascertain, Richard Condor, a Cambridgeshire football hardy, testified that he came to faith as a result of the declaration's publication. He explained that,

When I was a young man, I was greatly addicted to football playing; and as the custom was in our parish and many others, the young men, as soon as church was over, took a football and went to play. Our minister often remonstrated against our breaking of the sabbath which however had little effect, only my conscience checked me at times, and I would sometimes steal away and hide myself from my companions. But being dexterous at the game, they would find

[50] Thomas Wentworth, *The Earl of Strafforde's Letters and Dispatches*, edited by William Knowler, 2 vols. (London, 1739), I, 166.
[51] SP/16/267, no. 6.
[52] See also SP/16/267, no. 90; SP/16/278, no. 45, 45i; SP/16/294, no. 68; SP/16/280, no. 54; SP/16/287, no. 31; *CSPD: 1638–39*, p.362; Prynne, *Doome*, pp.149–52.

me out, and get me again among them. This would bring on me more guilt and horror of conscience. Thus I went on sinning and repenting a long time, but had no resolution to break off from the practice; til one sabbath morning, our good minister acquainted his hearers, that he was very sorry to tell them, that by the order of the King and Council, he must read them the following paper, or turn out of his living. This was the Book of Sports forbidding the minister or church-wardens or any other to molest or discourage the youth in their manly sports and recreations on the Lord's Day etc. When our minister was reading it, I was seized with a chill and horror not to be described. Now, thought I, iniquity is established by a law, and sinners are hardened in their sinful ways! What sore judgments are to be expected upon so wicked and guilty a nation! What must I do? Wither shall I fly? How shall I escape the wrath to come? And God set in so with it, that I thought it was high time to be in earnest about salvation. And from that time I never had the least inclination to take a football in hand, or to join my vain companions any more. So that I date my conversion from that time; and adore the grace of God in making that to be an ordinance to my salvation, which the devil and wicked governors laid as a trap for my destructon.[53]

In the 1630s, even the village footballer had strong convictions about sabbath observance; for many, if not most Englishmen included sabbath observance in their definition of good Christian practice. While recreations after evening prayer had long been allowed by ecclesiastical authorities, there was much popular opinion against their use. Precisionists are blamed for this emphasis, and there is certainly truth in that conclusion; however, numerous ecclesiastical documents supported the conviction that strict sabbath discipline was part of the Church's teaching. Many regarded the episcopal endorsement of the Book of Sports as a challenge to this commonly held belief, and pledged themselves in defence of the Sabbath, resisting the declaration and condemning it as an edict which clashed with God's moral law.

THEOLOGICAL CONTROVERSY: 1634–40

With widespread opposition to the Book of Sports, Church leaders reacted by suppressing those who preached against the declaration and stopped the licensing of sabbatarian works. A few of Laud's supporters produced works which stigmatized their opponents with the label of 'puritan'; and in the face of both protestant and Catholic teaching, claimed that the doctrine sabbatarians defended was an innovation and had no place in Christian theology. A

---

[53] Margaret Spufford, *Contrasting Communities* (Cambridge, 1974), pp.231–2.

similar problem had been encountered earlier in 1633 – in the notorious altar-table controversy at St Gregory's, when the king himself joined with Laud to brand as innovatory a practice stipulated by Canon 82.[54] No doubt the king acted in good faith. The same can hardly be said of Peter Heylyn, who became the chief apologist for the anti-sabbatarian cause, and dealt with tradition by falsifying it. Heylyn's first ploy was a stunning piece of deception, for he used the work of John Prideaux against judaizing sabbatarians to serve the need at hand, publishing the first English translation in February 1634. In an anonymous preface which introduced the work, Heylyn grossly distorted the conclusions of Prideaux's study, asserting that the Regius Professor had denied the morality of the fourth commandment and the imperative to keep one day in seven holy. He also claimed that Prideaux argued that the Lord's day was an ecclesiastical institution and that the Church had the authority to change the day. Citing Calvin, Bullinger, Bucer, Chemintz, and others as supporters of these positions, Heylyn observed,

The judgement and the practice of so many men and of such several persuasions in the controverted points of the Christian faith, concurring so unanimously together: the miracle is the greater, that wee in England should take up a contrary opinion, and thereby separate our selves from all that are called Christian. Yet so it is, I skill not how it comes to passe, but so it is, that some amongst us have revived again the Jewish Sabbath, though not the day it selfe yet the name and thing. Teaching that the Commandment of sanctifying every seventh day, as in the Mosaicall Decalogue, is naturall, morall, and perpetuall.[55]

Heylyn noted Thomas Rogers' account of the sabbatarian extremists, and reported that he had 'heard it preached in London, that the Law of Moses, whereby death temporall was appointed for the Sabbath-breaker, was yet in force'. He also related accounts of judaizers who refused to prepare food on Sunday, noting that 'these are the ordinary fruits of such dangerous Doctrines'. Heylyn observed that 'against these and such as these, our author in this following Treatise doth addresse himselfe, accusing them that entertaine the former doctrinalls, everywhere, of no lesse than Judaisme'. Heylyn went on to explain that

When I had seriously observed how much these fancies were repugnant both to the tendries of this church, and judgements of all kinde of Writers, and how

[54] See Judith Maltby, 'The Altar Controversy in the Church of England: 1547–1640' (unpublished B.A. thesis, University of Illinois, 1979), *passim*.
[55] John Prideaux, *The Doctrine of the Sabbath*, Translator's Preface.

unsafe to be admitted, I thought I could not go about a better worke, than to exhibite to the view of my deare countrymen this following Treatise…The rather, since of late the clamour is encreased, and that there is not any thing now more frequent in some Zelots mouthes, (to use the Doctors words) than that the Lords day is with us licentiously, yea sacrilegiously prophaned.[56]

The propaganda value of this work was enormous, for it was not only quickly dispatched, but written by a man respected in all quarters. While Heylyn's preface distorted the measured argument of Prideaux, his attacks on judaizing sabbatarians, taken out of context, appeared to condemn those currently defending the scholastic interpretation. His comments on recreations also seemed to support Laudian policy, for he claimed that 'wee are permitted Recreations (of what sort so ever) which serve lawfully to refresh our spirits, and nourish mutuall neighbourhood amongst us'.[57] In his concluding remarks Prideaux had stated that

Unto all these, Recreations, or Entertain-ments, Feastings, and other indifferent customes; it only appertaineth to the Religious Magistrates to prescribe bounds and limits: Not to the rashe zeale of every one, which out of a Schismaticall Stoicisme, not suffering people eyther to use a Fanne, or to kill a Flea, relapse to Judaisme.[58]

Given the circumstances in which Prideaux's work appeared in 1622, these comments against judaizing sabbatarians were quite appropriate and reasonable. However, in the context of 1634, such remarks could only be regarded as a condemnation of those who preached against the Book of Sports. This work was a devastating blow to sabbatarians who opposed the declaration. George Vernon, Heylyn's biographer, noted that this ploy 'not only justifie[d] his Majesties proceedings, but abated much of that opinion, which Dr. Prideaux had amongst the puritanicall Faction in those days'.[59] By distorting and misrepresenting the position held by Prideaux, Heylyn had precluded the possibility of appealing to this 'orthodox' divine for support.

The prosecution of Theophilus Brabourne in 1634 also proved invaluable in the campaign against sabbatarians. Brabourne was the son of a Norwich hosier, who was ordained in 1628, though

---

[56] *Ibid.*, Translator's Preface.   [57] *Ibid.*, p.39.   [58] *Ibid.*, p.41.
[59] George Vernon, *Life of Heylyn* (London, 1682), p.63. Heylyn's troubled relations with Prideaux over his doctoral defence in previous years suggests that malice also motivated his actions. (*Ibid.*, pp.58–62.)

he had no university training. In the same year he published his *Discourse upon the Sabbath Day*, in reaction to Broad's *Three Questions Answered*. Expressing doubts that Sunday was the lawful successor to the Saturday Sabbath, he asserted that 'when it can be shown me, that in scriptures account, any day of the week save Saturday, the last day of the week, was called the seventh day, then may I be brought to think the fourth commandment may be understood of some other seventh day besides Saturday, and not till then'.[60] In 1631, having debated the issue at length with ministers in Norwich diocese and arguing the matter with Bishop Francis White of Ely, he published his *Defence of the Sabbath Day*. Brabourne was not a schismatic, as Traske had been, for he dedicated his work to Charles, and appealed to the archbishops and bishops to recognize Saturday as the ancient Sabbath of the Church. This massive work included numerous arguments for the morality of the fourth precept and the continuance of the Saturday Sabbath.[61] Upon its publication, he was imprisoned in the Gatehouse at Westminster for nine weeks, then publicly examined before the High Commission in the presence of nearly a hundred ministers and hundreds of laymen. The king's advocate pleaded against him and Bishop White read a long discourse against his errors. One of the judges moved that the king should issue his writ '*de haeretico comburendo*', but Laud prevented this action. Instead, Brabourne was censured and sent to Newgate. In June 1634 Brabourne's case was reopened, being charged with 'maintayning and publishing hereticall, schismaticall and Judaicall Opinions touching the maintayneing [of] the Jewish Sabbath. And for compiling bookes and causing them to be printed and published in defense thereof'.[62] The long trial ended in February 1635 with Brabourne's submission, admitting that his assertion had been a 'rash and presumptuous error'.[63]

Bishop Francis White was commissioned by Charles to produce a work against Brabourne's errors. White's *Treatise of the Sabbath Day*, published in 1635, was dedicated to William Laud and argued against the moral and perpetual nature of the Saturday or Sunday

---

[60] Theophilus Brabourne, *A Discourse upon the Sabbath Day* (London, 1628), p.75.
[61] Theophilus Brabourne, *A Defence of that Most Ancient and Sacred Ordinance of Gods, the Sabbath Day* (London, 1631), *passim*.   [62] PRO, SP/16/261, fol. 73v.
[63] PRO, SP/16/261, fols. 69v–70r, 73v, 77r, 103r, 182v–183; *CSPD: 1634–1635*, pp.126–7, 547; *DNB* for Theophilus Brabourne.

Sabbath. In defence of this position, he cited selected portions of the rubrics of the Prayer Book, the *Homilies*, Canon 13, and Cranmer's *Catechism*, as well as John Frith, William Tyndale, and Robert Barnes. Bolstering his argument with quotes from twenty-six Greek and Latin Fathers, he claimed that his doctrine was that taught by the English Church, and was consonant with the teaching of the early Church.[64] White's selective use of authorized teaching, and his dependence on the works of early English reformers, distorted the position long established in the English Church. He condemned Brabourne's claim that the decalogue was purely and entirely moral, with no judicial or ceremonial parts, and went on to insinuate that Nicholas Bownde, John Dod, Richard Byfield, and Robert Cleaver were tainted with the same error.[65] However, White did concede that 'the comon and naturall equity of that Commandment is morall: to wit, That Gods people be obligated, to observe a convenient and sufficient time, for publike and solemne divine worship, for religious and Ecclesiastical duties'.[66]

White also argued that observance of the Lord's day and holy days was based on ecclesiastical tradition and authority, and warned that the Holy Ghost had given Christians a general law to obey those in authority. He did concede that there were many good reasons for observing Sunday, but denied that the moral law bound Christians to observe one day in seven and rejected the divine institution of Sunday.[67] He defended the use of moderate recreations, arguing that Old Testament sabbath laws did not bind Christians; and concluded the treatise with a reassertion of the Church's authority in establishing and regulating Sunday observance.

While Prideaux's work against Saturday sabbatarians had been misused, White's treatise was an attempt to rewrite the history of this doctrine, and was calculated to associate sabbatarians with judaizers. While acknowledging that the fourth precept was partly moral, he rejected the divine institution of Sunday and denied that uses of that day were based on the sabbath commandment. He stressed the role of the Church in instituting and regulating the Lord's day, and condemned those who failed to obey the ecclesiastical authorities. His work clearly was intended to justify

[64] Francis White, *A Treatise of the Sabbath Day* (London, 1635), pp.3–16.
[65] *Ibid.*, pp.17–90.   [66] *Ibid.*, p.90.   [67] *Ibid.*, pp.93–210.

the reissuing of the Book of Sports, and it condemned doctrines which generally were recognized as orthodox theology. Given the long history of the teachings which he condemned, it is little wonder that sabbatarians reacted sharply.

Henry Burton, rector of St Matthew's, London, responded quickly to White's tract. Burton had long been an opponent of Laud and his supporters, having lost his place at court after accusing Laud and Neile of popish tendencies, and had also taken a stand against Broad's anti-sabbatarian writings in 1631. Published without license in 1635, his *Brief Answer to a Late Treatise of the Sabbath Day* cited the *Homilies* as a source of authority which confirmed that Christians are bound to keep the fourth commandment. Contrary to White's claim, Burton asserted that the English Church disclaimed the power to prescribe the time and place of this observance, basing this practice on the sabbath precept, and argued that the Church taught the morality of one day in seven and the divine institution of Sunday.[68] Linking this doctrinal error with others White held, Burton noted that at Brabourne's trial he had heard White 'in open Court speake against Justification; that a man might be justified to day, and damned to morrow, and against Election of some to eternal life', and against the sanctification of the Sabbath.[69] To the accusation of innovation, Burton was able to bring the devastating and perfectly accurate retort, 'What say you to the learned Hooker, and to the learned Dr. Andrewes? were these any way inclined unto the Disciplinarian Faction? or were they novell Sabbatarians?' He concluded his treatise with proofs against the use of recreations on Sunday, citing the Justinian Code and the Synod of Dort, as well as the *Bishops' Book*, the *Homilies*, the 1625 Sabbath Act, and other ancient and modern precedents.[70]

In this debate over the Church's teaching on the Sabbath, the evidence vindicated Burton rather than White. Although the *Homilies* were ambiguous on the institution of Sunday as the Lord's day, it did base the observance of one day in seven on the fourth precept and endorsed the application of strict sabbatarian discipline. The writings of Hooker and Andrewes provided undeniable proof that what Burton claimed was true – and he was not alone in his defence of the Sabbath.

[68] Henry Burton, *A Brief Answer to a Late Treatise of the Sabbath Day* (n.p., 1635), pp.4–9.
[69] *Ibid.*, p.12.   [70] *Ibid.*, pp.22–31.

In the same year, George Walker, rector of St John, Watling Street, preached a series of sermons on the sabbath doctrine. Affirming the morally binding nature of the fourth precept and the divine institution of Sunday, Walker explained that 'this is the doctrine of many of the best learned heretofore in our Church, and divers godly divines do rest in this opinion which for the maine matter and substance of it is pious and godly and approved by Aquinas the great Schoolman'.[71] In describing the observance required of believers by the fourth precept, Walker stated,

I could bring more arguments and proofs both out of Scripture, alsoe out of the writings of the learned and cleare testimonies which shew the consent of all Godlie Orthodox writers of all ages: Yet because I will leave no occasion or colour to such sonnes of Beliall as doe intrude into our assemblies, to catch calumniate and report my words safely and to accuse my Doctrine, except they will harden their...malicious hearts, and put on brasen faces with whorish foreheads to accuse the holy Scriptures, and the Doctrine published in the booke of Homilyes, and by law established in this Church of England whereof we are members: therefore I will only commend to your consideration the publick Doctrine of our Church in the verie words of the Homilies.[72]

The frustration for men like Burton and Walker must have been enormous, for prelates of the Church were denying a doctrine enshrined in authorized teaching; and while doing so, accusing them of innovation. Burton and Walker were precisionists, but their use of precedents found through the centuries, and their appeal to the authorized teaching of the English Church, distances them from any accusation of bibliolatry. Their attitudes towards recreations were stricter than any demanded in those precedents; but the same views had often been expressed in parliament. On the more fundamental points of the Church's express doctrine, they were undeniably in the right.

However, Laud's supporters had barely begun their campaign. On 17 August 1635 John Pocklington, a noted ritualist and a man wholly loyal to Laud, preached on the history of 'sabbatarian novelty' before Bishop John Williams at Lincoln. Pocklington explained that the first day of the week, afterwards known as the Lord's day, was set aside by the Church during the time of the apostles. This institution derived from the apostles and apostolic

---

[71] George Walker, *The Doctrine of the Sabbath* (Amsterdam, 1638), p.53.
[72] *Ibid.*, p.147.

men – meaning bishops. The 'holy Fathers' of the Church required that men should leave all their worldly business on saints' days, and especially on the Lord's day to give themselves wholly to God's service. For 1,554 years Sunday had been used reverently and known as the 'Lord's day' in both the Latin and Greek tradition.[73] Pocklington explained that this tradition had been broken by John Knox and William Whittingham during the Frankfort troubles, when they referred to Sunday as the 'Sabbath' in a letter to Calvin. However, it was over thirty years before 'their children could turne their tongues from Sunday to hit on Sabbath'. Their fervour had become such that if this 'Sabbath' was allowed, there would be no Prayer Book and no holy days, and all would be reduced to preaching on Sunday. It was little wonder that they disallowed lawful sports.[74]

Pocklington argued that this ran counter to Christian tradition, which allowed men to use ordinary labours outside of service time on Sunday and encouraged believers to use it as a feast day. He asserted that the fourth commandment was to be treated figuratively and not literally,[75] and claimed that the sabbath question was in fact a cloak for the enemies of the Church's liturgy and discipline. Yet Pocklington explained that 'with us the Sabbath is Saturday, and no day else...no learned man, Heathen or Christian tooke it otherwise from the beginning of the world till the beginning of their schisme in 1554'.[76] Men of worth who used the word should not be blamed, for they were misled by

these pretenders to pietie, who for their own ends have for a long time deceived the world with their zealous and most ignorant or cunning clamours, and rung the name of Sabbath so commonly into all mens eares, that not Clerkes onely, but men of judgement, learning and vertue...doe likewise suffer the same often to scape the doore of their lips.[77]

Pocklington directed his hearers to observe the Lord's day by receiving the Eucharist, participating in public worship, and hearing preaching, though he noted that afternoon sermons were not an absolute necessity.[78] Profaners of this holy day were not those who 'use harmelesse recreations, or do some small usefull chore, or perhaps take a nap on the Lord's day'. Transgressors of that day were those who slept in church, refused to come to

---

[73] John Pocklington, *Sunday No Sabbath* (London, 1636), pp.4–6.
[74] *Ibid.*, pp.6–8. [75] *Ibid.*, pp.12–18.
[76] *Ibid.*, pp.20–1. [77] *Ibid.*, p.21. [78] *Ibid.*, pp.25–37.

church till the sermon began, forced the priest to curtail divine service, or sang after their own fancy and not antiphonally.[79]

Pocklington's sermon was published in 1636 under the title *Sunday No Sabbath*, but was superseded in the same year by Peter Heylyn's *History of the Sabbath*. Heylyn had set the tone for anti-sabbatarian polemics in 1634, and White and Pocklington had expanded his arguments. Yet it was Heylyn's work in 1636 that became the keystone of anti-sabbatarian propaganda. This massive work purported to be a comprehensive study of scriptural and historical evidence against sabbatarian claims to orthodoxy. However, like his introduction to Prideaux's work, Heylyn distorted and misrepresented works to support his anti-sabbatarian position, and to justify the issuing of the Book of Sports. Heylyn attempted to make the sabbatarian tradition seem as recent as possible, for unlike Pocklington, he traced the origins of 'sabbatarian errors' to Bownde's *Doctrine of the Sabbath*. Adopting Rogers' account, he explained that

In the yeere 1595, some of that faction [presbyterians] which before had laboured with small profit, to overthrow the Hierarchy and government of this Church of England, now set themselves on worke to ruinate all the orders of it: to beate downe at one blowe all dayes and times, which by the *wisdome* and *authority* of the Church, had beene appointed for Gods service, and in the steed thereof to erect a Sabbath, of their owne devising.[80]

Heylyn expressed regret that some ministers were 'so setled in the opinion of a Sabbath day, a day not heard of in the Church of Christ 40 yeeres ago, that they chose rather to deprive the Church of their paines, and ministerie, then yield unto his Majesties most just Commands'. Noting that 'our private pathes do leade us often into errour', Heylyn encouraged 'all those who have offended in that kinde, to lay aside their passions, and their private interests... [and] not to shut their eyes against those truths, which are presented to them for their information: that so the King may have the honour of their due obedience; the Church, the comfort of their labours, and conformable ministery'.[81]

Heylyn and Pocklington denied the morality of the fourth precept, asserting that it was abrogated by Christ. While the observance of Sunday was a laudable practice, it was a human convention, established by the Church and regulated by its

---

[79] *Ibid.*, p.37.
[80] Heylyn, *History of the Sabbath*, p.250.   [81] *Ibid.*, pp.269–70.

bishops. The works of these men were clearly intended to support episcopal authority, to establish their anti-sabbatarian views as ancient 'catholic' teaching, and rebut the arguments of those who claimed that the new rulers of the Church were innovators. However, Laud's defenders were not co-ordinated in their efforts to rebut the charge of innovation; for they were faced with the task of reinterpreting the long-established sabbatarian doctrine and discipline of the English Church. Three works which also appeared in 1636 exposed the lack of consensus among Laudian apologists.

The works of David Primrose, Robert Sanderson, and Christopher Dow concurred with the assertions of Pocklington and Heylyn that Sunday was not a divine institution and that recreations could be used on that day. However, they also endorsed the scholastic interpretation.[82] Sanderson explained that

the substance of the fourth Commandment in general (viz. that some certaine time should be set apart from secular employments, to be sanctified to a holy rest for the better attending on God's publick and solemne worship) is Morall and perpetuall; and of Divine Right as a branch of the law of Nature, whereto Christians under the Gospel are still bound.[83]

Dow, vicar of Battle, Sussex, went even further, rebuking those who denied the sabbath precept's place in the moral law. Instead he argued that while all the precepts of the decalogue were moral, some had ceremonials added to them, 'which haply God thought good to place among the *moral precepts*, to intimate the perpetuall necessity of having some *ceremonies* in the Church'.[84] While dissenting from his opponents' view that one day in seven is part of God's immutable law, Dow acknowledged that Christians are bound by the fourth commandment to dedicate some time to God's worship and service, citing the *Homilies* in support of this claim. He summarized his position by stating that 'this Commandment extends to us Christians, as well as to the Jewes, in as much as to consecrate some part of our time to God, is *morall*, and a *seaventh* part, though not *morall*, yet *fitly chosen*, and appointed by God, and observed by the *Church of Christ* (not as simply immutable, yet) as most worthy to be retayned'.[85] Like Nicholas

---

[82] David Primrose, *A Treatise of the Sabbath and the Lords Day* (London, 1636), p.138; [R. Sanderson], *A Soveraigne Antidote against Sabbatarian Errours* (London, 1636), p.11; Christopher Dow, *A Discourse of the Sabbath and Lords Day* (London, 1636), p.10.
[83] Sanderson, p.11.   [84] Dow, *Discourse*, p.10.   [85] *Ibid.*, p.25.

Estwick and Samuel Ward, Dow stated that 'I know no reason why honest recreations, moderate feasting, and such like expressions of rejoicing, may not fitly be counted a part of the externall observance and sanctification of this day.'[86]

No other evidence more conclusively exposes the false nature of the claims made by Heylyn and Pocklington. While their position was to be bolstered with a second treatise by Bishop White and a work by Gilbert Ironside in 1637, it remains evident that Laudians were combating sabbatarian attacks with two mutually incompatible arguments: one asserting that the fourth commandment was a ceremonial law and abrogated by Christ; the other defending the scholastic interpretation. Both positions were declared to be the teaching of the Church, ancient and modern.[87] While Dow and other Laudian apologists espoused the same doctrine defended by Burton, Walker, and many others, Heylyn and Pocklington had used anti-sabbatarian polemics to justify the Book of Sports, and defend episcopal authority in regulating Sunday observance. Yet it was Heylyn's 'history' which was to establish itself in the eyes of both friends and foes as the official Laudian position.

LAUDIAN PERSECUTION AND SABBATARIAN VINDICATION

While the Laudians may have had access to the presses 'by authority', Burton and Prynne still managed to publish their works. During 1636, they produced four works rebutting anti-sabbatarian propaganda. Prynne published an enlarged version of Burton's *Brief Answer*,[88] and both are credited with *A Divine Tragedy Lately Acted* and *News from Ipswich*. *A Divine Tragedy* cited examples of God's judgements in the two years since the Book of Sports had been issued. The author noted the tribulations of clergy 'who now unjustly suffer through the malice of ungodly persecutors, and raging prelates, for refusing to joine with others in spurring on the people to the greedy pursuite of this cryinge dangerous Syn, to the ruine of their soules, their bodies, and the shame of our religion'. He went on to assert that these abuses were

[86] *Ibid.*, p.69.
[87] Francis White, *An Examination and Confutation of a Lawlesse Pamphlet* (London, 1637); Gilbert Ironside, *Seven Questions of the Sabbath Briefly Disputed* (Oxford, 1637).
[88] [William Prynne], *The Lords Day, the Sabbath Day* (n.p., 1636).

'a Syn, yea and a crying Syn too, as all our writers, (yea and our Prelates generally), till now of late have unanimously defined, and the whole State in Parliament'.[89] Fifty-five examples of God's judgement on sabbath-breakers were cited from all parts of the country, with dates, places, and often names being given. Such a mass of information required considerable co-operation and sympathy. He reported that on 25 January 1634, 'being the Lords day, in time of the last great Frost, 14 young men presuming to play at football upon the yce on the river Trent, neere to Ganisborrow, coming altogether in a scuffle, the yce suddainly broke, and they were all drowned'.[90] An Oxford carpenter, deciding to finish on Sunday the stage for a play at St John's College on Monday, 'fell backward from the Stage, being not farre from the ground, and broke his neck, and so ended his life in a fearful Tragedy'.[91] In the epilogue, Pocklington's sermon was attacked, the author daring him to call the 'learned and pious compilers of them [the *Homilies*], a pack of Puritans' or to call them 'Novell Sabbatarians', as Bishop White had described defenders of the Sabbath.[92]

News from Ipswich was equally critical. The author began by lamenting the censureship of their times, noting that 'presses formerly open only to Truth and Piety, are closed up against them both of late, and patent for the most part, to nought but error, superstition, and profanesse'. He drew attention to 'those many prophane, erronious, impious books, printed within these 3 yeares by the authority (point-blanke against the established doctrine of the Church of England, and his Majesties pious Declarations) in defence of Arminianisme, Popery and Popish ceremonies; and which is yet more impious and detestable, against the very morality of the Sabbath, and 4. Commandment: the devine institution, title and intire religious sanctification of the Lords day SABBATH'.[93] Recounting the changes that were being forced on the Church and recalling Charles' promise to stand firm against any innovation in the Church, made in the last parliament, the author called upon the king to 'behold these desperate inno-vations, purgations, and Romish practices, of thy Prelates in open affront of these thy Declarations'.[94]

[89] [H. Burton], *A Divine Tragedy Lately Acted* (n.p., 1636), 'To the Christian Reader'.
[90] *Ibid.*, p.11.   [91] *Ibid.*, p.12.   [92] *Ibid.*, p.32.
[93] [W. Prynne], *News from Ipswich* (n.p., 1636), no pagination.   [94] *Ibid.*, no pagination.

By 1636 the sabbath doctrine had been appropriated by those who opposed Laudian innovations, and was an integral part of their agenda against Laud and his supporters. On 5 November 1636, Guy Fawkes day, Henry Burton preached two sermons against the innovations of the Laudians. These sermons, later published under the title *For God, and the King*, called on Charles to put an end to what he saw as the havoc caused by Laud and his supporters. He charged them with the introduction of novelties that amounted to a popish plot and urged the king to take action against them. He refused to believe that Charles had authorized the enforcement of the Book of Sports, citing the king's promise; but declared that changes nevertheless had been introduced, explaining that,

the reading of this Booke by the Ministers is to bring in...a mighty innovation of the unity or Doctrine concerning the Sabbath, which hath been ever since the Reformation, and so from the Raigne of Queene Elizabeth of famous memory, constantly, universally and unanimously maintayned in the church of England, untill this late faction of Anti-Sabbatarians started up, to cry downe all sanctification, all power and purity of Religion. And indeed the innovation of the Doctrine of the Sabbath bring with it an universall innovation of all religion, as experience is an eye-witnesse.[95]

Burton asserted that Laud was responsible for the reissuing of the Book of Sports, explaining that

the Prelates, with their Learned Doctors, and heires apparent, have pulled their wits, broken their braines and sleep, spent many precious howers, and dayes, and moneths in compiling and setting forth Treatises, Histories, Sermons, and such like, and all to overturne the fourth Commanndment, with the Sanctification of the Sabbath day, and so bring in Libertinisme and all profanesse into the Church, thereby exposing our Religion to the reproch and scorne of the Papists themselves.[96]

While Burton was not a man noted for his moderation, his complaints against the Laudians in this matter, as well as the altar controversy and other issues, were legitimate grievances. The archbishop and his supporters *were* altering the doctrine and discipline of the Church. Burton and Prynne were extremists, but their arguments were filled with assertions in defence of the established teaching of the English Church. Although Burton's accusation of popery was unjust, the Laudians were clearly guilty of innovation.

[95] Henry Burton, *For God, and the King* (n.p., 1636), pp.56–7.   [96] *Ibid.*, p.60.

However, given Laud's commitment to restoring the 'catholic' traditions of the Church, this was a point he could not and would not concede. Shortly after his Guy Fawkes sermons, Burton was summoned to the High Commission to answer articles charging him with sedition. He refused to answer the charges and appealed to the king. Burton remained in his house for fear of arrest, and prepared his sermons for publication, together with an appeal to Charles. Fifteen days after failing to appear at another, special High Commission, he was suspended from his living and orders for his apprehension were issued. On 2 February 1637, the Sergeant at Arms and Sheriff of London broke down Burton's door, arresting him and ransacking his study. He was soon joined in the Fleet by William Prynne and John Bastwick, one of his parishioners. The three were charged with producing books which slandered the hierarchy. The Star Chamber trial was conducted without counsel for the defendants, for no lawyer would take up their case, and their testimonies were not admitted as evidence. Noted in general for his imposition of harsh penalties, Laud pressed for particularly severe measures against these men. Burton was deprived of his benefice, degraded from the ministry and his academic degrees, and fined 5,000 pounds. In addition, he was to be set in a pillory at Westminster where his eares were to be cut off, and imprisoned at Lancaster Castle for life. Prynne and Bastwick received similar penalties.[97] At their sentencing on 14 June, Laud delivered a speech denying the charges of innovation and defending the authority of the episcopate. He insinuated that Burton's actions were less than sincere, implying that Burton was motivated by malice and frustration over losing his place at court in 1625. Laud explained that 'the main scope of these libels is to kindle a jealousy in men's minds that there are some great plots in hand, dangerous plots, (so says Mr. Burton expressly,) to change the orthodox religion established in England, and to bring in, I know not what, Romish superstition in the room of it'.[98] Laud denied that he introduced innovations, claiming that 'I have done nothing, as a prelate, to the uttermost of what I am

---

[97] For accounts of Burton's arrest and trial see: Henry Burton, *A Narration of the Life of Mr. Henry Burton* (London, 1643), pp.10–13; William Prynne, *A New Discovery of the Prelates Tyranny* (London, 1641), *passim.*; Prynne, *Doome*, pp.110–14; Heylyn, *Cyprianus Anglicus*, pp.339–43; Laud, *Works*, IV, 105–11; *DNB* for Henry Burton.

[98] Laud, *Works*, VI, 44.

conscious, but with a single heart, and with a sincere intention for the good government and honour of the Church, and the maintenance of the orthodox truth and religion of Christ, professed, established and maintained in this Church of England'.[99]

Much to Laud's distress, Burton, Prynne, and Bastwick faced a sympathetic crowd when they went to pillory at Westminster. After his wounds had healed, Burton was sent to Lancaster Castle. His journey from London on 28 July was that of a departing hero, for George Garrard reported to Wentworth that there was a

strange flocking of the People after Burton, when he removed from the Fleet towards Lancaster Castle. Mr. Ingram, Sub-Warden of the Fleet told the King, that there was not less than one hundred thousand People gathered together to see him pass by, betwixt Smithfield and Brown's Well, which is two miles beyond Highgate, his Wife went along in a Coach, having much Money thrown at her as she passed along.[100]

In his autobiography, Burton reported that

On the day appointed I passed on horseback from the Fleet through Smithfield, where for throng of people all along I could not passe, but very slowly, though the Keeper hastened all he could, who fretted to see so many all the way we went, he reckoned the number to be forty thousand. By the way so many taking me by the hand, pressed the very blood out at my finger ends...I rid to St Albans that night, being accompanied all the way with above five hundred horse of loving friends.[101]

This display of support and sympathy for Burton stands in stark contrast to the malice directed at Laud; for protests were nailed to the doors of St Paul's and caricatures were found in public places. The archbishop reported to Wentworth on 17 September that a board had been found 'hung upon the Standard in Cheap...a narrow board with my speech in the Star Chamber nailed at one end of it, and singed with fire, the corners cut off instead of the ears, a pillory of ink with my name to look through it'. Below the drawing was the comment, 'The man that put the saints of God into a pillory of wood, stands here in a pillory of ink... The author deserves to be used thus as well as the book'.[102]

Laud's attempt to defend his policies and the episcopate had only created more opposition, with open displays of support for those he persecuted and angry threats to bring down the hierarchy. To justify his actions, Laud commissioned Peter Heylyn and

[99] *Ibid.*, p.42.
[100] Wentworth, II, 114.
[101] Burton, *Narration*, p.14.
[102] Laud, *Works*, VII, 371–2.

Christopher Dow to write against Burton's *For God, and the King* and *Apology of an Appeal*. These works appeared in print during July 1637 and should have presented a uniform case for the Laudians. However, once again, Heylyn and Dow clashed in their description of the authorized teaching of the Sabbath, exposing the inconsistencies of the Laudian position and confirming the claims of Burton and others.

In his *Briefe and Moderate Answer*, Heylyn chastized Burton for his charge that Laud was responsible for the Book of Sports, observing that there was 'no reason to charge that on my Lord Archbishop, as if it were a matter of his procuring: or if it were, to reckon it amongst his faults'.[103] Heylyn asserted that the reissue was necessary to 'represse your follies: who under pretence of hindering recreations upon that day, had in some parts, put downe all feasts of dedications of the Churches, commonly called Wakes, which they which did it, did without authority'. Church leaders had done this to preserve the Lord's day 'from being overcome with Judaisme or superstition. And you might see how some out your principles came to have as much if not more of the Jew then the Christian in them, about the time when the declaration came forth.' Heylyn insisted that Laud was simply following the king's command in issuing and enforcing the Book of Sports.[104]

In response to Burton's charge that the sabbath doctrine had been changed, Heylyn claimed that 'there is indeed a mighty alteration in it, I could wish there were not: but it was made by you and yours, who little more then 40 yeeres agone, first broached these Sabbath-speculations in the Church of England; which now you press upon her for her ancient doctrine'.[105] He concluded his treatment of the sabbath doctrine with a personal testimony of his sincerity and desire to reveal the true nature of this doctrine. He stated that

For my part...I have dealt with all ingenuitie and sinceritee: and make this protestation before God and men, that if in all the scriptures, Fathers, Councells, moderne writers, or whatever monument of the church I met within so long a search, I had found any thing in favour of that doctrine which you so approve; I would not have concealed it, to the suppression of a truth, for all the world. How ever you accuse me, yet my conscience doth not.[106]

[103] Peter Heylyn, *A Briefe and Moderate Answer* (London, 1637), p.80.
[104] *Ibid.*, p.81.
[105] *Ibid.*, p.130.   [106] *Ibid.*, p.130.

If Heylyn's conscience did not convict him, the arguments used by Christopher Dow did. In rebutting Burton's charge of innovation, Dow condemned his libellous assertions against Laud and his supporters, accusing him of 'grosse and palpable ignorance and malice'. Dow asserted that the leaders of the Church 'acknowledge the appointing of set times and dayes, to the publick and solemn worship and service of God, to be not only *divine*, but *morall* and perpetuall: and that the common and naturall equity of the *fourth Commandment* obligeth all man-kinde to the end of the world'. He went on to explain that 'they grant, that the *resting from labour* on the Lords day, and Christian holy dayes...is both grounded upon the law of nature, and the perpetuall equity of the fourth Commandment'. He stated that 'they grant a *special sense* of that Commandment of perpetuall obligation: so that they have not absolutely removed the institution of the Lords day from the foundation of divine Authority: Nor is the fourth Commandment wholly abolished, as he falsely and unjustly clamours'. Explaining that the Church acknowledged the same ceremonial parts Burton found in the sabbath precept, Dow noted that while 'they deny the fourth Commandment to be wholly morall, so doth M. Burton'. He went on to observe that 'they deny the morality and perpetuall obligation of that Commandement, as it concerns the seventh day from the creation, which is our Saturday...which M. Burton also granteth'. Describing the strictness of the Jewish sabbath rest as another abrogated ceremony, he concluded that 'this also M. Burton must needs grant'.[107]

The contentious issues Dow highlighted were the institution of Sunday and the manner of observing that day. While denying 'that there is any Commandment given in the *New Testament* for the observation of the *Lords day*', Dow explained that they acknowledge 'sufficient ground there to warrant the Churches institution and observation of that day'. Concerning the regulation of Sunday observance, he stated that it was commonly understood 'that the Church hath liberty, power and authority thus to do', and claimed that 'Christians are in conscience bound to observe these precepts of the Church'.[108] Concluding that Burton's complaints against the authorities were groundless, Dow condemned him for 'railing against his opposers, and traducing the doctrine which he knowes

---

[107] Christopher Dow, *Innovations Unjustly Charged upon the Present Church and State* (London, 1637), pp.68–70.   [108] *Ibid.*, pp.70–1.

not how to confute'. He denied that the authorities had devised a new doctrine, affirming that they espoused the orthodox teaching of the Church, which Burton sought to defend.[109]

Dow did not openly repudiate the anti-sabbatarian arguments promoted by Heylyn and Pocklington, but his silence and failure to cite their works indicates that there was a conflict in ideology. While Dow staunchly defended Bishop White's first work on the Sabbath and attempted to vindicate Laud's actions, he made no references to Burton's bitter attacks on Heylyn and Pocklington. It is difficult to say which position Laud actually supported; however, Heylyn proved a much more successful propagandist than his associate. Although the Church's teaching and the convictions of many Laudian supporters confirmed the orthodoxy of the scholastic interpretation, Heylyn not only managed to identify Laudians with anti-sabbatarian views, but also provided what was ultimately the most influential, as well as the most misleading, account of the origins, nature, and meaning of English sabbatarianism.

But nemesis was now upon the Laudian party, and the structure which Heylyn's ingenious and specious arguments had been designed to support was about to tumble round the archbishop's head. Heylyn's triumph was in the future. On Sunday, 15 November 1640, Henry Burton received news that the House of Commons had dropped the charges against him and ordered him home. He regarded the receipt of this news on the Lord's day to be a sign and a blessing. Noting that he had defended the day 'both by preaching and writing against the malignant and profane adversaries of the sanctification thereof, and of its morality', Burton was certain that these sabbath tidings were 'a gracious reward of mercy from God, whose day I had formerly stood for against all the adversaries thereof'.[110] On his journey to London Burton was met by his wife at Bagshot, 'who came accompanied with many loving friends, and worthy Citizens of London'. He reported that they stopped at Egham, 'where every house brought forth a light to light us to our lodging, where we were most nobly entertained by multitudes of friends, that from London met us there'.[111] While Laud had meant to make an example of Burton

---

[109] *Ibid.*, p.72.
[110] Burton, *Narration*, p.38.   [111] *Ibid.*, p.40.

and his associates, they became instead symbols of resistance to Laudian innovations. The most obvious vindication of their struggle was their defence of the Sabbath – which became the standard of those who soon ruled the nation.

CONCLUSION

During the parliament of 1621, the crypto-papist Thomas Shepard charged that the supporters of the sabbath bill were attempting to subvert the king's will, set forth in the Declaration of Sports, and accused them of puritanism.[112] John Pym, in his maiden speech before parliament uttered words that were to prove prophetic. He denounced Shepard's attempt to

> devide us amongst our selves, exasperatinge one partie by that odious and factious name of Puritans; Or at least would make the world believe we were devided, which as it may breede in the Comon adversarie boldnes to attempt soe it may nourish among us jeolosye and suspicion in defence of our selves. And it hath been often seene that small seedes of Tumult and sedition growe upp into great dangers, even to the overthrowe of States.[113]

Nineteen years later, attitudes towards sabbath recreations were indeed one of the clearest means of determining religious and political allegiances.

Yet it is not enough to point to rigorous attitudes towards Sunday recreations as a source of this division; or to Laud as the chief protagonist who justly suffered for his narrow and oppressive use of authority. The underlying tensions were more fundamental and critical for both sides. Laud's pressing agenda was to restore the 'catholic' traditions of the English Church. He acted compulsively in protecting episcopal jurisdiction, preserving long-neglected rituals and festivals, and re-establishing the importance of the Church's sacramental life and aesthetics in worship. The 1633 controversy touched two of his concerns: episcopal jurisdiction and a traditional church festival. Despite the personal antagonisms that complicate the situation, Laud's defence of these principles was consistent with his desire to preserve the 'catholic' nature of the English Church.

However, Laud's agenda fed the long-standing fears of many English protestants. The Jacobean consensus was decidedly reformed in doctrine and practice. Laud's patronage of Arminians,

[112] See Chapter 6, Parliament: 1621–9. [113] *Commons Debates, 1621*, IV, 62–5.

his affection for practices that many considered 'popish', led his adversaries to believe that he was part of a Catholic conspiracy, despite his protestations.[114] In her study of Charles' court, Dr Caroline Hibbard has isolated two important themes in the religious and political controversies of the late 1630s. First, there was a firm belief among Laud's opponents that the subversion of religion and subversion of government were inextricably connected, for 'threats to English religion evoked fears for English liberties, and vice versa'. She also found that the charge of subversion by division was a common theme in the parliaments of the 1620s and particularly evident in the allegations against Strafford and Laud.[115]

Given these fears, it is understandable that the charges and counter-charges of innovation in sabbatarian doctrine and discipline were to prove so volatile. It is little wonder that Laud's supporters laboured so strenuously to deflect the charge of innovation onto their sabbatarian opponents. However, Heylyn's fraudulent summary of sabbatarian history, in defence of episcopal jurisdiction and Church-appointed festivals, fueled the suspicions of those who feared alterations in both religion and government.

In 1641, Richard Bernard observed that 'books upon books have been written, and by license passed the Presse, to take away the morality of the fourth Commandment, never, in an age, heretofore, doubted of... calling such as set the whole day apart for holy uses, *Sabbatarians* and *Judaizers*, thus reproaching, and in their sense, belying those that more truly honour Christ than they doe'.[116] George Abbot pressed the charge of conspiracy more explicitly, stating that

The plot of the times has beene against the power of Godlines, which could never bee pulled downe whilest the *Sabbath* stood upright, and therefore our Patrons of impiety have rightly projected to take that out of the way which stood so much in theirs... that so they might bring all to a level, by paring away *Sabbaths* and

---

[114] The growth of this paranoia was evident by 1626. In a parliamentary speech against Buckingham, Christopher Sherland asked, 'Why are Arminians that have sought the ruin of the Low Countries allowed here? They run in a string with papists and flatter greatness to oppress the subject'. John Hampden went even further, asserting that attempts to alter religion or the government amounted to 'no less than a subversion of the whole state'. (Russell, *Parliaments and Politics: 1621–1629*, pp. 379–80.)

[115] C. Hibbard, *Charles I and the Popish Plot* (Chapel Hill, 1983), p.14, also see pp. 7, 233; and see Conrad Russell, 'The Theory of Treason in the Trial of Strafford', *English Historical Review*, 80 (1965), 30–50.

[116] Richard Bernard, *Threefold Treatise of the Sabbath* (London, 1641), sig. A2v.

Sermons, which was the only way to mount them to the height of their designe of bringing Godlines to a forme, and all things (but Episcopacy) from *jus Divinum* to *jus Humanum*, that they might be all in all.[117]

Pym's speech before parliament on 7 November 1640 demonstrated the broader political fears raised by the recent religious controversies. Declaring that there was 'a design to alter the kingdom both in religion and government', he charged that the hierarchy 'cannot amount to the height they aim at without a breach of our law' and implied that they had joined with Catholics in a conspiracy against the English Church and State.[118]

While it is all too easy to pass judgement or take sides, the motives and fears of the Laudians and their opponents call for conclusions in shades of grey rather than black or white. However, on the sabbatarian issue there can be no doubt. Laud's opponents were justified in their charge of innovation in doctrine and practice. Heylyn's promotion of a fraudulent anti-sabbatarian tradition confirmed the fears and suspicions of many, and provided a focus for the polarization of religious and political attitudes throughout the nation. The assumption that this doctrine was a unique characteristic of puritanism must be revised, for sabbatarianism did not become a 'puritan *cause célèbre*' until a few Laudians made it so.

[117] George Abbot, *Vindiciae Sabbathi* (London, 1641), sig. A4.
[118] Kenyon, *Constitution*, p.204, n. 2; also see Anthony Fletcher, *The Outbreak of the English Civil War* (London, 1981), xxii-xxiv.

Epilogue

It is not surprising that, given the opportunity, Laud's opponents reasserted this doctrine and provided for strict sabbatarian discipline. Yet their rebuttal of anti-sabbatarian propaganda and firm measures in support of the Sabbath did not meet with resounding success; for the abuses they found in 1641 were still a source of concern in 1662.

This was not for want of effort. Although no sabbatarian books had been legally published since 1633, no less than nine works appeared in 1641.[1] All seem to have been written prior to 1640 and stress a common theme: the orthodoxy of the scholastic interpretation and the importance of strict sabbatarian discipline. Many other works were to follow, most notably the massive work of Daniel Cawdrey and Herbert Palmer, both members of the Westminster Assembly.[2] These theological labours were not directed simply at proving the biblical basis for sabbatarian doctrine and discipline, but also defended the place of this teaching in English Church tradition. Their assertions that recreations traditionally had been prohibited were exaggerated at best and often wrong. However, given the polarization of attitudes in the 1630s, it is little wonder that sabbatarians resorted to such claims, asserting what had been attempted, but never accomplished in the Jacobean Church.[3]

With power now in their hands, Laud's opponents lost little

[1] George Abbot, *Vindiciae Sabbathi*; Richard Bernard, *A Threefold Treatise of the Sabbath*; William Gouge, *The Sabbaths Sanctification*; George Hakewill, *A Short, but Cleare, Discourse, of the Institution, Dignity, and End of the Lords-day*; Authur Lake, *Theses de Sabbato* (published posthumously and attached to Twisse's work); Hamon L'Estrange, *Gods Sabbath Before the Law, Under the Law and Under the Gospel*; John Ley, *Sunday a Sabbath*; William Twisse, *Of the Morality of the Fourth Commandment*; George Walker, *The Doctrine of the Holy Weekly Sabbath*.
[2] Daniel Cawdrey and Herbert Palmer, *Sabbatum Redivivum* (Part I published in 1645, Parts II, III, IV published in 1652). For references to other works of this period, see Cox, *The Sabbath Question*, I 223-71; and Dennison, *Market Day of the Soul*, pp. 95-138.
[3] See Chapter 4 'Parliament'.

time in establishing strict sabbatarian discipline. On 8 September 1641, the Commons resolved that, 'the Lord's day should be duly observed and sanctified; that all dancing, or other sports either before or after divine service be forborne and restrained; and that the preaching [of] God's word be promoted in the afternoon'.[4] On 5 May 1643, parliament ordered that the *Declaration of Sports* be publicly burned by the hangman in Cheapside and required that all copies of the declaration be surrendered to the authorities for burning.[5]

During November 1644, the Assembly of Divines debated the sabbatarian provisions for the *Directory*, including a strict measure for 'a holy cessation or resting all day, from all unnecessary labor, and an abstaining not only from all sports and pastimes, but also from all worldly words and thoughts'.[6] Earlier that year parliament passed a sabbatarian act. Fines were increased, all recreations were prohibited, and the *Declaration of Sports* and all anti-sabbatarian works were to be seized and publicly burned. While these provisions were changes in the established order, what is most striking is how closely the rest of the bill resembles the measures found in episcopal injunctions and visitation articles of previous decades. Equally important were the provisions included to prevent the rise of judaizing scruples.[7] Even more detailed provisions were passed by parliament in 1650 and 1657; however, they did not deviate from the established pattern.[8]

While it is not possible here to explore the effectiveness of this legislation, the additional measures and increased detail found in the 1650 and 1657 acts suggest that puritans, possessing the power of enforcement, suffered the same fate as the Elizabethan and Jacobean bishops and secular officials. The gap between regulations and enforcement apparently remained quite wide. Perhaps the most striking evidence in support of this suggestion is found in provisions issued by Charles II in 1662. In his *Directions Concerning Preachers*, Charles forbade preachers to explore or

---

[4] Daniel Neal, *The History of the Puritans* (London, 1822), II, 419.
[5] Neal, *Puritans*, III, 37.
[6] John Lightfoot, *The Whole Works* (London, 1824), XIII, 327-30; A. H. Lewis, *A Critical History of Sunday Legislation* (New York, 1888), p.141; C. H. Firth and R. S. Rait, (eds.), *Acts and Ordinances of the Interregnum: 1642-1660*, 3 vols. (London, 1911), I, 598-9.
[7] *Ibid.*, pp. 420-22; Lewis, *Sunday Legislation*, pp. 115-120.
[8] *Ibid.*, pp. 121-40; Firth and Rait, II, 383-7, 1162-70.

expound on controversial doctrinal or political issues. However, in his concluding statement, Charles required that,

for the better observing of the Lord's day, too much neglected of late, they [preachers] shall, as by often and serious admonitions, and sharp reproofs, endeavour to draw off people from such idle, debauched, and profane courses, as dishonour God, bring a scandal on religion, and contempt on the laws and authority ecclesiastical and civil...[and] the minister shall exhort those, which are in authority in their several parishes and congregations, carefully to look after all such offenders...that they may be proceeded against according to the laws and quality of their offences, that all such disorder may for the time to come be prevented.[9]

In 1676 Charles signed into law an act that bore remarkable similarities to the measure passed in 1644. While the act excluded the prohibition of all recreations and issues particular to the 1640s, it increased the fine imposed on offenders and closely paraphrased several portions of the 1644 act.

Although it would be unwise to push the implications of these documents too far, it does suggest that after the tensions of the 1630s and 1640s had diminished, Restoration England returned to the sabbatarian consensus that had existed during the Jacobean period. Disputes continued over sabbath recreations, the divine institution of Sunday, and anti-sabbatarian propaganda. However, the sabbatarian doctrine and discipline of the pre-Laudian Church were to play an important role in English religious life during the next three centuries. Certainly in this matter, the Restoration Church was, as Professor Collinson has described it, 'a true successor to the Jacobean Church'.[10] Yet it is perhaps even more accurate to say that Restoration sabbatarianism was part of a recurring pattern in the history of the English Sabbath, reasserting and reaffirming the doctrine and discipline that had been part of English religious life for centuries.

[9] Edward Cardwell, *Documentary Annals*, II, 258-9.
[10] Collinson, *Religion of Protestants*, p. 283.

Appendix

Table 1a

Ely Diocese – Wisbech and Ely Deaneries

Years	Sexual offences (%)	Community faults (%)	Sabbath offences (%)	Holy-day offences (%)	Other (%)
1576–80	403 (43)	182 (19)	149 (16)	12 (1)	193 (21)
1588–92	554 (36)	265 (17)	354 (23)	34 (2)	341 (22)
1593–1600	941 (34)	454 (16)	629 (22)	77 (3)	692 (25)
1600–6	671 (33)	363 (18)	331 (16)	77 (4)	586 (29)
1608–17	699 (21)	600 (19)	856 (26)	232 (7)	870 (27)

Note: In Tables 1a and 3, the category 'Community faults' refers to presentments for brawling, defaming neighbours, drunkenness, and the detention of public and church dues, as well as not receiving communion, failing to be catechized, or other forms of religious non-conformity. The category 'Other' includes the faults of parish officers and clergy, and other miscellaneous cases.

The figures given are the totals of *types* of presentments, and are not a reflection of the number of individuals presented to the courts.

Table 1b

Type	1576–80 (%)	1588–92 (%)	1593–1600 (%)	1600–6 (%)	1608–17 (%)
Attendance	71 (48)	124 (35)	260 (41)	136 (41)	183 (21)
Work	20 (13)	62 (17)	130 (21)	58 (18)	311 (37)
Alehouse activities	7 (5)	28 (8)	46 (7)	31 (9)	95 (11)
Pastimes	0 (–)	20 (6)	70 (11)	40 (12)	69 (8)
Trading	0 (–)	2 (1)	11 (2)	6 (2)	75 (9)
Other	51 (34)	118 (33)	112 (18)	60 (18)	123 (14)
Total	149	354	629	331	856

Table 2

Chichester Diocese

Type	1586–89 (%)	1603–6 (%)	1606–9 (%)	1609–12 (%)
Attendance	124 (71)	88 (45)	75 (37)	78 (30)
Work	16 (9)	37 (19)	31 (16)	50 (19)
Alehouse activities	7 (4)	40 (20)	45 (23)	69 (26)
Pastimes	7 (4)	8 (4)	25 (12)	33 (13)
Trading	0 (–)	13 (7)	23 (12)	11 (4)
Other	20 (12)	11 (5)	1 (–)	22 (8)
Total	174	197	200	263

Table 3

Chester Diocese:
Blackburn, Chester, Leyland, Manchester, Warrington Deaneries

Years	Sexual offences (%)	Community faults (%)	Sabbath offences (%)	Holy-day offences (%)	Other (%)
1580–82	164 (54)	38 (13)	19 (6)	0 (–)	83 (27)
1592–3	324 (31)	238 (22)	215 (21)	2 (–)	271 (26)
1598–9	653 (34)	789 (42)	235 (12)	1 (–)	226 (12)
1605 (06)	531 (16)	2258 (69)	266 (8)	13 (–)	234 (7)
1611	634 (45)	395 (28)	175 (12)	6 (–)	203 (15)
1614	448 (40)	319 (28)	121 (11)	4 (1)	231 (20)

Bibliography

VISITATION ARTICLES AND INJUNCTIONS
The bibliographical references for these documents may be found in *The Short-Title Catalogue: 1475–1640* (2nd ed.), vol. 1.

Blank – 1558, 1559, 1560–1, 1560, 1597, 1616, 1621, 1624, 1633, 1634.
Bangor – 1634, 1640.
Bath and Wells – 1630, 1636.
Bristol – 1585, 1603, 1631, 1637, 1640.
Dorset – 1624.
Canterbury – 1556, 1557, 1560, 1563, 1566, 1573, 1576, 1580, 1582, 1605, 1610, 1615, 1619, 1621, 163-, 1635, 1638.
Canterbury – 1636.
Carlisle – 1627, 1629, 1632.
Chester – 1580, 1604, 1605, 1617, 1634, 1637.
Chichester – 1586, 1600, 1606, 1628, 1634, 1637.
Chichester – 1635, 1638, 1640.
Coventry and Lichfield – 1537, 1565, 1584, 1609, 1610, 1620, 1632, 1639.
Durham – 1577, 1613, 1640.
Durham – 1636.
Northumberland – 1639.
Ely – 1571, 1573, 1579, 1610, 1613, 1638.
Exeter – 1579, 1599, 1625, 1627, 1630–1, 1638.
Deanery of St Peter – 1609.
Exeter – 1612.
Barnstaple – 1617.
Gloucester – 1551–2, 1556, 1631, 1634, 1640.
Gloucester – 1618, 1624, 1629, 1635.
Hereford – 1586, 1592, 1634, 1635, 1640.
Hereford – 1620.
Lincoln – 1552, 1571, 1574, 1577, 1585, 1588, 1591, 1598, 1601, 1604, 1607, 1613, 1614, 1618, 1622, 1625, 1627, 1628, 1630.
Bedford – 1629, 1636, 1640.
Buckingham – 1627, 1630, 1639.
Leicester – 1611, 1613, 1622.
Lincoln – 1627, 1637.
Llandaff – 1603, 1640.

London – 1550, 1554, 1555, 1571, 1577, 1586, 1598, 1601, 1604, 1605, 1607, 1612, 1615, 1618, 1621, 1627, 1628, 1631, 1634, 1636, 1637, 1640.

Colchester – 1607, 1631, 1635.

Deanery of Arches – 1632.

Deanery of St Paul's – 1632.

Essex – 1610, 1615, 1625, 1635, 1638, 1639.

London – 1584, 1585, 1620, 1625, 1626, 1640.

Middlesex – 1582, 1616, 1620, 1631, 1634.

Norwich – 1549, 1561, 1567, 1569, 1613, 1619, 1620, 1627, 1629, 1633, 1636, 1638.

Norfolk – 1608, 1625, 1630, 1632, 1633, 1636, 1637, 1640.

Norwich – 1606, 1618, 163-.

Sudbury – 1624, 1627, 1639.

Suffolk – 1618, 1625, 1633, 1636, 1638, 1639, 1640.

Oxford – 1619, 1622, 1628, 1629, 1632, 1635, 1638.

Peterborough – 1594, 1623, 1631, 1639.

Huntingdon – 1624.

Rochester – 1565, 1605.

Rochester – 1608, 1632.

St Asaph – 1637.

St David's – 1583, 1622.

Salisbury – 1538, 1581, 1614, 1616, 1628, 1631, 1635.

Berkshire – 1595, 1615, 1626, 1631, 1635, 1638.

Winchester – 1570, 1574–5, 1584, 1597, 1606, 1612, 1619, 1625, 1628, 1633, 1635, 1636, 1639.

Surrey – 1619, 1621, 1625, 1626, 1635, 1638.

Worcester – 1551–2, 1569, 1577, 1607, 1626, 1632, 1635.

Worcester – 1615, 1634, 1638.

York – 1538, 1571, 1578, 1590, 1607, 1623, 1629, 1633, 1636, 1640.

Derby – 1630.

Nottingham – 1599, 1605, 1610, 1639.

York – 1635.

MANUSCRIPTS

Bodleian Library

MS Oxf. Dioc. Papers d.4
MS Oxf. Dioc. Papers d.5
MS Oxf. Dioc. Papers d.6
MS Rawlinson C.218
MS Rawlinson D.896(14)
MS Rawlinson D.1346
MS Rawlinson D.1350
MS Rawlinson Letters 89
MS Tanner 65
MS Tanner 71
MS Tanner 279

British Library

Additional MS 4160
Additional MS 18007
Additional MS 38492
Cott. MS Cleop. C.4
Harleian MS 1926
Harleian MS 2339

Harleian MS 6534
Harleian MS 7038
Lansdowne MS 115
British Library Loan 29/202
Stowe MS 362

Cheshire Record Office

EDVI/6d
EDVI/10
EDVI/12a
EDVI/13
EDVI/14
EDVI/17
EDVI/19

Corporation of London Record Office

Repertory 34
Repertory 36
Repertory 38

East Sussex Record Office

467/7/9

Herefordshire Record Office

AL 19/16

John Rylands Library

Rylands English MS 524
Rylands English MS 874

Lambeth Palace Library

MS 943

Manchester Central Library

MS 347.96.M2

Public Record Office

Assizes 24/20
SP/12/222
SP/12/244
SP/12/283

SP/12/235
SP/14/17
SP/14/159
SP/14/122
SP/14/96
SP/14/113
SP/14/165
SP/16/255
SP/16/247
SP/16/250
SP/16/96
SP/16/395
SP/16/538
SP/16/267
SP/16/269
SP/16/278
SP/16/159
SP/16/261
SP/16/72
SP/16/73
SP/16/294
SP/16/280
SP/16/287

Somerset Record Office

D/D/VC 74
DD/PH 222
Quarter Session, Minute Book 1613–20
    Minute Book 1620–7
    Session Rolls, 2
    Session Rolls, 61,i
    Session Rolls, 70

University Library, Cambridge

Additional MS 6380
MS Ff.5.25
EDR B/2/4
    B/2/5
    B/2/10
    B/2/11
    B/2/12
    B/2/14
    B/2/15
    B/2/17

B/2/18	*West Sussex Record Office*
B/2/20	
B/2/21	Ep 1/15/1/11
B/2/22	Ep 1/15/2/19
B/2/27	Ep 1/15/MP 977
B/2/28	Ep 1/17/6
B/2/29	Ep 1/17/11
B/2/30	Ep 1/17/12
B/2/34	Ep 1/17/13
B/2/35	Ep 1/17/15
D/2/5	Ep 1/17/25
D/2/8	
D/2/10	*Dr Williams Library*
D/2/10a	MS Morrice BI
D/2/17a	MS Morrice BII
D/2/18	MS. 28.1
D/2/23	

THESES

Carter, J. K., 'Sunday Observance in Scotland, 1560–1606', University of Edinburgh unpublished Ph.D. thesis (1957).

Curtis, T. C., 'Some Aspects of the History of Crime in Seventeenth Century England', University of Manchester unpublished Ph.D. thesis (1973).

Dent, C. M., 'Protestants in Elizabethan Oxford', University of Oxford unpublished D.Phil. thesis (1980).

Houlbrooke, R., 'Church Courts and People in the Diocese of Norwich, 1519–1570', University of Oxford unpublished D.Phil. thesis, (1970).

Hunt, W. A., Jr, 'The Godly and the Vulgar: Puritanism and Social Change in Seventeenth Century Essex, England', Harvard University unpublished Ph.D. thesis (1974).

Jones, J. B. H., 'Puritanism and Moral Legislation before the Civil War', University of Wales unpublished M.A. thesis (1954).

Lake, P., 'Laurence Chaderton and the Cambridge Moderate Puritan Tradition', University of Cambridge unpublished Ph.D. thesis (1978).

Leaper, W. A., 'The Growth of Sabbatarianism in England from 1558–1658', National University of Ireland unpublished M.A. thesis (1919).

Maltby, Judith, 'The Altar Controversy in the Church of England: 1547–1640', University of Illinois unpublished B.A. thesis (1979).

Parker, Kenneth L., 'The English Sabbath, 1558–1640', University of Cambridge unpublished Ph.D. thesis (1984).

Peake, T. H., 'The Somerset Clergy and the Church Courts in the Diocese of Bath and Wells, 1625–1642', University of Bristol unpublished M.Litt. thesis (1978).

Richardson, R. C., 'Puritanism in the Diocese of Chester to 1642', University of Manchester unpublished Ph.D. thesis (1968).

Shipps, K. W., 'Lay Patronage of East Anglian Puritan Clerics in Pre-Revolutionary England', Yale University unpublished Ph.D. thesis (1971).

Tyacke, N. R. N., 'Arminianism in England, in Religion and Politics, 1604–1640', University of Oxford unpublished D.Phil. thesis (1968).

Wrightson, K., 'The Puritan Reformation of Manners', University of Cambridge unpublished Ph.D. thesis (1973).

ARTICLES

Avis, P. D. L., 'Moses and the Magistrate: A Study in the Rise of Protestant Legalism', *Journal of Ecclesiastical History*, vol.26, no.2 (1975), 149–72.

Axon, Ernest, 'The King's Preachers in Lancashire 1599–1845', *Transactions of the Lancashire and Cheshire Antiquarian Society*, vol.56, (1941–2), 67–104.

Baker, W. P., 'The Observance of Sunday', *Englishmen at Rest and Play*, edited by R. Lennard (Oxford, 1931).

Barnes, T. G., 'County Politics and a Puritan Cause Célèbre: Somerset Church-ales, 1633', *Transactions of the Royal Historical Society*, 5th series, vol.9 (London, 1959), 103–22.

Beresford, M. W., 'The Common Informer, the Penal Statutes and Economic Regulations', *Economic History Review*, vol.10, no.2 (1957), 221–38.

Bossy, John, 'The Counter-Reformation and the People of Catholic Europe', *Past and Present*, no.47 (1970), 51–70.

Brinkworth, E. R. 'The Study and Use of Archdeacons' Court Records: Illustrated from the Oxford Records (1566–1759)', *Transactions of the Royal Historical Society*, 4th series, vol.25 (London, 1943), 93–119.

Cate, J. L., 'The Church and Market Reform in England during the Reign of Henry III', *Medieval and Historiographical Essays in Honor of James Westfall Thompson*, edited by Cate and Anderson (Chicago, 1938), pp. 27–65.

'The English Mission of Eustace of Flay', *Etude d'histoire dédiées à la mémoire d'Henri Pirenne* (Brussels, 1937), pp. 67–89.

Collinson, Patrick, 'The Beginnings of English Sabbatarianism', *Studies in Church History*, vol.1 (London, 1964), 207–21.

'Cranbrook and the Fletchers: Popular and Unpopular Religion in the Kentish Weald', *Reformation Principle and Practice: Essays in Honour of Arthur Geoffrey Dickens*, edited by P. N. Brooks (London, 1980), pp. 171–202.

'John Field and Elizabethan Puritanism', *Elizabethan Government and Society*, edited by S. T. Bindoff, J. Hurstfield, and C. H. Williams (London, 1961), pp. 127–62.

'The "nott conformytye" of the young John Whitgift', *Journal of Ecclesiastical History*, vol.15 (1964), 192–200.

'Sir Nicholas Bacon and the Elizabethan Via Media', *Historical Journal*, vol.23, no.2 (1980), 255–73.

Curtis, M. H., 'Hampton Court Conference and its Aftermath', *History*, vol. 46 (1961), 1–16.

'The Trials of a Puritan in Jacobean Lancashire', *The Dissenting Tradition:*

Essays for Leland H. Carlson, edited by C. R. Cole and M. E. Moody (Athens, Ohio, 1975), pp. 3–38.

Donaldson, G., 'The Scottish Church 1567–1625', *The Reign of James VI and I*, edited by A. Smith (London, 1973), pp. 40–56.

Elton, G. R., 'Enacting Clauses and Legislative Initiative, 1559–71', *Bulletin of the Institute of Historical Research*, vol.53, no.128 (1980), 183–91.

'Parliament in the Sixteenth Century: Functions and Fortunes', *Historical Journal*, vol.22, no.2 (1979), 255–78.

Fines, J., '"Judaising" in the Period of the English Reformation – The Case of Richard Bruern', *Transactions of the Jewish Historical Society of England*, vol. 21 (1968), 323–6.

Fisher, R. M., 'Privy Council Coercion and Religious Conformity at the Inns of Court, 1569–84', *Recusant History*, vol.15, no.5 (1981), 305–24.

Graves, M., 'Thomas Norton the Parliament Man: An Elizabethan M.P., 1559–1581', *Historical Journal*, vol.23 (1980), 17–35.

Greaves, R. L., 'The Origins of English Sabbatarian Thought', *Sixteenth Century Journal*, vol.12, no.3 (1981), 19–34.

Haigh, Christopher, 'Puritan Evangelism in the Reign of Elizabeth I', *English Historical Review*, vol.92, no.362 (1977), 30–58.

'The Continuity of Catholicism in the English Reformation', *Past and Present*, 93 (1981), 37–69.

Hill, J. E. C., 'Puritans and "the Dark Corners of the Land"', *Transactions of the Royal Historical Society*, 5th series, vol.13 (London, 1963), 77–102.

'Seventeenth Century English Society and Sabbatarianism', *Britain and the Netherlands*, edited by J. S. Bromiley and E. H. Kossman (Groningen, 1964), pp. 84–108.

Kent, Joan, 'Attitudes of Members of the House of Commons to the Regulation of "Personal Conduct" in Late Elizabethan and Early Stuart England', *Bulletin of the Institute of Historical Research*, vol.46 (1973), 41–71.

Knappen, M. M., 'The Early Puritanism of Lancelot Andrewes', *Church History*, vol.2 (1933), 95–104.

Møller, J. G., 'The Beginnings of Puritan Covenant Theology', *Journal of Ecclesiastical History*, no. 14 (April, 1963), 46–67.

Owst, G. R., 'The People's Sunday Amusements in the Preaching of Medieval England', *Holburn Review*, n.s., vol.17 (1926), 32–45.

Parker, Kenneth L., 'Thomas Rogers and the English Sabbath: The Case for a Reappraisal', *Church History*, vol.53, no.3 (1984), 332–47.

Phillips, H., 'An Early Stuart Judaising Sect', *Transactions of the Jewish Historical Society of England*, vol.15 (1939–45), 63–72.

Prest, W., 'The Art of Law and the Law of God: Sir Henry Finch (1558–1625)', *Puritans and Revolutionaries*, edited by D. Pennington and K. Thomas (Oxford, 1978), pp. 94–117.

Primus, John, 'Calvin and the Puritan Sabbath', *Exploring the Heritage of John Calvin*, edited by D. E. Holwerda (Grand Rapids, Michigan, 1976), pp. 40–75.

Richardson, R. C., 'Puritanism and the Ecclesiastical Authorities: The Case of the Diocese of Chester', *Politics, Religion, and the English Civil War*, edited by B. Manning (London, 1973), pp. 3–33.

Rupp, Gordon, 'Andrew Karlstadt and Reformation Puritanism', *Journal of Theological Studies*, n.s., vol.10 (1959), 308–26.

Russell, Conrad, 'The Theory of Treason in the Trial of Strafford', *English Historical Review*, 80 (1965), 30–50.

Schama, Simon, 'The Unruly Realm: Appetite and Restraint in Seventeenth Century Holland', *Daedalus*, 108 (Summer, 1979), pp. 103–23.

Shriver, F., 'Hampton Court Re-Visited: James I and the Puritans', *Journal of Ecclesiastical History*, vol.33, no.1 (January, 1982), 48–71.

Sprunger, Keith, 'English and Dutch Sabbatarianism and the Development of a Puritan Social Theology, 1600–1660', *Church History*, vol.51, no.1 (March, 1982), 24–38.

Tait, James, 'The Declaration of Sports for Lancashire', *English Historical Review*, vol.32 (1917), 561–8.

Thurston, H., 'The Medieval Sunday', *The Nineteenth Century*, vol.46 (July, 1899), 36–50.

Tupling, G. H., 'The Causes of the Civil War in Lancashire', *Transactions of the Lancashire and Cheshire Antiquarian Society*, vol.65 (1955), 1–32.

Tyacke, N., 'Puritanism, Arminianism, and the Counter-Revolution', *Origins of the English Civil War*, edited by C. Russell (London, 1973), pp. 119–43.

White, B. R., 'John Traske (1585–1636) and London Puritanism', *Transactions of the Congregational Historical Society*, vol.20, no.7 (1968), 223–33.

Williams, D. A., 'Puritanism in the City Government 1610–1640', *Guildhall Miscellany*, vol.1, no.4 (1955), 3–14.

Wrightson, Keith, 'Alehouses, Order and Reformation in Rural England 1590–1660', *Popular Culture and Class Conflict, 1590–1914*, edited by E. and S. Yeo (Sussex, 1981), pp. 1–27.

Wrightson, Keith and Walter, John, 'Dearth and Social Order in Early Modern England', *Past and Present*, no.71 (1976), 22–42.

PRIMARY SOURCES

Abbot, George, *An Exposition upon the Prophet Jonah* (London, 1600).

Abbot, George, *Vindiciae Sabbathi* (London, 1641).

Adams, Thomas, *The Happiness of the Church* (London, 1618).

Ames, William, *The Marrow of Sacred Divinity* (London, 1642).

Andrewes, Lancelot, *Works*, 11 vols. (Oxford, 1841–54).
    The Moral Law Expounded (London, 1642).
    Ninety-Six Sermons, 5 vols. (Oxford, 1841).
    XCVI Sermons (London, 1629).
    A Patterne of Catechisticall Doctrine (London, 1630).

Aquinas, Thomas, *Summa Theologica*, 61 vols. (London, 1964–81).

Assheton, Nicholas, *Journal of Nicholas Assheton*, edited by F. R. Raines, (Manchester, 1848).

Axon, Ernest (ed.), *Oliver Heywood's Life of John Angier of Denton* (Chetham Society, 1937).

Manchester Sessions (n.p., 1901).

Babington, Gervase, *Certaine Plaine, Briefe and Comfortable Notes upon Genesis* (London, 1596).

' A Sermon at Paules Cross ' in *An Apology for Brotherly Love*, edited by Richard Hill (London, 1798).

A Very Fruitfull Exposition of the Commandements (London, 1583).

The Workes of Gervase Babington (London, 1615).

Balmford, James, *Three Posicions Concerning the Aucthoritie of the Lordes Daye* (London, 1607).

Barker, Peter, *A Judicious and Painefull Exposition upon the Ten Commandments* (London, 1624).

Barnes, Robert, *Supplycacion* (London, 1534?).

Barnes, T. G. (ed.), *Somerset Assize Orders, 1629–1640* (Somerset Record Society, 1959).

Barrow, Henry, *The Writings of Henry Barrow*, edited by Leland H. Carlson (London, 1962).

Bateman, Stephen, *The New Ariual of the Three Graces, into Anglia, Lamenting the Abuses of this Present Age* (London, 1580?).

Bayly, Lewis, *The Practice of Piety* (London, 1632).

Beard, Thomas, *The Theatre of Gods Judgements* (London, 1597).

Becon, Thomas, *A New Postil* (London, 1566).

Catechism, edited by J. Ayre (Cambridge, 1844).

The Demaundes of Holy Scripture (London, 1577).

Bedel, Henry, *A Sermon Exhorting to Pitie the Poore* (London, 1573).

Bernard, Richard, *A Double Catechisme* (Cambridge, 1607).

A Threefold Treatise of the Sabbath (London, 1641).

Bible [Bishops' Version] (London, 1568).

Bible [Geneva Version] (Geneva, 1560).

Bird, Samuel, *A Friendlie Communication or Dialogue between Paul and Demas* (London, 1580).

Boas, Frederick (ed.), *The Diary of Thomas Crosfield* (London, 1935).

Bolton, Robert, *Some General Directions for a Comfortable Walking with God* (London, 1638).

Two Sermons (London, 1639).

Bownde, Nicholas, *The Doctrine of the Sabbath* (London, 1595).

Sabbathum Veteris et Novi Testamenti, or The True Doctrine of the Sabbath (London, 1606).

Brabourne, Theophilus, *A Defence of that Most Ancient and Sacred Ordinance of Gods, the Sabbath Day* (London, 1631).

A Discourse upon the Sabbath Day (London, 1628).

Bradford, John, *Godly Meditations uppon the Ten Commaundements* (London, 1567).

Bradshaw, William, *A Protestacion of the Kings Supremacie* (n.p., 1605).

Bramston, John, *The Autobiography of Sir John Bramston* (London, 1845).

Brathwait, Richard, *Barnabees Journall* (London, 1932).

Brereton, William, *Travels in Holland, the United Provinces, England, Scotland and Ireland,* edited by Edward Hawkins ([Manchester], 1844).

Brerewood, Edward, *A Second Treatise of the Sabbath* (Oxford, 1632).

Brerewood, Edward, and Byfield, Nicholas, *A Learned Treatise of the Sabbaoth* (Oxford, 1630).

Bridges, John, *A Sermon Preached at Paules Crosse on the Monday in Whitson Weeke 1571* (London, 1571).

Broad, Thomas, *Three Questions Concerning the Obligations of the Fourth Commandment* (Oxford, 1621).

Tractatus de Sabbato (n.p., 1627).

Bucer, Martin, *Common Places of Martin Bucer,* translated and edited by by D. F. Wright (Abingdon, 1972).

'De Regno Christo', in *Melanchthon and Bucer,* translated by Wilhelm Pauck (Philadelphia, 1969).

Bulkeley, Edward, *A Sermon Preached at Bletsoe* (London, 1586).

Bullinger, Henrie, *Fiftie Godlie and Learned Sermons* (London, 1577).

A Hundred Sermons upon the Apocalips (London, 1561).

Bunny, Edmund, *The Whole Summe of Christian Religion* (London, 1576).

Burton, Henry, *A Brief Answer to a Late Treatise of the Sabbath Day* (n.p., 1635).

The Law and Gospel Reconciled (London, 1631).

A Narration of the Life of Mr. Henry Burton (London, 1643).

A Divine Tragedie Lately Acted [also attributed to William Prynne] ([Amsterdam], 1636).

Burton, William, *An Abstract of the Doctrine of the Sabbaoth* (London, 1606).

'The Anatomie of Belial' in *Works* (London, 1602).

Byfield, Richard, *The Doctrine of the Sabbath Vindicated* (London, 1631).

The Light of Faith: and Way of Holinesse (London, 1630).

Calendar of State Papers, Domestic.

Calvin, John, *Institutes of the Christian Religion,* 2 vols. (Philadelphia, 1975).

The Whole Doctrine of Calvin about the Sabbath and the Lord's Day, edited by Robert Cox (Edinburgh, 1860).

Cardwell, Edward, *A History of Conferences* (Oxford, 1840).

Documentary Annals, 2 vols. (Oxford, 1839).

Synodalia, 2 vols. (Oxford, 1842).

Carew, Richard, *The Survey of Cornwall* (London, 1769).

Carleton, Dudley, *Letters, January 1615/16 to December 1620* (London, 1780).

Cartwright, Thomas, *A Confutation of the Rhemists Translation* ([Leyden], 1618).

Cawdrey, Daniel, and Palmer, Herbert, *Sabbatum Redivivum,* Part I (London, 1645).

Sabbatum Redivivum, Parts II, III, IV (London, 1652).

Chaderton, Laurence, *A Fruitful Sermon upon the 3, 4, 5, 6, 7 and 8 Verses of the 12 Ch. of the Ep. to the Romanes* (London, 1584).

Chamberlain, John, *The Letters of John Chamberlain,* edited by N. E. McClure, 2 vols. (Philadelphia, 1939).

Christie, James (ed.), *Some Accounts of Parish Clerks*, (1893).

Clark, Andrew (ed.), *Register of the University of Oxford* (Oxford Historical Society, 1885).

The Shirburn Ballads 1585–1616 (Oxford, 1907).

Clay, William K. (ed.), *Liturgical Services Set Form in the Reign of Queen Elizabeth* (Cambridge, 1847).

Cleaver, Robert, *A Godly Form of Householde Governement* (London, 1598).

A Declaration of the Christian Sabbath (London, 1625).

Commons Debates, 1621. See W. Notestein, F. Relf and H. Simpson.

Cooper, Thomas, *An Admonition to the People of England* (London, 1589).

Corpus Juris Canonici (Graz, 1959).

Corrie, G. E. (ed.), *Homilies* (Cambridge, 1850).

Cosin, John, *The Works*, 5 vols. (Oxford, 1843–55).

Cox, J. C. (ed.), *The Records of the Borough of Northampton*, 2 vols. (Northampton, 1898).

Cranmer, Thomas, *Miscellaneous Writings and Letters*, edited by John Cox (Cambridge, 1846).

Crashawe, William, *Milke for Babes, or A North-Countrie Catechisme* (London, 1618).

The Sermon Preached at the Cross Feb. 14, 1607 (London, 1608).

Dalton, Michael, *The Countrey Justice* (London, 1618).

Dasent, J. R. (ed.), *Acts of the Privy Council* (London, 1890-).

Deacon, John, *A Treatise, Intituled, Nobody is My Name, which Beareth Everi-bodies Blame* (London, 1585).

Dent, Arthur, *The Plaine Mans Pathway to Heaven* (London, 1601).

Dering, Edward, *Works* (London, 1597).

D'Ewes, Simonds, *The Autobiography and Correspondence of Sir Simonds D'Ewes*, edited by J. O. Halliwell, 2 vols. (London, 1845).

A Compleat Journal (London, 1693).

Journals of all the Parliaments during the Reign of Queen Elizabeth (London, 1682).

Dives and Pauper, edited by Priscilla H. Barnum, 2 vols. (London, 1976).

Dod, John, *A Plaine and Familiar Exposition of the Ten Commandments* (London, 1604).

Dow, Christopher, *Innovations Unjustly Charged upon the Present Church and State* (London, 1637).

A Discourse of the Sabbath and the Lord's Day (London, 1636).

Downame, John, *Guide of Godlinesse* (London, 1629).

Earwaker, J. P. (ed.), *The Court Leet Records* (Manchester, 1884).

Elton, Edward, *A Forme of Catechizing* (London, 1616).

Emmison, F. G., 'Abstract of the Act Book of the Archdeacon of Huntingdon's Court' in *Transactions of the East Huntingdonshire Archeological Society* VIII (1928–9), 26–42.

Erasmus, *Praise of Folly and Letter to Martin Dorp: 1515* (Harmondsworth, Middlesex, 1971).

Estye, George, *Certaine Godly and Learned Expositions* (London, 1603).

A Most Sweete and Comfortable Exposition upon the Tenne Commandements and upon 51 Psalmes (London, 1602).

Eusebius, *The Ecclesiastical History and the Martyrs of Palestine* (London, 1927–8).

Falconer, J., *A Briefe Refutation of John Traskes Judaical and Novel Fancyes* (n.p., 1618).

The Farington Papers, edited by Susan Ffarington (Chetham Society, 1856).

Fénélon, Bertrand de Salignac de la Mothe, *Correspondance Diplomatique 1568–1575*, edited by A. Teulet, 7 vols. (Paris, 1838–40).

Fenner, Dudley, *Certain Godly and Learned Treatises* (Edinburgh, 1592).

Fetherstone, Christopher, *A Dialogue agaynst Light, Lewde and Lascivious Dauncing* (London, 1582).

Field, John, and Wilcox, Thomas, *Admonition to the Parliament* (London, 1572).

Field, John, *A Caveat for Parsons Howlet* (London, 1581).

A Godly Exhortation by Occasion of the Late Judgement of God, Showed at Paris-Garden (London, 1583).

Firth, C. H., and Rait, R. S., *Acts and Ordinances of the Interregnum: 1642–1660*, 3 vols. (London, 1911).

Fleming, Abraham, *The Footpath to Felicitie* (London, 1581).

Force, Peter (ed.), *Tracts and Other Papers* (New York, 1947).

Formularies of Faith, (Oxford, 1825).

Foster, Elizabeth Read (ed.), *Proceedings in Parliament, 1610*, 2 vols. (London, 1966).

France, R. Sharpe (ed.), *A Lancashire Miscellany* (Blackpool, 1965).

Frere, W. H., *Visitation Articles and Injunctions 1536–1558*, 3 vols. (London, 1910).

Frere, W. H. and Douglas, C. E. (eds.), *Puritan Manifestoes* (London, 1954).

Gee, Alexander, *The Ground of Christianitie* (London, 1584).

Gerard, John, *John Gerard: The Autobiography of an Elizabethan* (London, 1951).

Gibbens, Nicholas, *Questions and Disputations* (London, 1601).

Gibson, Edmund, *Codex Juris Ecclesiastici Anglicani* (London, 1713).

Gifford, George, *A Catechisme* (London, 1583).

Gilby, Anthony, *A Pleasaunt Dialogue betweene a Souldier of Barwicke and an English Chaplaine* (n.p., 1581).

Gosson, Stephen, *The Schoole of Abuse* (London, 1579).

Gouge, William, *Workes* (London, 1627).

The Sabbaths Sanctification (London, 1641).

Greenham, Richard, *The Works* (London, 1599).

Grindal, Edmund, *The Remains* (Cambridge, 1843).

Groombridge, M. J. (ed.), *Calendar of Chester City Council Minutes 1603–1642* (Blackpool, 1956).

Gualter, R. *An Hundred, Threescore, and Fiftene Sermons uppon the Actes of the Apostles* (London, 1572).

Hacket, John, *Scrinia reserata* (London, 1693).

Hakewill, George, *A Short, but Cleare, Discourse, of the Institution, Dignity, and End of the Lords-day* (London, 1641).

Hale, W. H., *A Series of Precedents and Proceedings in Criminal Causes* (London, 1847).

Hales, John, *Golden Remains* (London, 1659).

Hall, H. (ed.), 'Some Elizabethan Penances in the Diocese of Ely', in *Transactions of the Royal Historical Society*, 3rd Series, vol.I. (1907), 263–77.

Hall, John, *Works*, 10 vols. (London, 1808).

Hamilton, A. H. A., *Quarter Sessions From Queen Elizabeth to Queen Anne* (London, 1878).

Harland, John (ed.), *The Lancashire Lieutenancy under the Tudors and Stuarts*, 2 vols. (Chetham Society, 1844).

Harrison, William, *The Difference of Hearers; or an Exposition of Certayne Sermons, at Hyton, in Lancashire* (London, 1614).

Hartley, T. E. (ed.), *Proceedings in the Parliaments of Elizabeth I* (Leicester Univ. Press, 1981).

Hening, W. W. (ed.) *Statutes at Large of All the Laws of Virginia*, 13 vols. (New York, 1823).

Heylyn, Peter, *Cyprianus Anglicus* (London, 1671).
  A Briefe and Moderate Answer (London, 1637).
  Extraneus Vapulans (London, 1656).
  The History of the Sabbath (London, 1636).
  Microcosmos (Oxford, 1627).

Hill, Adam, *The Crie of England* (London, 1595).

Historical Manuscripts Commission Reports.

Holland, Thomas, *A Sermon Preached at Paul's in London the 17th of November Ann. Dom. 1599* (Oxford, 1601).

Homilies. See G. E. Corrie.

Hooker, Richard, *The Works* (Oxford, 1836).

Hooper, John, *A Declaration of the Ten Holy Commaundements* ([Zurich], 1548).
  Early Writings (Cambridge, 1843).

Houlbrooke, Ralph A. (ed.), *The Letter Book of John Parkhurst* (Norwich, 1975).

Howson, John, *A Sermon Preached at St Maries in Oxford, the 17 Day of November, 1602* (Oxford, 1602).

Hughes, Lewis, *Signes from Heaven* (London, 1642).

Hughes, Paul, and Larkin, J. F. (eds.), *Tudor Royal Proclamations*, 3 vols. (London, 1964–9).

James I, *The Kings Majesties Declaration to his Subjects, Concerning Lawful Sports to Be Used* (London, 1618).

Jeaffreson, John C. (ed.), *Middlesex County Records*, 4 vols. ([1886]–92)

Jenkyns, Henry (ed.), *The Remains of Thomas Cranmer*, 4 vols. (Oxford, 1833).

Jones, Richard, *A Briefe and Necessarie Catechisme* (London, 1583).

Journals of the House of Commons.

Journals of the House of Lords.

Kennedy, W. P. M., *Elizabethan Episcopal Administration*, 3 vols. (London, 1924).

Kenyon, J. P. (ed.), *The Stuart Constitution, 1603–1688* (Cambridge, 1966).

Kethe, William, *A Sermon Made at Blanford Forum* (London, 1571).

King, John, *Lectures upon Jonas, Delivered at Yorke 1594* (Oxford, 1597).

Knappen, M. M. (ed.), *Two Elizabethan Puritan Diaries* (Chicago, 1933).

Knewstub, John, *The Lectures of John Knewstubs Upon the Twentieth Chapter of Exodus and Certain Other Places of Scripture* (London, 1577).

Lambard, W., *The Duties of Constables* (London, 1583).

Larkin, J. F. and Hughes, P. L. (eds.), *Stuart Royal Proclamations 1603–1625* (Oxford, 1973).

Laud, William, *Works*, 7 vols. (Oxford, 1847–60).

Leighton, Alexander, *Speculum Belli sacri* (Amsterdam, 1624).

L'Estrange, Hamon, *Gods Sabbath before the Law, under the Law and under the Gospel* (London, 1641).

   The Reign of King Charles (London, 1656).

Ley, John, *Sunday a Sabbath* (London, 1641).

Lovell, Thomas, *A Dialogue between Custom and Veritie* (London, 1581).

Luther, Martin, *Luther's Works*, edited by J. Pelikan (St Louis, 1955-).

McNeill, John T., and Gamer, H. M. (eds.), *Medieval Handbooks of Penance* (New York, 1938).

Manningham, John, *Diary of John Manningham 1602–03* (Westminster, 1868).

Mannyng, Robert, *Handlyng Synne* (London, 1862).

Martin, Charles T. (ed.), *Journal of Sir Francis Walsingham* (London, 1870).

Martyr, Peter, *The Commonplaces* (London, 1583).

Mayer, John, *English Catechism Explained* (London, 1623).

Meads, Dorothy M. (ed.), *Diary of Lady Margaret Hoby 1599–1605* (London, 1930).

Mirk, John, *Mirk's Festial: A Collection of Homilies* (London, 1905).

   Instructions for Parish Priests (London, 1868).

More, Thomas, *The Complete Works of St. Thomas More* (New Haven, 1963-).

   The Workes of Sir Thomas More (London, 1557).

Munday, Anthony, *A Second and Third Blast of Retrait from Plaies and Theatres* (London, 1580).

Musculus, Wolfgang, *Commonplaces* (London, 1563).

Nichols, John G. (ed.), *The Diary of Henry Machyn* (London, 1848).

Norden, John, *The Pensive Mans Practise* (London, 1594).

   A Progress of Piety (Cambridge, 1847).

   A Sinfull Mans Solace (London, 1585).

Northbrooke, J., *A Treatise wherin Dicing, Dauncing, Vaine Playes or Enterluds, with Other Idle Pastimes Commonly Used on the Sabbath Day, are Reproved* (London, 1579?).

Notestein, Wallace, Relf, F. H., and Simpson, H. (eds.), *Commons Debates, 1621*, 7 vols. (New Haven, 1935).

Nowell, Alexander, *A Catechism* (Cambridge, 1853).

O'Keeffe, J. G., 'Cain Downaig' in *Ériu: Journal of the School of Irish Learning, Dublin*, vol.II (Dublin, 1905), 189–214.

– 'Poem on the Observance of Sunday' in *Ériu*, vol.III (Dublin, 1907), 143–7.

Orme, William, *Remarkable Passages in the Life of William Kiffin* (London, 1823).

Overall, John, *The Convocation Book of* MDCVI (Oxford, 1844).

Palmer, W. M. (ed.), *Episcopal Visitation Returns for Cambridgeshire 1638–1665* (Cambridge, 1930).

Parker, Matthew, *Correspondence of Matthew Parker* (Cambridge, 1853).

Parsons, Robert, *A Brief Discours Contayning Certayne Reasons Why Catholiques Refuse to Goe to Church* (Doway, 1580).

Peel, A. (ed.), *The Seconde Parte of a Register*, 2 vols. (Cambridge, 1915).

Perkins, William, *Works*, 3 vols. (London, 1631).

    A Commentarie or Exposition upon the Five First Chapters of the Epistle to the Galatians (Cambridge, 1604).

    A Godly and Learned Exposition of Commentarie upon the Three First Chapters of the Revelation (London, 1606).

    A Golden Chaine (Cambridge, 1591).

    The Whole Treatise of the Cases of Conscience (Cambridge, 1606).

    The Work of William Perkins (Abingdon, 1970).

Perry, G. G. (ed.), *English Prose Treatises of Richard Rolle* (London, 1866).

Peter, Hugh, *A Dying Fathers Last Legacy to an Onely Child* (London, 1660).

Peyton, Sidney A. (ed.), *The Churchwardens' Presentments in the Oxfordshire Peculiars of Dorchester, Thames and Banbury* (Abingdon, 1928).

Pilkington, James, *The Works of James Pilkington* (Cambridge, 1842).

Pocklington, John, *Sunday No Sabbath* (London, 1636).

Powicke, F. M., and Cheney, C. R. (eds.), *Councils and Synods: AD 871–1313*, 2 vols. (Oxford, 1964–1981).

Poynet, John, *A Short Catechisme* (London, 1553).

Prideaux, John, *The Doctrine of the Sabbath, Delivered in the Act at Oxon, Anno 1622* (London, 1634).

Priebsch, R. (ed.), ' The Chief Sources of Some Anglo-Saxon Homilies ', *Otia Merseliana*, vol. 1 (London, 1899), 129–47.

Propositions and Principles of Divinitie, translated by John Perry (Edinburgh, 1591).

Prynne, William, *Canterburies Doome* (London, 1646).

    The Antipathie of the English Lordly Prelacie (London, 1641).

    A New Discovery of Prelates Tyranny (London, 1641).

    News from Ipswich (n.p., 1636).

    Histrio-Mastix (London, 1633).

Raines, F. R. (ed.), *Chetham Miscellanies*, vol.v (Chetham Society, 1875).

Ramus, Peter, *Commentariorum de Religione* (Frankfurt, 1576).

Reeve, Edmund, *The Communion Book Catechisme Expounded* (London, 1636).

Roberts, Humphrey, *An Earnest Complaint, of Divers Vain, Wicked and Abused Exercises, Now Commonly Practised on the Saboth Day* (London, 1572).

Rogers, John, *The Displaying of an Horrible Secte . . . the Familie of Love* (London, 1578).

    The Summe of Christianitie ([London] 1580?).

Rogers, Richard, *Seven Treatises* (London, 1603).

Rogers, Thomas, *The Catholic Doctrine of the Church of England* (Cambridge, 1854).

Royster, J. F. (ed.), 'A Middle English Treatise on the Ten Commandments', *Studies in Philology*, vol.vi (Chapel Hill, 1910), 1–39.

Rushworth, J., *Historical Collections*, 8 vols. (London, 1680–1701).

[Sanderson, Robert], *A Soveraigne Antidote against Sabbatarian Errour* (London, 1636).

Saunders, H. W. (ed.), *The Official Papers of Sir Nathaniel Bacon 1580–1620* (London, 1915).

Sclater, William, *The Ministers Portion* (Oxford, 1612).

Shutte, Christopher, *A Compendious Forme and Summe of Christian Doctrine* (London, 1581).

Skaife, R. H. (ed.), 'Extracts from the Visitation Books at York', *Yorkshire Archeological Journal*, xv (Leeds, 1900), 224–43.

Some, Robert, *A Godly Treatise* (London, 1588).

Southwell, Robert, *Two Letters and Short Rules of a Good Life* (Charlottesville, 1973).

Sprint, John, *Propositions Tending to Proove the Necessarie Use of the Christian Sabbaoth, or Lord's Day* (London, 1607).

Stephens, A. J. (ed.), *The Statutes Relating to the Ecclesiastical and Eleemosynary Institutions of England*, 2 vols. (London, 1845).

Stockwood, John, *A Very Fruiteful Sermon Preached at Paules Crosse the Tenth of May Last, Being the First Sunday in Easter Term* (London, 1579).

Strype, John, *Annals of the Reformation*, 7 vols. (Oxford, 1824).

  John Aylmer (Oxford, 1821).

  Ecclesiastical Memorials, 6 vols. (Oxford, 1822).

  Edmund Grindal (Oxford, 1821).

  The Life and Acts of Matthew Parker, 3 vols. (Oxford, 1821).

  The Life and Acts of John Whitgift, 3 vols. (Oxford, 1822).

Stubbes, Philip, *The Anatomie of Abuses* (London, 1583).

Sutton, Christopher, *Disce vivere. Learne to Live* (London, 1604).

Tait, J. (ed.), *Lancashire Quarter Session Records*, vol. 1 (Manchester, 1917).

Tanner, J. R. (ed.), *Constitutional Documents of the Reign of James I, 1603–1625* (Cambridge, 1960).

Terry, John, *The Triall of Truth* (Oxford, 1600).

Thoresby, John, *Instruction for the People*, edited by Thomas F. Simmons and H. E. Nolloth (London, 1901).

Thorpe, Benjamin, *Ancient Laws and Institutes of England* (London, 1840).

Townshend, Heywood, *Historical Collections* (London, 1680).

Traske, John, *A Treatise of Libertie from Judaisme* (London, 1620).

Turnbull, Richard, *An Exposition upon James* (London, 1592).

Twisse, William, *Of the Morality of the Fourth Commandement* (London, 1641).

Tyndale, William, *An Answer to Sir Thomas More's Dialogue* (Cambridge, 1850).

Tyndale, Frith, and Barnes, *The Whole Workes of W. Tyndall, John Frith, and Doctor Barnes* (London, 1573).

Udall, John, *Obedience to the Gospell* (London, 1584).

Ursinus, Zacharias, *The Summe of Christian Religion* (Oxford, 1587).

Usher, Roland G. (ed.), *The Presbyterian Movement in the Reign of Queen Elizabeth* (London, 1905).

Ussher, James, *The Judgement of the Late Archbishop of Armagh and Primate of Ireland* (London, 1657).

Vaughan, William, *The Golden-grove* (London, 1608).

Vaux, Laurence, *A Catechisme* (Antwerp, 1574).

Viret, Pierre, *A Christian Instruction* (London, 1573).

Walker, George, *The Doctrine of the Holy Weekly Sabbath* (London, 1641).

The Doctrine of the Sabbath (Amsterdam, 1638).

Wallington, N., *Historical Notices*, vol. 1 (London, 1869).

Walsall, John, *A Sermon, Preached at Pauls Crosse* (London, 1578).

Wentworth, Thomas, *The Earl of Strafford's Letters and Dispatches*, vol. 1 (London, 1739).

Whitaker, William, *A Disputation on the Holy Scripture against the Papists* (Cambridge, 1849).

White, Francis, *An Examination and Confutation of a Lawless Pamphlet* (London, 1637).

A Treatise of the Sabbath Day (London, 1635).

White, John, *The Way to the True Church* (London, 1608).

White, Thomas, *A Sermon Preached at Pawles Crosse on Sunday, the Thirde of November 1577 in the Time of the Plague* (London, 1578).

Whitelock, D., Brett, M., and Brooke, C. N. L. (eds.), *Councils and Synods: A.D.871–1204*, 2 vols. (Oxford, 1981).

Whitford, Richard, *A Werke for Housholders* (London, 1530)

Whitgift, John, *Works*, 3 vols. (Cambridge, 1851).

Widley, George, *The Doctrine of the Sabbath* (London, 1604).

Wilkins, David, *Concilia Magnae Britanniae et Hiberniae*, 4 vols. (London, 1737).

Williams, Griffith, *The True Church* (London, 1629).

Williams, John F. (ed.), *Bishop Redman's Visitation 1597*, vol. 18 (Norfolk Record Society, 1946).

Willis, Arthur (ed.), *A Hampshire Miscellany: Metropolitical Visitation of the Archdeaconry of Winchester of 1607–08* (Kent, 1963).

Willis Bund, John W. (ed.), *Worcestershire County Records: Calender of the Quarter Sessions Papers*, 2 vols. (Worcester, 1900).

Willson, David H. (ed.), *The Parliamentary Diary of Robert Bowyer* (New York, 1971).

Wolphius, Johannes, *Chronologia* (Zurich, 1585).

Woolton, John, *The Castell of Christians* (London, 1577).

Wright, Leonard, *A Summons for Sleepers* (n.p., 1589).

Yonge, Walter, *Diary of Walter Yonge*, edited by George Roberts (London, 1848).

Zurich Letters, The, edited by H. Robinson (Cambridge, 1842).

SECONDARY SOURCES

Allen, John W., *English Political Thought, 1603–1660* (London, 1938).

Bacchiocchi, S., *From Sabbath to Sunday* (Rome, 1977).

Bailey, Derrick S., *Thomas Becon* (Edinburgh, 1952).

Baines, E., *The History of the County Palatine and the Duchy of Lancaster*, 2 vols. (London, 1868–70).

Barnes, Thomas, *Somerset 1625–1640* (London, 1961).

Barwick, John, *A Summarie Account of the Holy Life of Thomas Late Lord Bishop of Dureseme* (London, 1660).

Beckwith, Roger, and Stott, W., *This Is the Day* (London, 1978).

Boas, Frederick S., *University Drama in the Tudor Age* (Oxford, 1914).

Breslow, Marvin, A., *A Mirror of England: English Puritan Views of Foreign Nations, 1618–1640* (Cambridge, Mass., 1970).

Brewer, John, and Styles, J. (eds.), *An Ungovernable People* (London, 1980).

Bridgett, T. E., *History of the Holy Eucharist in Great Britain*, 2 vols. (London, 1881).

Burnet, Gilbert, *The History of the Reformation* (Oxford, 1865).

Caiger-Smith, Alan, *English Medieval Mural Paintings* (Oxford, 1963).

Carson, Donald A. (ed.), *From Sabbath to Lord's Day* (Grand Rapids, 1982).

Carter, Alice, *English Reformed Church in Amsterdam in the Seventeenth Century* (Amsterdam, 1964).

Chambers, E. K., *The Elizabethan Stage*, 4 vols. (Oxford, 1923)

Chandler, George, *Liverpool Under James I* (Liverpool, 1960).

Clark, P., and Slack, P., *English Towns in Transition 1500–1700* (London, 1976).

Collier, Jeremy, *An Ecclesiastical History of Great Britain*, 9 vols. (London, 1852).

Collinson, Patrick, *English Puritanism* (London, 1983).
 A Mirror of Elizabethan Puritanism; The Life and Letters of 'Godly Master Dering' (London, 1964).
 Religion of Protestants: The Church in English Society 1559–1625 (Oxford, 1982).
 The Elizabethan Puritan Movement (London, 1967).
 Archbishop Grindal 1519–1583 (London, 1979).

Commons. 3 vols. See Hasler.

Cooper, Charles H., *Annals of Cambridge*, 5 vols. (Cambridge, 1842–1908).

Coulton, G. G., *Five Centuries of Religion*, 4 vols. (Cambridge, 1923–50).
 The Medieval Village (Cambridge, 1925).

Cox, Robert, *The Literature of the Sabbath Question*, 2 vols. (Edinburgh, 1865).
 Sabbath Laws and Sabbath Duties (Edinburgh, 1853).
 The Whole Doctrine of Calvin about the Sabbath and the Lords Day (Edinburgh, 1860).

Darby, H. C., *The Medieval Fenland* (Cambridge, 1974).

Davids, T. W., *Annals of Evangelical Nonconformity in the County of Essex* (London, 1863).

Dennison, James, *The Market Day of the Soul* (Lanham, Maryland, 1983).

Dent, Christopher M., *Protestant Reformers in Elizabethan Oxford* (Oxford, 1983).

Denton, W., *England in the Fifteenth Century* (London, 1888).

Dickens, Arthur G., *English Reformation* (New York, 1974).

Edwards, Mark U., *Luther and the False Brethren* (Stanford, 1975).

Elton, Geoffrey R., *Reform and Reformation, England 1509–1558* (Cambridge, Mass., 1977).

Eusden, John D., *Puritans, Lawyers, and Politics in Early Seventeenth Century England* (New Haven, 1958).

Fletcher, Anthony, *The Outbreak of the English Civil War* (London, 1981).

Frere, W. H., *English Church in the Reign of Elizabeth and James I* (London, 1924).

Fuller, Thomas, *The History of the Worthies of England*, 3 vols. (London, 1840).
The Church History of Britain, 3 vols. (Oxford, 1868).

Gardiner, Samuel R., *History of England*, 10 vols. (London, 1883).

George, C. H. and K., *The Protestant Mind of the English Reformation, 1570–1640* (Princeton, N.J., 1961).

Gough, J. W., *Fundamental Law in English Constitutional History* (Oxford, 1955).

Govett, Lionel A., *The King's Book of Sports* (London, 1890).

Greaves, Richard, *Society and Religion in Elizabethan England* (Minneapolis, 1981).

Haigh, Christopher, *Reformation and Resistance in Tudor Lancashire* (Cambridge, 1974).

Haller, William, *The Rise of Puritanism* (New York, 1938).

Halley, Robert, *Lancashire: Its Puritanism and Non Conformity* 2 vols. (Manchester, 1869).

Hart, A. Tindal, *The Country Clergy* (London, 1958).

Hasler, P. W. (ed.), *The House of Commons, 1558–1603*, 3 vols. (London, 1981).

Haugaard, William, *Elizabeth and the English Reformation* (Cambridge, 1968).

Hessey, J. A., *Sunday, its Origins, History, and Present Obligation* (London, 1860).

Hey, David G., *An English Rural Community, Myddle, under the Tudors and Stuarts* (Leicester, 1974).

Hibbard, Caroline, *Charles I and the Popish Plot* (Chapel Hill, 1983).

Higham, Florence, *Catholic and Reformed* (London, 1962).

Hill, Christopher, *Society and Puritanism in Pre-Revolutionary England* (London, 1964).

Hill, J. W. F., *Tudor and Stuart Lincoln* (Cambridge, 1956).

History of King-Killers, The (London, 1719).

Hollingworth, R., *Mancuniensis* (Manchester, 1839).

Houlbrooke, R., *Church Courts and the People* (Oxford, 1979).

Jewett, Paul K., *The Lord's Day* (Grand Rapids, Michigan, 1971).

Jones, John, *Bishop Hall, His Life and Times* (London, 1826).

Jones, Norman L., *Faith By Statute* (London, 1982).

Katz, David S., *Philo-Semitism and the Readmission of the Jews to England: 1603–1655* (Oxford, 1982).

Kendall, R. T., *Calvin and English Calvinism to 1649* (Oxford, 1979).

Kevan, Ernest F., *Grace of Law* (London, 1964).

Knappen, M. M., *Tudor Puritanism: A Chapter in the History of Idealism* (Chicago, 1970).

Lake, Peter, *Moderate Puritans and Elizabethan Church* (Cambridge, 1982).

Levy, Max, *Der Sabbath in England* (Leipzig, 1933).

Lewis, A. H., *A Critical History of Sunday Legislation* (New York, 1888).

Lightfoot, John, *The Whole Works*, 13 vols. (London, 1822–4).

MacCaffrey, Wallace T., *Exeter, 1540–1640* (Cambridge, Mass., 1975).

Macfarlane, Alan, *The Family Life of Ralph Josselin* (Cambridge, 1970).

McGrath, Patrick, *Papists and Puritans under Elizabeth I* (London, 1967).

McIntosh, P. C., *Sport in Society* (London, 1963).

Macpherson, C. B., *The Political Theory of Possessive Individualism* (Oxford, 1962).

Maitland, Frederic, *Roman Canon Law in the Church of England* (London, 1898).

Maitland, William, *The History of London*, 2 vols. (London, 1756).

Manning, Bernard, *The People's Faith in the Time of Wyclif* (Cambridge, 1919).

Marchant, Ronald, *The Puritans and the Church Courts in the Diocese of York 1560–1642* (London, 1960).

Mitchell, William M., *The Rise of the Revolutionary Party in the English House of Commons 1603–1629* (New York, 1957).

Moorman, John R. H., *Church Life in England in the Thirteenth Century* (Cambridge, 1945).

Morgan, Irvonwy, *Puritan Spirituality* (London, 1973).

Neal, Daniel, *The History of the Puritans*, 5 vols. (London, 1822).

Neale, Edward V., *Feasts and Fasts* (London, 1845).

Neale, J. E., *Elizabeth I and Her Parliaments 1559–1601*, 2 vols. (London, 1953–7).

New, John F. H., *Anglican and Puritan, the Basis of their Opposition, 1558–1640* (London, 1964).

Nuttall, Geoffrey F., *The Holy Spirit in Puritan Faith and Experience* (Oxford, 1946).

   The Puritan Spirit (London, 1967).

Owen, Dorothy M., *The Records of the Established Church in England* (London, 1970).

Owst, G. R., *Literature and Pulpit in Medieval England* (Oxford, 1961).

   Preaching in Medieval England (Cambridge, 1926).

Pagitt, E., *Heresiography* (London, 1661).

Palliser, D. M., *Tudor York* (Oxford, 1979).

Pearson, A. F. S., *Thomas Cartwright and Elizabethan Puritanism* (Cambridge, 1925).

Porter, Harry C., *Reformation and Reaction in Tudor Cambridge* (Hamden, Conn., 1972).

Prest, W., *The Inns of Court under Elizabeth I and the Early Stuarts: 1590–1640* (London, 1972).

Read, Conyers, *Lord Burghley and Queen Elizabeth* (London, 1960).

Richardson, Roger, *Puritanism in North-West England: A Regional Study of the Diocese of Chester to 1642* (Manchester, 1972).

Rordorf, Willy, *Sunday* (London, 1968).

Rose, E., *Cases of Conscience* (Cambridge, 1975).

Rouse, E. Clive, *Discovering Wall Paintings* (n.p., 1980).

Rowse, A. L., *Raleigh and the Throckmortons* (London, 1962).

Russell, Conrad, *The Crisis of Parliaments* (London, 1971).
    Parliaments and English Politics 1621–1629 (Oxford, 1979).

Schiller, Gertrud, *Iconography of Christian Art*, 2 vols. (London, 1971–2).

Schuecking, Levin L., *The Puritan Family* (London, 1969).

Seaver, Paul S., *The Puritan Lectureships: The Politics of Religious Dissent 1560–1662* (Stanford, 1970).

Serjeantson, R. M., *History of the Church of All Saints, Northampton* (Northampton, 1901).

Sharpe, Kevin (ed.), *Faction and Parliament* (Oxford, 1978).

Sheils, W. J., *The Puritans in the Diocese of Peterborough 1558–1610* (Northampton, 1979).

Solberg, Winton, *Redeem the Time: The Puritan Sabbath in Early America* (London, 1977).

Spufford, Margaret, *Contrasting Communities* (Cambridge, 1974).

Tanner, J. R., *English Constitutional Conflicts of the Seventeenth Century: 1603–1689* (Cambridge, 1928).

Thomas, Keith, *Religion and the Decline of Magic, Studies in Popular Beliefs in Sixteenth and Seventeenth Century England* (Harmondsworth, 1973).

Trevelyan, W. B., *Sunday* (London, 1903).

Trevor-Roper, H. R., *Archbishop Laud* (London, 1962).

Trimble, William R., *The Catholic Laity in Elizabethan England, 1558–1603* (Cambridge, Mass., 1964).

Tristram, E. W., *English Wall Paintings of the Fourteenth Century* (London, 1955).

Troeltsch, Ernst, *The Social Teaching of the Christian Churches*, 2 vols. (London, 1956).

Usher, Roland G., *The Rise and Fall of the High Commission* (Oxford, 1913).
    The Reconstruction of the English Church, 2 vols. (London, 1910).
    The Presbyterian Movement in the Reign of Queen Elizabeth (London, 1904).

Venn, J.A., *Alumni Cantabrigiensis* (Cambridge, 1927).

Vernon, George, *Life of Heylyn* (London, 1682).

Welsby, Paul A., *George Abbot, the Unwanted Archbishop* (London, 1962).
    Lancelot Andrewes (London, 1958).

Whitaker, W. B., *Sunday in Tudor and Stuart Times* (London, 1933).

Willey, Basil, *The Seventeenth Century Background* (London, 1950).

Williams, George Huntston, *The Radical Reformation* (London, 1962).

Willson, D. Harris, *King James VI and I* (London, 1956).

Woodeforde, Christopher, *The Norwich School of Glasspainting in the Fifteenth Century* (London, 1950).

Wrighton, Keith, and Levine, David, *Poverty and Piety in an English Village, Terling 1525–1700* (London, 1979).

Wylie, James, *The Reign of Henry V*, 3 vols. (Cambridge, 1914).
    History of England under Henry the Fourth, 4 vols. (London, 1884–98).

Index